DIGITAL
AT
Snapshots from the
first thirty-five years
WORK

DIGITAL AT WORK

Snapshots from the
first thirty-five years

WORK

**Edited by
Jamie Parker Pearson**

Digital Press

Trademark products mentioned in this book are
listed on page 208.

Printed in the United States of America

9 8 7 6 5 4 3 2 1

Order number EY-J826E-DP

The publisher offers discounts on bulk orders of
this book. For information, please write:

Special Sales Department
Digital Press
One Burlington Woods Drive
Burlington, MA 01803

Design and Production: Janice Moore and
Laraine Armenti, Quantic Communications, Inc.
Typesetting: Lee Ann Bartow, Margaret Burdine,
and Nancy Jones, Quantic Communications, Inc.
Editing and Proofing: Terri Autieri, Quantic
Communications, Inc.
Copy Editing: Ann Hall, Editorial, Inc.

Views expressed in this book are those of the
editors, not of the publisher. Digital Equipment
Corporation assumes no responsibility for any
errors that may appear in this book.

Library of Congress Cataloging-in-Publication Data

Digital at work: snapshots from the first thirty-five years / edited
    by Jamie Parker Pearson.
        p.   cm.
    Includes bibliographical references and index.
    ISBN 1-55558-092-0
    1. Digital Equipment Corporation—History. 2. Computer industry—
United States—History. I. Pearson, Jamie Parker.
HD9696.C64D5316 1992   92-6308
338.7′61004′0973—dc20   CIP

Contents

Foreword

The job of a leader is to be sure every task is assigned, budgeted and scheduled. Those tasks which no one else is going to do, the leader must do. He must never claim credit for them, he is supposed to be getting everybody else to work, and if you pick up some of the pieces, you should never brag about it.

When people are tempted to brag about what they did, I tell them a fable that used to be in *The Second Grade Reader,* called "The Turtle that Wanted to Fly." A turtle talked some crows into putting a stick between their mouths. He then held onto the center of the stick with his mouth and flew with them. Once, someone on the ground said, "That's a clever idea. Who thought of it?" The turtle couldn't keep his mouth shut, and had to say, "It was me."

My advice to people who want to be leaders is, the task of a leader is not to claim credit, but to be the leader and get the job done.

This is a book about Digital, written by some people who have worked at Digital and gotten the job done. There are many others.

— Ken Olsen
   April 1992

Preface

This is a book about many people, written by many people.

When we discussed the idea of a book about Digital, it seemed that the best and most honest way to show what working at Digital was like would be to let people tell their own stories, in their own words.

This is not a formal history, a systematic account, or a comprehensive analysis. Elements of analysis are here, and the raw material of history. Words and remembrances provide insight into Digital's culture and help to explain how it became the company it is today. We conducted more than three hundred interviews for this book. Some people were close at hand, still working at Digital. Others were several careers away. All, regardless of their roles, knew personally what it is to work at Digital. We gathered far more material than we could possibly use, and found that many people remembered different things, differently. Yet they all talked about the same things, many having shared common experiences. We hope it presents a candid picture of Digital's working environment.

In developing what may be considered the first volume, we felt there were some separate areas of the story worth researching: the roots of the company, the development of the style of interactive computing, the initial contact with customers and the early days of sales and service, how we have manufactured over the years, our engineering philosophy, and how the company is organized and how it operates.

At the beginning of each part of the book is an illustrated section, providing a visual history of the product and business milestones of the period. Part I covers the period from the 1950s through the introduction of Digital's first computer, the PDP-1, in 1960. Part II spans the growth years, from the mid-1960s through the late 1980s, introducing the PDP-11 and the VAX family of systems. Part III looks at the development and internal use of Digital's family of networking products, linking the use of the network to the dynamic operating environment.

I am grateful to many people who supported this effort. It has offered me a rare opportunity to look closely at Digital. In particular, I would like to thank Ken Olsen, Win Hindle, and John Sims. For their roles as advisors and sounding boards, I would like to acknowledge Henry Crouse, Russ Doane, Gary Eichhorn, Jim Fleming, Peter Jancourtz, Ann Jenkins, Ted Johnson, Peter Kaufmann, Dallas Kirk, Bob Kucharavy, Randy Levine, Linda Lindgren, Al Mullin, Richard Seltzer, Geoff Shingles, Tom Siekman, and Ron Smart, who reviewed drafts and ideas, offering insight and advice.

The collective creativity of the team who produced this effort was extraordinary. For the writing, I would like to acknowledge the late Bob Hofmann, Bob Lindgren, Bob Lynch, and Patrick Pierce, who weaved together many people's words and provided the chapters. Patti Polisar and Patrick Murphy were careful and ruthless editors. Janice Moore and Laraine Armenti collaborated on the design, providing an elegant format for the words and pictures. Mark Sniffen handled print production, keeping us honest with our budget. Two students from WPI, Ken Spark and Aran Anderson, provided the glossary, a valuable source for readers. Digital Press provided editorial advice and publishing experience.

Through the efforts of many people who generously shared in this telling emerges a mosaic of hundreds of points of view. I would like to thank all concerned. By knowing the past, we gain an understanding of the present, and a basis for moving into the future.

— Jamie Parker Pearson
    April 1992

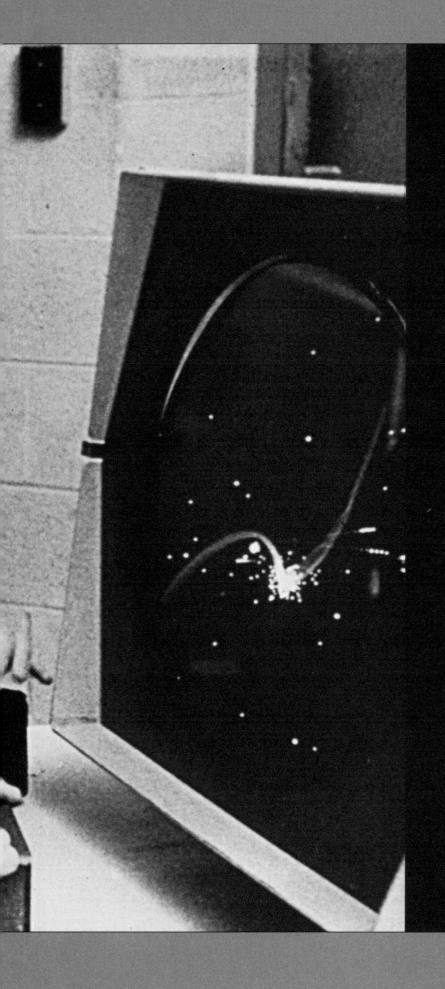

Part I

Digital's Beginnings

An icon of interactive computing: Spacewar!, developed in 1960 by Steve Russell, J.M. Graetz, and Wayne Wiitanen of MIT, and played on Digital's PDP-1.

Massachusetts Institute of Technology, Cambridge, Massachusetts

1

Foundations of Interactive Computing

It was 1950, the beginning of the transistor revolution. Only four years earlier the first electronic digital computer had been unveiled at the University of Pennsylvania. To calculate artillery-aiming tables for the U.S. Army, ENIAC, also known as "the electronic brain," manipulated decimal rather than binary numbers. The actual storing of programs was still a long way off.

Earlier, from British universities in Manchester and Cambridge came the Williams tube, which made random access memory practical, while from Bell Labs in New Jersey came the point-contact transistor that forever changed electronics and computer design.

The magnetic drum soon offered greater storage capacity than delay lines and Williams tubes, and the first short programs, called subroutines, were stored on punched paper tape on the EDSAC computer. By 1951, UNIVAC was used to predict U.S. presidential results, and the junction transistor replaced vacuum tubes and revolutionized electronics.

When Digital opened its doors, computers were a mystery to the general public—a steel-cased UNIVAC that dwarfed Walter Cronkite on the evening news. For years they remained a mystery to all but a corps of specialists who could operate them. Even scientists who spoke of approaching one directly were eyed with suspicion.

But the engineers who formed Digital were among those who saw it differently. If you could make these machines approachable, it would make the difference between a diatribe and a conversation.

Fortune magazine's report in the late 1950s that no money was to be made in computers suggested the word itself be avoided in Digital's first business plan. No mention was made of modules, a staple of electronics manufacturing and the building blocks of computers of the day. So Digital began with a plan it could back with confidence, to produce modules until the new venture turned a profit. At that moment, the new company would begin putting its proven commodity into the riskier business of manufacturing interactive computers.

In 1959, Digital hired a young hardware engineer named Ben Gurley to design the company's first computer. Three and a half months later, the prototype of Digital's first Program Data Processor, the PDP-1 system, was complete. "Kind of spectacular" is how Ed Fredkin—an engineering master in his own right who bought the first PDP-1—describes this achievement.

The PDP-1 reflected the MIT tradition, with system modules patterned directly after the circuits of Lincoln Laboratory's TX-0 and TX-2, two of the earliest transistorized computers.

Computer room construction

Specifications
Whirlwind

Operational
1950

Word Length
16 bits

Speed
16 microseconds, maximum

Primary Memory
2K word addressable core

Secondary Memory
Revolving drums, tapes

Instruction Set
32 instructions

Input/Output
I/O initiation and
completion testing by bits

Size
50′ × 50′ × 20′

Software
Assembly/machine language
Programmed primarily in OCTAL

Number Produced
1, originally at MIT's
Digital Computer Laboratory

Architecture
Fixed word machine

Technology
First generation
15,000 vacuum tubes

Power
150,000 watts

History
Begun in 1947,
completed in 1957

MIT and the Whirlwind Tradition

The Whirlwind project, initiated at MIT in 1944 to develop a simulator to help train naval flight crews, progressed far beyond its original goals. By 1953, the design team, led by Jay Forrester and Robert Everett, had built a high-speed digital computer to control an air defense system.

The Whirlwind computer occupied 2,500 square feet on the second floor of MIT's Barta Building. So great was this computer's appetite for electrical power that when it was turned on, the lights in Cambridge were said to have dimmed.

Whirlwind was the first large-scale, real-time control system. From early work tracking aircraft by digital computer, an experimental Cape Cod system linked a network of 16 radar sites. Each site could feed data to and interact simultaneously with the Whirlwind as the control element. The Whirlwind computer was one of the first practical applications of time-sharing and originated techniques that were incorporated into the SAGE (Semi-Automatic Ground Environment) air defense system.

Few on the Whirlwind project team could have guessed that their efforts would help transform the computer from a highly specialized scientific instrument to a tool as practical and popular as the typewriter.

The Barta Building at MIT

The computer room in 1952

Jay Forrester with magnetic core memory

Storing Information

For primary storage, some early computers relied on magnetic core memory. Each tiny doughnut-shaped core could store one bit, or unit, of information. Storing large amounts of information required thousands of cores, which took up considerable space in the system. To store 12,000 characters of information, for example, a system needed 96,000 cores: 8 for each character, or byte, of information.

The expense of production was not in the cores themselves but in the labor required to manufacture the complete memory. Cores were strung together on fine wire by hand and mounted on a frame or board. By 1974, core memory would be replaced by the semiconductor chip.

Whirlwind pioneered the use of electronic core memory. The first bank of core storage—with a capacity of 2,048 words—was wired-in in August of 1953. The two banks that were ultimately added gave Whirlwind a total of 6K words of memory.

The invention of core memory is credited to Jay Forrester. Faster and more reliable than other memory devices of the time—mercury delay lines, electrostatic tubes, and rotating magnetic drums—magnetic cores reduced access time on the Whirlwind from 25 microseconds (with tube storage) to 9 microseconds.

Norman Taylor (behind panel), Bob Everett, and J.A. O'Brien at the Whirlwind control matrix

TX-0 operator's console

Specifications

TX-0

Lincoln Test-Experimental
Computer Model 0

Operational
1957

Word Length
18 bits

Speed
83,000 additions/second
Programmed multiply and divide

Primary Memory
64K word magnetic core memory
Additional parity bit
6 microseconds read-rewrite time

Instruction Set
3 addressable instructions
1 programmable instruction

Input
250 lines/second photo reader;
manual Flexowriter and toggle switch

Output
10 characters/second Flexowriter;
CRT display

Size
200 square feet

Number Produced
1, originally installed at Lincoln Laboratory

Technology
3,500 Philco L-5122
surface-barrier transistors

Power
1,000 watts

History
An experimental digital computer
used to test advanced design techniques,
including very large core storage
and transistor circuitry

Whirlwind's Descendants

The TX-0 and the TX-2 computers were among the most advanced machines of their time. Developed at MIT's Lincoln Laboratory government-sponsored research center in Lexington, Massachusetts, by members of the Whirlwind team, the TX-0 was designed to verify the feasibility of building a 64K word core memory and to test a new type of transistor circuitry. Although the Philco SBT100 surface-barrier transistors were expensive at $80 each, they simplified transistor circuit design significantly.

The TX-0 was followed by the large-scale 36-bit TX-2 computer. The short word length, high-speed operation and interactive features of Whirlwind and both TX-0 computers greatly influenced early minicomputer design at Digital. When they joined Digital in the early 1960s, some of the engineers and programmers who had built these systems brought with them the lessons they learned.

TX-0 programmers with Gordon Bell (center)

Testing Memory

The Memory Test Computer, known as Ken Olsen's first computer, was designed to test Whirlwind's newly invented core memory.

I was given the job of building the computer just as soon as my thesis was done. It cost a million dollars. I remember being impressed at how much work it took to spend a million dollars. Now I'm impressed at how little effort it takes to spend a million dollars. My way of showing off was to build it in a room in a straight row of racks with a console in front of it, with enough room for the photographer to stand back and take pictures of it. We naively showed off by saying, "Look how easy it is." That's kind of the young academic approach. The first night it ran, my wife was out of town. We stayed late in the lab. Everybody else went home. I stayed there and listened to it work. We put a loudspeaker on every computer we built because you always wanted to be able to play music or do other things. I had the computer on the loudspeaker, and as long as the tone was constant I knew it was working. So I went in the ladies lounge and lay down on the sofa with the door open and fell asleep with my ear tuned to that sound, so I knew it went all night long without a glitch. That was a significant test.

— Ken Olsen

A Machine That Matched the Characteristics of a PC Today

When I was given the opportunity to work on a transistor computer, the idea was new and exciting. The rules were I could hire no one and have no space. I found all the loopholes. I somehow was able to get three or four people to work with me. We discovered that the hallway was not considered space, so we moved my office into the hall and put walls around it. We then traded that space for space in the basement which was less desirable but bigger. With that we were able to do our work. We asked for additional light, brightly colored walls, and a new floor. Then we set out to make a computer that would attract attention. Our experience with the Memory Test Computer told us that blah-looking computers never attract attention. So we set out to make as modern a design as we could. It had rakish lines, like race cars were supposed to have. We picked a color that was opposite the traditional black wrinkle finish from World War II. Brown and beige seemed like a dramatic change. It turned out to be the place where the laboratory brought visitors.

The cathode ray tube was automatically built into the computer. We used the light pen, which is the equivalent of today's mouse. We used Japanese model-railroad lamp bulbs, one for every flip flop. We joked that we probably confused the industry watchers there with that order! The circuitry in this computer was built around the Philco surface-barrier transistor, a magnificent piece of design. It was very expensive but very fast, very intolerant of power or spark or discharge.

The TX-0 was designed to be a demonstration of the reliability and the capability of transistor circuitry, and making a fast, inexpensive, low-powered computer. It really could do what a personal computer does today, limited only by the fact that the memory was small. You could draw pictures on the cathode ray tube, read your program in, take it home, play games—all the things you can do today.

— Ken Olsen
Smithsonian Interview
September 1988

General Doriot (left) with Ken Olsen

"Ken Olsen had a product that he could make the next day and that was important. But Ken also had a view of the future. He had a family of products in mind. Ken was taking a risk, but it was a thought-out risk, the kind of risk I favor. I was impressed Ken had the ability to sense the evolution of the market. He redeveloped or reinvented products in some cases, always following the market. Ken had the desire to do something useful, constructive, and imaginative."

— General Georges Doriot

"The Kind of Risk I Favor"

Georges Doriot (known as "General" since his tour of duty in the French army) headed one of the first venture capital firms in America, American Research and Development (AR&D), which helped launch 150 companies. In the course of 35 years on the Harvard Business School faculty, he taught his students as much about the value of ethics and integrity in business as about industrial management.

To Digital, he is best known as the man who, in 1957, loaned Digital President Ken Olsen $70,000 to launch a new company.

General Doriot often told a story about three men who were breaking stones. When asked what he was doing, one said he was breaking stones, the second said he was making a living. The third said he was building a cathedral. It was people like the third man, individuals with a dream, whose companies he prized.

The Manufacturing course General Doriot taught at Harvard was an inspiration to thousands of students who became successful business leaders. William McLean, Philip Caldwell, and Arnaud de Vitry, among them, were later to join Digital's Board of Directors.

AR&D advised on the selection of directors of the newly incorporated company. Seated left to right at an early board meeting are: Harry Hoagland, Jack Barnard, Jay Forrester, Bill Congleton, Harlan Anderson, Ken Olsen, Dorothy Rowe, Vernon Alden, Arnaud de Vitry, and Wayne Brobeck.

Digital's Board Members Pay Tribute

"Whatever a problem needed [General Doriot] would give day and night. He expected the same of his students. He brought the practical side of his life to the classroom, interpreted not just in terms of the individual company, but in how you live, how you work, how you serve your company. His was a commonsense message about the world, stressing many old-fashioned, simple virtues, such as frugality, willingness to stand up and be counted, courage and innovation."

— William McLean

"Sometimes you wonder what lessons you learned from your professors. It would be fair to say that the course we took was manufacturing. What we learned was philosophy."

— Philip Caldwell

"General Doriot felt it was important for [the wives] to understand that their husbands should work very, very hard, but never take themselves too seriously. Even if they were to become wealthy it should be a by-product of doing good work. One should never be proud of earning money, but of doing good work."

— Arnaud de Vitry

First product: laboratory module

Kenneth H. Olsen
Resume of Experience

I am 31 years old and have a B.S. and M.S. from MIT in electrical engineering. For 12 months I attended the U.S. Navy radar school and had somewhat less than a year's experience in the fleet. Before that I studied machine shop practice and worked in a tool shop.

. . . for seven years I have worked at MIT Lincoln Lab. My M.S. thesis resulted in the first demonstration of a magnetic core memory. The circuits and techniques developed during this thesis are now commonly used in most large digital computers.

For 13 months I was in residence at IBM as the MIT representative and the Air Force quality-control engineer during the manufacture of the first SAGE computer. Here I had the opportunity to observe the production and organizational techniques of a large well-run company.

. . . in 1955 I organized a group to develop and build computers using the then-new Philco surface-barrier transistors. In just over two years, we developed a complete set of circuits and packaging techniques with which we have completed one computer and have well under way a computer that for some time will be the world's most capable computer.

Ken Olsen (left) with Harlan Anderson

A Proposal to American Research and Development from Digital Computer Corporation

On May 27, 1957, the objective of Digital Computer Corporation was to manufacture and sell electronic test equipment and high-speed electronic digital computers. Emphasis was placed on developing products that could be general purpose and would have a wide variety of applications.

American Research and Development directors cautioned that the "exceedingly active" field of digital computing would see "substantial competition develop in the future . . . successful survival will depend upon outstanding creative technological competence, an aggressive sales effort, high-quality precision manufacturing, and adequate financial support." AR&D's grant of a quarter-million dollars backed their confidence in the formation of a "speculative and daring" undertaking.

As outlined in Ken Olsen's and Harlan Anderson's proposal, the plans for starting Digital Computer Corporation were divided into two phases. The primary goal of Phase I was to design, produce, and sell transistorized digital test equipment. The secondary goal was to design on paper the general-purpose computer that would be built in Phase II and to obtain military study contracts that would lead to procurement of this type of equipment. Phase II would be entered after the test-equipment business was operating at a profit, or a firm purchase order for a general-purpose computer had been obtained.

A PROPOSAL TO AMERICAN RESEARCH AND DEVELOPMENT CORPORATION 27 MAY 1957

ESTIMATED PROFIT AND LOSS STATEMENT AND BALANCE SHEET (PHASE I)

	Initial	1st quarter	2nd quarter	3rd quarter	4th quarter
Profit and Loss Statement					
Net Sales		0	40,000	65,000	80,000
Manufacturing Cost					
Materials		13,000XXX	12,000XXX	22,000XXX	30,000XXX
Labor		13,560XXX	18,000XXX	23,000XXX	26,000XXX
Overhead		7,040XXX	8,000XXX	10,000XXX	11,000XXX
Change in Inventory		13,000XXX	4,000XXX	5,000XXX	8,000XXX
		20,600	34,000	52,000	59,000
Gross Profit		−20,600	6,000	13,000	21,000
Tax		0	0	0	5,000
Net Profit		−20,600	6,000	13,000	16,000
Balance Sheet					
Assets					
Current					
Cash	91,200XXX	40,000XXX	40,000XXX	40,000XXX	40,000XXX
Inventory		13,000XXX	17,000XXX	22,000XXX	30,000XXX
Fixed					
Equipment		7,600XXX	9,600XXX	17,600XXX	25,600XXX
Total	91,200	60,600	66,600	79,600	95,700
Liabilities					
Net Worth					
Common Stock	91,200XXX	60,600XXX	66,600XXX	79,600XXX	91,200XXX
Earned Surplus					4,500XXX
Total	91,200	60,600	66,600	79,600	95,700

The same general circuits that would be used in the test-equipment line would be used in the computer. Therefore, the test-equipment business could be considered a stepping stone . . . the computer's capacity and speed would be in excess of computers available at the time, while the price (about $400,000) would be significantly less.

Testing laboratory modules

Harlan E. Anderson
Resume of Experience

I am 27 years old and was born and raised in the Midwest. I attended the University of Illinois from 1947 to 1952 receiving a B.S. in Engineering Physics and an M.S. in Physics. In June 1952, I joined the staff of the Digital Computer Laboratory of MIT and soon thereafter joined the Lincoln Laboratory staff.

My initial work was concerned with the logical design of a high-speed electronic digital computer used to test the new magnetic core memory. Next, circuit development work associated with a high-speed electronic switch for use with magnetic drums was undertaken . . . then I became a member of the Lincoln Laboratory systems office, which was responsible for specifications for the IBM production of the SAGE computer. I assumed administrative responsibilities for eight engineers, most of whom were older than myself.

During the last year and a half I have been active in the field of systems planning for new systems to be associated with the SAGE system. This work has broadened my contact with the Air Force at many levels and has brought me into close working contact with such organizations as RAND Corporation and Boeing.

Photographs courtesy Maynard Historical Society

"One day [around 1960] we walked out to the end of Building 12, and we went up a little ramp, and there was a kind of wire-screen fence. We pressed our noses against the fence, and Dick [Best] said, 'We might expand into this space.' That was a new idea to me—this company might grow! After a while I got used to the idea. . . ."

— **Russ Doane**
Joined Digital 1960

Getting Started: New Quarters in an Old Mill

In 1957, with seven years of experience on engineering projects at MIT's Lincoln Laboratory in Lexington, Massachusetts, and a year as MIT representative and Air Force quality-control engineer in residence at IBM, Ken Olsen started a company in nearby Maynard with engineering colleague Harlan Anderson. The new company, Digital Equipment Corporation, took over 8,680 square feet of leased space in a nineteenth-century mill that once produced blankets and uniforms for soldiers who fought in the Civil War.

The spacious, idiosyncratic Mill was a home that suited a growing engineering company. The space could be renovated for a fraction of the cost of constructing new facilities, and the challenge of negotiating the byways of connecting floors and buildings still satisfies the "Mill rats," engineers who work heartily to solve any problem that whets their curiosity.

In 1974, Digital took exclusive ownership and occupancy of the sprawling 19-building complex.

"We had no problems on weekends, we knew exactly what we were going to do. We were going to the plant to clean. Everybody in the family. Our kids looked forward to it because the watchman would give them a nickel.

They would clean the coffee cups, I would clean the bathrooms, Ken would clean the work area. It was regular physical work that we did for the first three years."

— Aulikki Olsen

Space for Rent

On July 9, 1957, two young men came into my office: Ken Olsen and Harlan Anderson. We were about 90 percent occupied. They thought the second floor of Building 12 would suit their purposes. On August 20, they returned, agreeing to take the floor consisting of 8,680 square feet at a monthly rental of $300. Before I could prepare the lease, there would be a delay until their corporate name was approved by the State House in Boston. The three-year lease was signed on August 27, 1957.

Digital was the first company to come in that painted their own area. I remember hearing Howard Prescott, a local paint manufacturer, recall that Digital had called him for advice on paint. Howard doubted what they wanted could be hand painted, but Ken, his brother Stan, and Harlan worked all weekend. On the following Monday, Ken called to order some paint. Howard called me to inquire about their credit. I told him we were going with them, so he did, too.

For the next 17 years, the relationship between Maynard Industries and Digital was as compatible as two businesses could be. We had mutual respect for one another; honesty and fair play took precedence over everything else. Cooperation was a requirement when occupying buildings that, by virtue of their age, carried with them complexity and quirkiness. I recall Ken's assistance when a main water pipe burst, Stan's offer to help when a boiler tube let go, hurricanes causing window panes to burst, snow on desks in the morning after a storm!

In June of 1974, after occupying more and more buildings of the Mill as the company steadily grew, Digital purchased the complex for $2.25 million in stock. No cash was involved. And I, after having watched and worked with Digital during that time, accepted an offer to join them to manage new facilities—none with the challenge of the Mill.

— Irving Burg
Property Manager of the Mill

Digital system modules

"We initially thought we were going to use circuits we had developed at MIT, but just as we started, we had to make a difficult business decision because a new transistor had just come out. We decided to go with the new transistor, design all new circuitry, start from scratch. It was a much better one, but a terrible gamble.

"They cost $12.50 each and we bought a thousand of them. So, out of $70,000, $12,500 went into one little box you could hold in your hand.

"Before we used any of them, the price went down to around $8 . . . we had a $4,000 inventory loss before we did anything.

"By planning everything and doing it carefully, we were able to design and build modules that sold well. For a while we had a monopoly. Not much of a market, but a monopoly."

— Ken Olsen

1982 Address to the Newcomen Society, founded in 1923 to recognize achievement and prosperity attained under the free-enterprise system

Nothing Like It in the Market

In 1957, Digital Equipment Corporation consisted of three men, $70,000 in capital, 8,680 square feet of rented space in a woolen mill in Maynard, Massachusetts, and a single product—modules.

Because *Fortune* magazine had reported that no one was making any money on computers, General Doriot, of American Research and Development, recommended avoiding the word *computer* in Digital's first business proposal. To honor his counsel, the first Digital products were called "modules," the building blocks of computers.

Making Modules

The first Digital Laboratory modules were intended to sit on an engineer's workbench or be mounted in a scientist's equipment rack. To simplify the construction of logic systems, the modules were connected by simple cords with banana plugs.

Digital Laboratory modules were supplemented by the Digital system modules, which later were incorporated in the PDP-1 computer. Identical in circuitry, signal levels, and speed range, the system modules had a higher packing density and fixed backplane wiring. Many different types of system modules were developed and used for computers, memory testers, and other complex systems of logic.

Dick Best

Modules Timeline

1957   100 series Lab Modules (5 MHz)

1959   1000 series System Modules (500 kHz)

1960   3000 and 5000 series Lab Modules (10 MHz)

1961   4000 series System Modules (500 kHz–1 MHz)
        6000 series System Modules (10 MHz)

1963   8000 series Modules (30 MHz)

1964   Blue Flip Chip Modules (10 MHz)

1965   Red Flip Chip Modules (1 MHz)

1967   K series Industrial (100 kHz)

1969   M series modules for computers using small,
        medium, and large integrated circuits

1970   Register Transfer Modules (RTM)

1973   MPS (8008, microprocessor-based)

By 1964, while the cost of semiconductors decreased, system module mounting hardware and wiring were still expensive. To offset the expense, Digital engineers developed a new type of module. The flip chip—a printed circuit card with a color-coded plastic handle—was the first module to facilitate automating the wiring of the module mounting blocks using automatic Gardner-Denver wire-wrap equipment. Flip chip modules were also the first Digital products to incorporate printed integrated circuits made at the Maynard Mill.

Ted Johnson

"The first products were modules enclosed in an extruded aluminum wave guide. They were indeed rugged. The circuits were negative logic built with surface-barrier germanium transistors, which could run at 5 megahertz. There was nothing in the market like that then. The transistors were the most expensive item, so we figured out the cost of anything by counting the number of transistors on the boards."

— Dick Best
Joined Digital 1959

Specifications

PDP-1

Word Length
18 bits

Speed
5-microsecond
cycle time

Primary Memory
4K word core

Instruction Set
Memory address instruction
Operate class, I/O class

Input/Output
Typewriter, paper tape
Cathode ray tube
Options: Light pen, magnetic tape,
ultrahigh-precision scope

Size
4 cabinets: 8′ × 2⅓′ × 6′

Software
Diagnostics, assembler, debugger,
Editor, conversion routines
for punching tapes

Number Produced
50

Price
$120,000

Digital system module

Nothing as Affordable at the Time

Its short word length and high speed suited the PDP-1 to laboratory and scientific control applications that required its computation ability and real-time control. Lawrence Livermore Laboratory first used the PDP-1 for peripheral support processing for their large scientific calculators and for graphics input and output. Atomic Energy of Canada used a PDP-1 for pulse-height analysis and Van de Graaff generator experiment control, and International Telephone and Telegraph used PDP-1 computers in message-switching systems.

Digital brought the prototype PDP-1 to demonstrate at the Joint Computer Conference in Boston in December of 1959.

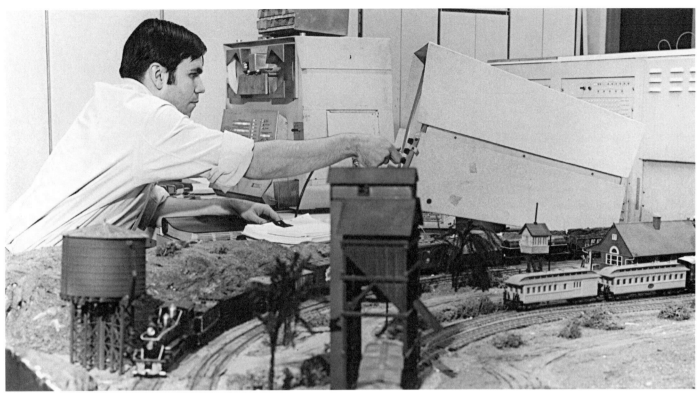

PDP-1 in use at Tech Model Railroad Club, MIT

"We had a dream for interactive computing. Normal computing was considered big, expensive, awesome, beyond ordinary people. Interactive computing was exciting and fun, and people could interact directly with the computer. We had demonstrated the usefulness of this at MIT. It was our dream to show the world what it could do."

— Ken Olsen

1960 *Corporate Profile*

Employees	Revenues	Location	Highlights
117	$1.3 million	The Mill Maynard, Massachusetts	Introduction of the PDP-1, Digital's first computer

PDP-1 production model

"Digital had brought the prototype PDP-1 to demonstrate at the 1959 Joint Computer Conference in Boston. The whole show was buzzing about this fledgling company and its little machine which cost less than $150,000. Nothing was that affordable at the time. Bolt Beranek and Newman recognized the importance of the machine and bought the prototype right off the floor."

— Bert Singer

Consistent from the First

The 18-bit PDP-1 and the PDP-4, PDP-7, PDP-9, and PDP-15 computers that followed were all designed with the common goals of interactivity, low cost, simplicity, and reliability. And with each new computer came more software programs and peripheral hardware options to simplify work in nuclear physics, chemical instrumentation, biomedicine, process and industrial control, and data communications.

Ken Olsen unveiling PDP-1 at BBN

The Beginnings of Timesharing

The PDP-1 sale to Bolt Beranek and Newman (BBN) was one of the events that led to the development of sharing computing time. A number of computer scientists at MIT and BBN believed interactive access to computers was the only way to make real progress based on accurate information. The only way to make this interactive access economically viable was for users to share the computer simultaneously. The BBN timesharing system began operation in September of 1962.

18-Bit Family Timeline

1960 PDP-1, Digital's first 18-bit computer

1963 PDP-4

1964 PDP-7, uses flip chip modules; used by Ritchie and Thompson to develop UNIX

1966 PDP-9, program compatible with PDP-7

1969 PDP-15 replaces PDP-9

1972 MUMPS-15 (Massachusetts General Hospital Utility Microprogramming System), PDP-15-based timesharing system designed to handle medical records, still in use

1979 PDP-1 with working Spacewar! game installed at The Computer Museum, Boston

1988 A PDP-1 system (serial no. 44) is saved from a barn in Wichita, Kansas, and donated to the Digital Historical Collection

"The first systems we made were Memory Test Systems, to check the core stacks that were the memories used at the time. We used that technology to build memories for the PDP-1, our first computer. Ken and I jointly patented many of the circuits that were involved there."

— Dick Best

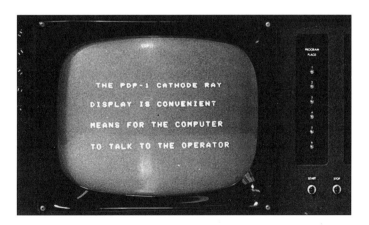

Archeological Find

In rescuing some ancient manuscripts from the trash, I was reminded of having heard that the DECUS symbol is based on a front view of the old "TYPE 30" point-scope (note the object labeled A7 on the diagram). There are pages in the saved document dated as early as 28 November 1961, and there are references to the PDP-1.

In the old days we spent many hours staring at this contraption, into what appeared to be a surplus radar scope dueling across the void of space with simulations of heavily armed spaceships. We were utterly amazed and enthralled and we wondered whether the general public would ever see such an expensive toy, much less own one.

Little did we know.

Sincerely,
James A. Mahaffey, Ph.D.

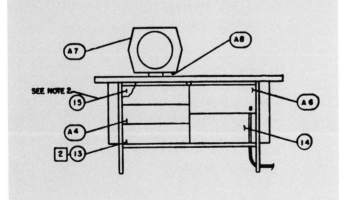

DECUS collectibles

DECUS: Sharing Information About a New Machine

Soon after Digital's first computer was introduced, a group of PDP-1 users met in Lexington, Massachusetts, with the idea of starting a program library. Since 1961, DECUS (the Digital Equipment Computer Users Society) has grown to be the largest international society of computer users. Among the benefits of membership is the open exchange of information between user and manufacturer.

The impetus for DECUS was the need to share information and computer programs for the PDP-1. Because it had been typically used in dedicated applications, users had written their own programs. Most of the early DECUS members were programmers from MIT, Bolt Beranek and Newman, and other institutions with access to the PDP-1. Software they developed for the PDP-1 included a microassembler, a linking loader, and an interactive debugging program (DDT). By pooling resources with Digital, the DECUS program library has become a thriving institution. Today, DECUS holds semi-annual symposia, issues regular publications, and assembles special users' groups for a membership that exceeds 100,000, with activities and offices in 60 locations around the world.

Symposium attendees

"The Thin-Skinned Computer"

Like its ancestors at MIT, the PDP-1 brought computing out of the computer room and into the hands of the user. From an early edition of *DECUSCOPE*, the publication of the Digital Equipment Computer Users Society, comes this excerpt from the minutes of a DECUS meeting:

> [DECUS members] had much praise for the "thin-skinned" PDP-1 and its versatile "approachability" in terms of diverse and amenable software. Immediate feedback to the user was the advantage. The user could compare and rephrase his questions and modify his reasoning paths immediately at the console. This kind of man-machine interaction is not always possible with the "thick-skinned" computer installations frequently encased in unbreakable glass. The facility of learning "right now" at the console seemed better to him than waiting a day or two to learn the results. . . .

"To understand what motivated the programmers of the early 1960s, put yourself in their place: they were confronted with a computer that could and would do useful things but it took programmers to create the programs. Programming was a very tedious business, usually involving the creation of paper tapes. Individuals who could program were relatively few. They could simply not create all the programs that a given computer needed. It was a natural step to look for a mechanism to obtain programs that were already written and useful."

— **C.W. Goldsmith**
U.S. Chapter President DECUS, 1983–87

The console room in 1950, Jay Forrester and Bob Everett, standing

2

A Catalyst for Invention

**Working at MIT's
Digital Computer Lab**

*Edited by
Jamie Parker Pearson*

In 1989, two pioneers of the computer industry were awarded the National Medal of Technology, the United States' highest honor in technology. Although recognized for their work on MIT's Whirlwind computer project of the 1950s, Robert R. Everett and Jay W. Forrester in decades since have continued to spur innovation through technical competence and effective management.

Developed under contract to the Navy, Whirlwind began in 1944 as an idea for a universal flight trainer and aircraft simulator. It quickly became much more: the first general-purpose, high-speed, real-time parallel synchronous electronic digital computer. When first conceived, Whirlwind seemed almost unbelievable—a machine so fast and reliable, it could monitor and control physical processes, direct aircraft, and handle a vast range of general control tasks. The mini- and microcomputers that are its direct descendants have made such tasks commonplace.

Forrester, then director of MIT's Digital Computer Laboratory, and Everett, his associate director, worked on a research project that developed much of the fundamental technology of the first generation of computers, including Forrester's invention of the random-access, coincident-current, magnetic core storage memory and Everett's invention of a light-gun photocell system, the first interactive computer device.

Whirlwind pioneered the successful use of synchronous parallel logic design, significantly increasing the machine's speed, and techniques used to ensure the machine's reliability by providing self-checking capabilities. Another interactive feature—unknown to its peers of the decade—was the cathode ray tube it used to display information. In addition to real-time control, Whirlwind pioneered the concept of computer simulation of the real world, now commonplace. Techniques developed during Whirlwind have since contributed to such fields as numerically controlled tools, computer-aided manufacturing and design, and timesharing.

Whirlwind was operational by 1950, and Forrester and Everett went on to tackle its successor, a computer the Air Force would use for its new SAGE (Semi-Automatic Ground Environment) air defense system, and the Federal Aviation Administration would use for the nation's first air-traffic control system.

Two of the modern giants of the computer industry benefited from Whirlwind. IBM got the contract for the first 18 SAGE computers and incorporated Whirlwind innovations into its newly launched computer line. The Whirlwind legacy also formed the basis of Digital Equipment Corporation's emerging computing and design philosophy. In Ken Olsen's words, "Digital's computers and culture owe a great deal to MIT."

Passion for Truth

"Looking back at my days at MIT, I see something that was very important to our company. Science education then was left over from the 1930s, when there was a different attitude in science: scientists did everything themselves. They had this absolutely religious passion for truth and for accuracy, and they deplored exaggeration or misleading data. Today, science is some-what pragmatic: the need is to get results. But that old tradition has had a great influence on us at Digital."

— Ken Olsen

A Dialogue Between Jay Forrester and Bob Everett

In the dialogue that follows, Jay W. Forrester, Germeshausen professor emeritus, Massachusetts Institute of Technology, and Robert R. Everett, trustee, former president and chief executive officer, The MITRE Corporation, review their association as colleagues at MIT's Digital Computer Laboratory during the development of the Whirlwind computer project.

Recognized as gifted managers, Forrester's and Everett's styles and talents complemented each other. In addition to his technical contributions, Forrester was responsible for the administration of the project, selling it to sponsors at MIT and the federal government. Through careful and convincing research, he managed to keep funding alive for the risky and largely unproven project during a period of tight budgets. Everett created the basic system design for Whirlwind, made numerous technical contributions, and managed to instruct and guide a highly talented team for more than 10 years.

Jay Forrester: When we came out of World War II and began work on digital computers, the general atmosphere of wartime research still prevailed. The main objective was to get the job done, and get it done quickly. That was before the existence of barriers that gradually came into being when, in due course, enough people began to abuse the system. Although extremely inefficient, there are now more and more restraints of all kinds. I just read that 25 percent of all medical costs now go into paperwork. There was very little of that at MIT in the years following the war. When I first began to do wartime research, around 1940, MIT didn't have a purchasing department that dealt with what we wanted. It did not have a security or guard system. When I wanted to buy something, I would call up a supplier and order it, then take an MIT purchase order out of my desk and sign it and mail it to them. Because classified work required guards, and we didn't have guards, I got a Cambridge Police badge and pistol permit, which I still have somewhere.

Bob Everett: The work was new. In general, if you look at new organizations, they start out small, without large numbers, restraints, and restrictions and auditors. As time goes on, people put restraints and reviews in, partly as a reaction to, as Jay said, somebody doing something wrong. Instead of finding it and getting rid of the culprits, people put in a process to prevent the abuses from happening again. There are lots of people who impose such controls for a living. Organizations, as they age and grow, build up bureaucracies, which are difficult to remove after they've happened. You almost have to start over. I think the advantage we had is that we were able to essentially start over.

JF: If you're working at the front edge of an entirely new field, as we were in digital computers, there are not many people who presume to interfere because they don't see themselves as having the competence.

BE: There was a lot of interest, in both the United States and Great Britain, in electronic digital computers and a number of groups engaged in building computers. This came about for several reasons. There were some good ideas, like stored programs, which came out of the Moore School, von

Neumann, Eckert and Mauchly. There was the availability of technology and pulse circuits and storage devices, which came out of the war, that were developed for radar use. There were groups of capable people who were experienced in building things during the war, were excited about that, and wanted to continue to do so. Not least important, there were mechanisms and funds in place for supporting such work. There was a great opportunity, resources and technology, and the momentum left over from the war, making it possible for all these groups to work on digital computers. Today, one would be forced to write performance requirements and convince others they could be done. It would be very difficult to do that kind of innovating today. Things were different in those days, much more promising, as far as new development efforts were concerned.

JF: I have sometimes said that it was easier to design a North American air defense system in the late '40s and early '50s—in spite of the lack of any available technology—than it would be to do it today. Today, there would be 10 layers of people, all of whom would think they could do it as well or better.

BE: That's absolutely right. The atmosphere at the MIT Division of Sponsored Research, which did contract work with the government and outside agencies, encouraged bad news to flow uphill. There was the presumption that things were all right, and you didn't need to push good news uphill. With bad news flowing uphill, you knew there would be people to help out when there was a problem. The layers through Gordon S. Brown up to Nat Sage, Sr., the director of the Division of Sponsored Research, consisted of people who were there to help solve problems. This is very different from an organization in which, if there is a glimpse of bad news, pressures and criticisms, rather than help and assistance, come down from above.

JF: There were big differences among individual laboratories at MIT, and even within the Electrical Engineering department. There were laboratories which sent out research assistants who were not really very effective in the world. And there were ones like Gordon Brown's Servomechanisms Laboratory, which developed feedback control systems for military equipment during the war, where a very high percentage came out to have major roles in their later activities. Gordon Brown was my mentor and very largely responsible for my career, even up to the present moment. His laboratory was very effective in developing people's leadership and initiative. It was turbulent and demanding.

The postwar MIT environment had been shaped by the research laboratories of World War II. These had been freewheeling operations organized around a vision of what was to be done. They had considerable freedom to carry out that vision. More than in other institutions, and more than at MIT now, [MIT] was a free enterprise society in which people could do about anything they wanted as long as it was honorable and they could raise the money for it.

BE: "Honorable," meaning straightforward. They told you what they thought, you knew what they were about. You could argue with them,

An Innovation in Computer Memory

In the early years of Project Whirlwind, Jay Forrester recognized the limitations of the computer memory systems then available. Electrostatic storage tubes, magnetic drums, tapes, and disks lacked the speed and reliability required for the project. With Forrester's invention of random-access coincident-current core memory, information could be extracted immediately rather than searched for sequentially on tapes or disks.

Working with graduate student Bill Papian, Forrester's invention led to an array of ferrite magnetic materials for storing information. In his thesis, entitled "A Coincident-Current Magnetic Memory Unit" (1950), Papian described magnetic core memories, honeycombs of minute magnetic cores strung on wires, through which storage information was read to electronic circuits in the computer. This invention provided the speed and reliability the project required.

The first bank of core memory was installed in the Whirlwind on August 8, 1953. Computing speed doubled, and useful operating time increased to more than 90 percent. The same year, Raytheon, Remington Rand, and RCA shifted commercial machine storage emphasis to magnetic core storage, followed a year later by IBM. Although initially unappreciated except by the engineers, scientists, and researchers working on this new technology, its impact on the history of computing would be great.

Inventing

"... Jay took a bunch of stuff and went off in a corner of the lab by himself. Nobody knew what he was doing, and he showed no inclination to tell us. All we knew was that for about five or six months, he was spending a lot of time by himself working on something. The first inkling I got was when he came out of retirement and put Bill Papian to work on his little metallic and ceramic doughnuts. That was in the fall and winter of 1949–50."

— MIT Graduate Student

disagree, but you trusted them. I think that's the foundation of the word *honor* in my opinion. What do you say, Jay?

JF: Probably, it also carried the connotation of being useful, in the public interest, and within MIT, something that was innovative and not routine.

Working in that environment was very freewheeling. There was a multiplicity of projects. Gordon Brown himself was a project leader on a number of projects. You had to argue, stand up to the laboratory director to get resources for your projects in competition with his projects. He had great respect for people who would stand up, and he became helpful in proportion to your degree of independence. He encouraged people in their own individual projects without trying to either dominate those projects or closely monitor or direct them.

BE: Jay offered me a job. He was scraping the bottom of the barrel! It was the summer of '42. I graduated from Duke and came to MIT for graduate school. The war was on, and it was pretty clear either I went to work in the labs or I went to work in the Army.

JF: In hiring for the lab, we placed a high premium on initiative and courage. Also, open communication. We had biweekly reports where people regularly reported on what they'd been doing and shared information with other people. People moved around offices and sat in different places so they'd get a sense of what was going on in other areas.

There was always an ample number of problems and difficulties to discuss. Another characteristic of the organization was that, in addition to the idea of bad news flowing uphill, there was no necessity for information to go through channels. The director of the Division of Sponsored Research might drop in and talk to people that worked for me. Gordon Brown would talk to them. I would come in at the lab-bench level and look at what people were doing, talk to them about it, even though they worked for someone else.

BE: There were not the barriers to communication that one sees in a lot of organizations. Everyone had his task and knew where it fit into the final objective. If you did your work, and delivered, you were an honored member of the organization. You got plenty to do, you got invited to the director's Friday afternoon teas. You got told what was going on. There was never any question of cozying up to the boss. Nobody ever cozied up to Jay; it wouldn't have done him any good, anyway.

Ken Olsen, who was part of the team, speaks about the confidence that people in those days had; he says it's confidence that the management would look after them. I don't think so. I think it was that people had confidence in themselves. They had confidence that management was looking out for the outfit and that if they did their job they would be treated well.

JF: There was a core team: Bob and I and several others—Bob Wieser and Steve Dodd, for example—who had gone through several projects from basic research to end use in the field before we came to the big job on the SAGE air defense system. It was a team that knew what was likely to follow every step they were engaged in. Furthermore, they were expected to go through all the steps and be there at the end. This makes a very great difference to how you do business. If you are the recipient of what you're doing rather than just passing it off to someone else, it gives you a very different feeling for responsibility. Do it right, because if you don't, you will have to fix it later rather than turn it over to somebody else. This makes a tremendous difference in organizations. As organizations grow, there is an unnecessary tendency to subdivide into functional activities. There are people in research, design, development, tooling, production, and sales. They never come together. Every step is done blaming the people in the prior step and creating problems for the people in the next step. There's no one who has a sense of accomplishment when you're through. If it goes well, there's no identifiable hero; if it goes badly, there is no one who learns the lesson. Everyone says, "I wasn't involved." In fact, there was no one who was involved in all of it. So there's not much learning out of mistakes in many organizations. By contrast, I think we had an organization that had gone through that whole cycle as a team, and knew what it was like at the other end.

BE: It was very important that it was a team of people who had worked with each other for a long time, and understood each other's strengths and weaknesses, so that you automatically gave the right jobs to the right people, and you knew where to go to get help. It wasn't a fixed organization. It was a team. You expected the job to change. The job flowed by, and the team configured itself to do whatever had to be done at that time. That's a very different way of looking at it than most bureaucracies, where, as Jay says, the people own some particular job and they own some particular group, and nobody owns the thing as a whole except maybe somebody so far up that he hasn't got any grasp on what's going on at the bottom.

JF: The kind of team approach we had can still be effective in today's very different environment. I have been a proponent of a decentralized entrepreneurial form of organization for a long time. I wrote a paper in the mid-'60s called "A New Corporate Design" as part of my activity on the board of Digital Equipment. The paper was revised each year for two or three years as I discussed the ideas with the board. It eventually was published. [Forrester, *Collected Papers,* Productivity Press, Cambridge, MA.] Essentially, it's about bringing inside the corporation the legal structure of the outside world. You start by erasing the idea of the superior/subordinate relationship. A lot of people say that can't work. But there is no superior/subordinate relationship between your dentist and General Motors. There is no superior/subordinate relationship between any of the legal entities in the economy, so why should there be inside a subdivision of the economy? You can carry that same set of concepts inside in principle, and I think you can in practice. One sees occasional experiments in that direction. They can be quite dramatic, but it is hard to maintain that philosophy when you have so many people that have grown up in bureaucratic structures. One sees executives of major corporations giving impassioned speeches about entrepreneurship, and the free enterprise system, while they run some of the biggest socialist bureaucracies in the world. Another way of putting it is that every person wants to have authority decentralized down to his level, and centralized up to his level.

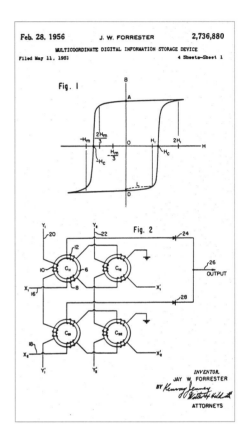

BE: That's clear. Let's make the proper distinction, though, between separable parts in the organization. Anybody who worked for Jay understood about somebody being the boss. The boss, the leader of Jay's organization, was Jay. This meant, among other things, that there was a clear vision of where we were going and what we were trying to do. The rest of the organization had to fit into that. The one thing a leader has to have is followers. If you're going to make an automobile, you can't tell George to build any kind of engine he wants. You can't build computers that way, either, and you can't build air defense systems that way. If you break it up in too many pieces and these pieces are in fact intertwined, then you run the risk that the conception as a whole will not come true.

JF: Except that if you do break it up, it tends to discipline the specifications of what you want from the different parts. Very often organizations begin to work on all the pieces of something before anybody has decided what the something is to be, or how the pieces are to go together.

BE: I absolutely agree with that. But it's the job of the person at the top to define what it is you're trying to do, and see that the goals are properly set up, and that people know what they're supposed to do. Pick the people. If that's done properly, then the thing will run. From then on, you just keep an eye on it and help each of them. It's critical to have a team of people who understand each other, and have been through things together. Then you can break it up, because the people know what they're doing, and they know what the problems are, and they see that the interfaces are properly defined. If you do not have a team, but just have a scattered group of people that you've brought in or that just appeared, and ask them to do the same thing, they wouldn't understand or trust each other. You're running the danger of getting into very serious troubles before you find out about it. But this is a real conflict, a need to make sure that you get the things that you need for the large part, and at the same time what you need for the pieces.

JF: Part of that freedom to get the job done is to run an organization that has a certain amount of slack in it—where there is money and space that isn't overcommitted. One can then allocate resources to match responsibility. The Digital Computer Laboratory provided support for what people were expected to do. People weren't in the position of feeling that they'd been given responsibility, but without the authority and resources to do it. That makes a very big difference. People are essentially frustrated by being given so-called freedom when they aren't given anything to exercise that freedom with. Then, in fact, they haven't been given freedom.

BE: That's right. It's very important to have slack. Lack of slack is one of the troubles big organizations get into. They end up with each group having too little money and too much commitment. It's a normal result of the way that jobs and money are divvied up. If somebody is smart and shrewd enough to squirrel off some money, people will come and take it away from him. "You are not supposed to have any extra money. You're undertaking this program and you don't know how to do it? You don't know what it's going to cost? You're spending the taxpayer's money, risking the lives of our fighting men, and you don't know what you're doing?!" Of course, the answer is "Yeah, I don't know what I'm doing." Nobody knows what he is doing when he's on the leading edge. Lack of slack results in cost overruns, because it costs more to build something if you've got less than the money you need, than if you had the money you needed at the beginning. You lack the resources to protect yourself, to put in backups, to try different things. You're forced to gamble that everything will be all right. It's never all right! When something turns wrong, you've got a big problem because there is no room to maneuver. It takes longer and it costs more money to have everything carefully planned and every scrap of surplus money taken out. That's the worst possible way of doing business. It's done as a normal thing in the Department of Defense, where most people don't understand that it's the most expensive way to get results.

JF: Another reason that it costs more and takes longer when there are not surplus resources is that a larger and larger percentage of time goes into fighting about the resources rather than doing the job.

Go back to the idea of teams. I think teams are tremendously important, but all the folklore is against the idea. Teams are called cliques. They're looked upon as bad. One reason effective teams are looked upon as bad is that a real team has great power.

One can have personal independence and entrepreneurship even within the goal of a clearly defined and articulated program. Independent action results from a match between responsibility, authority, and the specification of the task. Clear specification implies thought about what the whole project is to be before allocating parts. A lot of wasteful programs start before those decisions have been made. You can't create balanced authority, resources, and specifications without having given a lot of thought to the overall goal. With enough thought to goals and interfaces, one can challenge people. Then, what they accomplish is primarily a reflection of their ability, and not a reflection of how they have been impeded by other people. I think people do respond to a fair and challenging match of responsibility, authority, and resources. They like to work in such a setting.

BE: It's more than just thinking, in many cases. You have to do a lot of work and run a lot of experiments and try a lot of things, not only to find out what are the desirable characteristics of what you're doing and what kinds of fundamental materials and technologies, but also to determine the character of the people and the organization you've got doing these things. If you want a team, it's fundamental that the people really understand each other. You know how, in football, when they bring in the stars from all the teams to play together? It turns out that it's not as good as one of the teams, because there wasn't the time to really build understanding. "Team" implies that people understand each other.

JF: In this kind of frontier research and development, it probably takes 10 years to create such a team. It's not something that you do in six months or a year. One must see the mistakes and the shortcomings and the successes of the members and arrive at a point where the abilities of each person are shared. The person with a shortcoming must realize he has a shortcoming, other people know it, and everyone knows that the objective is to avoid having individual weaknesses become important. In other words, use each person's strength. We had individuals who were very good in outside political contacts, but not particularly good at developing people. We had individuals who were very good at developing people that we tended to keep away from the external world. If you can accentuate the strengths and essentially neutralize the weaknesses, you get a powerful organization. By contrast, there are organizations that accentuate the weaknesses, and neutralize the strengths—that leads to failures and disasters.

An organization is a tremendously powerful filtering process. It attracts the people that fit. Those that do come in get conditioned to fit. If they won't be conditioned, the organization repels them. The character of an organization and its internal attitudes become strongly self-perpetuating. An authoritarian organization, where the decisions are made at the top, results in the kind of atmosphere seen in many corporations, where people feel helpless.

BE: Raised as an engineer, like Jay, I believe that efficiency and economy and good work are important, and who gets what is not important. Others believe the other way around: who gets what is important; efficiency and economy are not important.

We had a very highly select team of people who had spent the war as radar officers, grown up in the process, and gone back to school on the GI Bill. They were really given an opportunity. They weren't sent off to solder for two years, and then sent off to do something else. There was so much to do that anybody who demonstrated some ability and initiative and willingness to work rapidly got all that he could possibly do. When we started working on the computer, there wasn't all this marvelous test equipment that people have nowadays. We had to do everything ourselves. You might think that's a drawback. If you had to design a modern computer with the tools we had, you couldn't do it. But to build the first computer was an eminently doable thing, partly because we could design something that we could build. We could build the thing that we've designed. This combination of marvelous raw materials, a really open environment, a wonderful job and the discipline to carry it out . . . that's a very unusual set of circumstances.

JF: There are many kinds of discipline. There's the kind of just looking over someone's shoulder and telling him every step to take. That's a very suppressive kind of discipline. The ideal kind of discipline exists where there is a clear goal. If the person succeeds in meeting the goal, there is an important, lasting consequence and contribution from it. It's not sufficient to meet a goal and then find it is unused or ineffective or doesn't fit with other people's plans. Such futile activity doesn't hold people's loyalty through many such cycles.

BE: That's true. You have to set that goal. You have to reach an agreement on what you're trying to do. I think the discipline at the lab was a two-way discipline. Once people committed themselves to do things, they had to do those things. They couldn't change their minds over a weekend. That wasn't allowed. The discipline worked down as well as up. If you told a guy to build a part of the computer, and if he built it right and it wasn't used, you had a tough time explaining to him why. It works both ways. It's like a contract.

But that contract has to be signed. Just having a contract and insisting that people live up to it doesn't work if the contract isn't signed. It has to be deliverable in the sense that the technology is at least possible, and it has to be deliverable in the sense that the people who are doing it are capable of doing it and they have adequate resources to do it. There also have to be mechanisms for changes, facing up to unforeseen difficulties when they happen. If you have a good, sound contract, that's good.

JF: Another characteristic of the laboratory was not feeling that we had to save face by sticking with our prior plans and commitments, because those plans and commitments did change many times. Successful research and development management often depends on knowing when to cut your losses and give up an approach that does not live up to early expectation. We were willing to say we were wrong, and here is what we will do instead. A lot of organizations won't admit to making a mistake, so they keep going down the road that is the mistake. A good example of plans that changed arose in the early design goal of the Whirlwind project. It specified an analog computer for an aircraft analyzer. It turned out to be a digital computer for a combat information center. There wasn't really anything that survived from the first plan.

BE: In the days when computing was such new territory, it was important to keep your plans flexible. It still is, but then it was even more so.

JF: We frequently ran across opposition to new ideas, which I would call part of the pioneering atmosphere. Since the days of Whirlwind, say from 1946 to 1956, there have been steady improvements in the computer but they've been fairly straightforward. Computers since that time have been a production process, production of incremental improvements. By 1956 the idea of a general-purpose, internally programmed computer was well established. After that, I expect the private desktop computer may be the thing that's going to have the greatest impact. It's pretty much essential to what we're now doing. It brings computers to the point where large numbers of people can use them. That may be the biggest break. Solid-state electronics were necessary to reach that point.

BE: MIT has had a long history of being a catalyst for invention. You have such transitions now going on in biology, which, I suppose, is the present version of the digital computer setting of fifty years ago. It's a new frontier that's not understood, not explored. It's not clear where it's going. It's still possible to start a computer company and have it grow very rapidly. I think they used to draw a picture of the computer business. You know the picture of the big fish eating the middle-sized fish eating the little fish? It's the other way around in the computer business. The big fish is being eaten by the middle-sized fish, who is being eaten by the little thing. My feeling about computers is that it was possible back in the '50s to get a picture of how the business was going to end up. It was going to end up with everybody with a computer and those computers networked together and connected to inter-mediate servers of some sort. Those, in turn, were hooked up to things which were big computers, file machines and such. As the technology has advanced, you can see it all moving in that direction. First, you could only afford a single, great big machine. Then, as machines got cheaper, minis appeared, and timesharing came along, which gave people a rough approximation of having their own machine. Little machines, like the PDP-8s, appeared. Eventually, personal computers and workstations appeared. Now we're in a position where people can afford their own machines and those machines are in fact networked structures, servers, and communications. I've run out of vision. That was as far as I could see. I'm not sure what's going to happen next, except that it's all going to improve. Personal computers are not at all user friendly, even the best of them. Fixing that is going to be a bottomless pit of innovation in processing and storage. Most people seem to be working on language inputs, allowing the user to talk to the machine. I don't think that's important. I think what's important is to have a machine that knows enough so that it can understand what you're talking about if you don't spell it out in every last detail. I usually talk about this using the analogy of asking my secretary, "You know that letter I wrote to Joe What's-his-name a couple of years ago?" She finds it! Computers have to do that.

JF: Mine now does that fairly well. If you just specify some words that might have been in it, like his name, and the subject, it will find the letter.

BE: They're making progress. But that's the kind of thing that's necessary. If the secretary treated the manager like a computer treats its owner, the relationship would break down almost instantaneously!

JF: Yes, like, "You told me to MAIL it to Joe Smith, you didn't tell me to write his address!"

3

A Distinguished Lineage

Interactive Computing with the PDP-1

Edited by Bob Hofmann from interviews with Edward Fredkin

Digital's PDP-1 was the direct descendant of the TX-0 computer, developed along with the larger TX-2 system at Lincoln Laboratory in the late 1950s. Designed by Wesley Clark, the TX-0 and TX-2 were among the first transistor-driven computers in the world.

With many of the features pioneered on the massive Whirlwind system—CRTs, consoles, paper-tape input and output—the TX-0 and TX-2 effected many advances in interactive computing.

The TX-2 was planned as a large-scale 36-bit system for advanced graphic display research. The smaller TX-0 was built first, to test the transistor circuitry and complex core memory of the larger system. That process produced the TX-0 Direct Input Utility System, a set of programs that made it possible to communicate directly with the computer with an online typewriter. This primitive operating system was the first ever developed for a real-time computer.

Soon the power of the TX-0 was applied to other tasks. A program to analyze electroencephalograph recordings for sleep research utilized the first moving window display ever to appear on a CRT. To create scientific characters on the display for mathematical equations, team member (and later PDP-1 architect) Ben Gurley developed a light pen. "The TX-0 could do everything a personal computer does today," remembers Ken Olsen, another member of the team, "limited only by the fact that the memory was small."

The much larger TX-2 was less limited, especially after 65K of memory from the TX-0 was added to it. At the first official meeting on interactive graphics, a young graduate student named Ivan Sutherland introduced his TX-2-based Sketchpad system, a new kind of simulation language that enabled the computer to translate abstractions into concrete visual forms. Many of Sketchpad's capabilities were sophisticated even by the workstation standards of the 1980s. "If I had known how hard it was to do," Sutherland said later, "I probably wouldn't have done it."

Stripped of most of its memory, the TX-0 was sent on a long-term loan to MIT, where it inspired a new generation of graphics pioneers. Assistant Professor Jack Dennis gave access to the system to members of the Signals and Power Subcommittee of the MIT Model Railroad Club, students who were to win fame as the first computer "hackers." Dennis himself designed a symbolic debugger for the system. Called FLIT, after a popular insecticide, this Flexowriter Interrogation Tape was the first of many playfully named but useful programs created by the group. The TX-0 was considered the ultimate in interactivity by the hackers—until the first PDP-1 arrived a few years later.

Plotting on PDP-1 CRT

A Machine Remembered: The PDP-1

A pioneer in the fields of artificial intelligence, physics, and computer science, Edward Fredkin is internationally known for his theories of cellular automata, which use computational models to explain physical phenomena. He has taught at MIT, CalTech, and Boston University, and has founded several companies, including Information International, Inc.

My conversion to the emerging doctrine of interactive computing came a few years before Dr. Licklider's [J.C.R. Licklider, 1915–90], because I was fortunate enough to encounter the handful of individuals who were creating the theories and systems that gave birth to the idea of interactivity in the 1950s. Given the chance, I very quickly joined their number.

After serving as an Air Force pilot and intercept controller, I was transferred in 1958 to the Air Proving Grounds Command. Every time the Air Force purchased something new, such as a B-47 bomber or a pair of combat boots, it was sent to the Air Proving Grounds Command to determine if it was suitable.

This time, the Air Force was purchasing a new computer system, designed to manage the interception of hostile aircraft for the entire United States. SAGE [Semi-Automatic Ground Environment] was developed at MIT's Lincoln Laboratory, the product of the most massive programming effort in history. When work on SAGE began, it was estimated it would take 1,000 man-years of programming to complete. At the time there were perhaps 500 computer programmers in the world. In the end, SAGE required 7,000 programming man-years to complete; for several years, most of the world's programmers were trained on the SAGE project.

Air Proving Grounds Command gave us one month to study this system before the test was to begin. We soon realized it would take a year, or possibly more. Fortunately, after training all those programmers, Lincoln offered a superb course of study in digital logic, software design, and the SAGE system itself. The Proving Grounds team decided to spend the year enrolled in these courses. About a week later everyone dropped out, except me.

For the next year, I received the best education in computer science then available. The SAGE system was an outgrowth of work on Project Whirlwind, the first true interactive computer ever developed. Many of that system's designers still worked at Lincoln: the developers of core memory, light pens, the first modem, the first graphics displays. Working with this group of uniquely gifted people converted me to the idea that direct, real-time interaction between human and computer was, in fact, the way to realize the real potential of computing.

This was not a widely shared idea. In fact, to 99 percent of the computing establishment at the time, it was the next thing to heresy. To them, using a computer meant waiting in line to feed it instructions on stacks of punch cards, then waiting hours or even days for an answer. If you mistyped a character on one of the cards, or left out a comma, or had a card out of sequence, the machine informed you at the end of the run that your offering had been rejected. Then you started the process again.

"Thirty years ago, the overwhelming majority of the people who designed, manufactured, programmed, and used computers shared a single idea . . . 'Computers are mysterious devices meant to be used for mathematical calculations.' You could count the people who took exception to this dogma on the fingers of one hand."

— Howard Rheingold
Tools for Thought

"We felt passionately that we had a better approach. We were too much scientists to say we invented anything or it belonged to us, or was uniquely ours. But we did have this missionary zeal to introduce these technologies to the world."

— Ken Olsen

"I guess you could say I had a kind of religious conversion."

— J.C.R. Licklider
upon using his first interactive computer, the PDP-1

"Lick"

Even before his "religious conversion" to interactive computing, Dr. J.C.R. Licklider was obsessed with the potential of "man-machine symbiosis" (as he called it in a seminal paper). A researcher in the perception of sound, Licklider conducted the first time-and-motion study of intellec-

tual investigation. "Although aware of the inadequacy of the sampling," he wrote, "I served as my own subject."

Licklider found that 85 percent of his "thinking" time was actually spent searching for information—plotting graphs for his acoustic research, for instance—instead of interpreting it. The path to reversing that imbalance seemed clearer to him when Licklider's group at Bolt Beranek and Newman acquired a true interactive computer: "The PDP-1 opened me up to ideas about how people and machines like this might operate together in the future."

In 1962, "Lick" (as he was known) was asked to manage the funding of computing research for the Defense Department's Advanced Research Projects Agency (ARPA). His budget was more than the total allocated to computer research by all other government-supported agencies.

The computer establishment criticized Licklider's ARPA program, arguing that timesharing was an inefficient use of machine resources. But ARPA-funded research helped prove the viability of commercial timesharing in the late 1960s, and led the way to networking in the early 1970s, with the famous ARPANET.

The basic argument for this approach was that computing power was costly and therefore precious. It could not be wasted to make the computer more accessible to mere mortals. Instead, a highly trained caste of operators was needed to formulate problems in a language the machine could understand. The processing efficiency of the hardware was everything: the efficiency of the human-machine interaction was something for the humans to worry about, by learning to understand the machine better.

To question this received truth made one highly suspect. In 1958, Jack Gilmore, who worked at Lincoln, gave a paper on a utility program he wrote for one of the Lab's smaller interactive machines to a computing conference at the University of Toronto. He was, he later reported, "almost kicked out of the room. The audience was livid with anger that I would waste their time with something that implied that a human being would stand in front of a computer and actually use it while all these fractions of MIPS were going by and being wasted."

Shortly after leaving Lincoln, I went to work for Dr. Licklider at the consulting firm of Bolt Beranek and Newman. Dr. Licklider was also concerned with waste, in his case the waste of the human mind's thinking potential. While Dr. Licklider was conducting basic research into psychoacoustics and human engineering, BBN had no computer to support his research.

There were, in fact, no computers available that could really do the job. Really powerful computers were far too expensive. Small scientific computers were being made by manufacturers like Bendix and Librascope, but these copied the long word lengths of the multimillion-dollar batch-processing machines. Their serial design and clumsy drum memories made them too slow to be really useful in laboratory applications.

In December 1959, the situation changed. At the Eastern Joint Computer Conference in Boston, a small module maker called Digital Equipment Corporation introduced a system that was to revolutionize the way scientists, and ultimately humans in general, used computers.

To me, this machine, the prototype of the PDP-1, was like a dream come true. For the first time a truly fast, powerful computing system was available at a price that brought it within reach of small research labs like ours.

It's difficult to appreciate from the perspective of the 1990s what this meant. Today, if a new workstation comes on the market with twice the speed of its predecessor, it's hailed as a great advance in price/performance. At a cost of $120,000, the PDP-1, with its 5-microsecond cycle time, could outrun every machine in the world priced less than a million dollars, and most of the systems priced just over a million. It beat the competition by a factor of ten.

Even more important, the PDP-1 offered all the wonderful interactive features of the research computers of the Whirlwind and SAGE projects. It had switches the user could manipulate, and a monitor for graphics. Instead of programming with boxes of punch cards, you fed programs to this machine on high-speed paper tape. You could make changes while the machine was running. For the first time in history, when you had an idea you could implement it in a few hours or a few days—projects that would take a team of people forever in a batch environment, or would just be impossible.

The PDP-1 was the world's first commercial interactive computer. It was the world's first "fun" computer. This one system was the foundation for everything that followed, from personal computers, to workstations, word processing, video games, microprocessor laboratory control—almost all the major advances in interactive computing over the next three decades.

It was also a very beautifully designed machine. At the Joint Computer Conference, I met the PDP-1's architect, Ben Gurley, whom I had known slightly at Lincoln Lab. I asked him what parameters he had been given for the system's design. He answered, jokingly, "To make it from inventory"; in other words, to use the system modules that were Digital's main product up until then. In fact, Gurley designed about half the modules of the PDP-1 from scratch. In one of the greatest tours de force in the history of computer design, Gurley created the entire system in three and one-half months.

It was anything but a rush job. By the time the PDP-1 was designed, the basic elements of an interactive computer—logical organization, addressing, sequencing control, I/O control—had all been invented. Building these elements into a piece of hardware suitable for commercial production was another matter. Ben Gurley, perhaps better than any other engineer of his time, had the right combination of technical brilliance and engineering conservatism to bring these ideas into reality. In those days, module failure was common, but Ben's modules failed very much less than other people's. He was a master of conservative design; when he drew something on paper, it worked exactly as drawn. There were no bugs in his logic.

To cite a small example: the Teletype paper-tape punch for the PDP-1 was rated to run at 120 characters per second. Ben examined the Teletype mechanism very carefully, ran it at various speeds, and concluded that it would operate more quietly and have a longer life if it ran at 63.3 characters per second. His philosophy was that it should not just work, but that it should keep working. The standard set by Ben Gurley on the PDP-1 helped establish Digital's long-standing reputation for very reliable, well-engineered products.

Of course, I recommended that BBN purchase a PDP-1, the first PDP-1 system ever sold, as it turned out. This was very exciting, because being the first customer gave us influence over how the machine changed and evolved as production increased. We were very willing guinea pigs, and Digital was very open to our suggestions. They were still a very small company, and most of their engineers had until recently been academic researchers themselves. Our relations had something of the give-and-take of the community of scholars; very different from the formal relationship between the large computing vendors and their customers.

For instance, we noticed the small fans at the base of the PDP-1 were rather noisy. I asked one of BBN's acoustics experts if the machine couldn't be cooled more quietly. At his recommendation, the small fans were replaced by a single large fan. In addition to redesigning the cooling system, we at BBN made a series of more significant hardware modifications, including adding the electronic typewriter for input and designing a keyboard for it.

It was a wide open, two-way street. Many of the PDP-1's improvements can be traced to the genius of its small band of enthusiastic users. Digital made it easy for us. The PDP-1's design was very fully articulated in a series of

Ben Gurley

Ed Fredkin, who bought the first PDP-1, expresses his admiration for the young engineer who designed the prototype for Digital's first computer in three and one-half months.

Speed is one thing, reliability another. According to Fredkin, Ben Gurley was an

engineering master whose work was as meticulous as it was imaginative: "When he put his pencil on the paper to design something, it worked when it was built.

He was one of the finest designers the world has ever seen," Fredkin said.

Before the PDP-1, Gurley proved the value of his cautious yet creative approach at MIT and Lincoln Lab, where he participated in developing the Memory Test Computer (MTC), the TX-0, and the TX-2. At a time when vacuum-tube memories had mean fault times of 20 minutes, a core memory based on the theoretical work of Jay Forrester and Ken Olsen's design was engineered by Gurley for the MTC. It was so successful, it was rushed onto the primary Whirlwind system, where it ran for a solid month before the first error.

Gurley left Digital in 1962 to serve as vice president of Information International, a consulting firm that won nationwide attention for its use of the PDP-1 in oceanography, film reading, man-machine interaction, and other applications. In 1963, Ben Gurley was murdered by a deranged former employee.

Expensive Typewriter

To those who think of the word processor as a cost-effective productivity tool, it may come as a surprise that the first successful word processing program permitted a $120,000 computer to work almost as well as a $200 electric typewriter.

"Expensive Typewriter" was the first of a series of "expensive" programs that permitted the PDP-1 to mimic the functions of rather less esoteric tools. There was "Expensive Mirror," which used the system's CRT to copy visual patterns. The star map used in the Spacewar! video game was dubbed "Expensive Planetarium." The PDP-1's three-pitch sound function led to the creation of "Expensive Tape Recorder" and something more: a program that played a Bach sonata in three voices. The music never stopped; it was programmed in an endless loop.

Unlike million-dollar computers, the PDP-1 didn't feature floating-point arithmetic, so it was a real challenge to develop "Expensive Desk Calculator." When this calculator's creator used it to do his homework, his professor reportedly said, "You used a computer? It can't be right!"

paperback handbooks, for which Digital later became justly famous. They were freely distributed to users and to potential users, and were popular even among those who couldn't afford to buy the machine. These handbooks spread the gospel of interactivity more effectively than any other medium.

Nowhere was the developmental role of the user more evident than in the area of software, because Digital's early policy was simply to supply the hardware, and leave the software to the customer. I designed an assembler for our PDP-1, which had a 1,024-word memory. It was the world's first variable-symbol assembler, as far as I know. The third PDP-1, which had a larger memory than the BBN machine, was given by Digital to MIT's school of electrical engineering. Six MIT students, including Alan Kotok and Peter Samson, bet Jack Dennis, who ran the PDP-1, that they could come up with their own assembler in a single weekend. The wrote and debugged it in 250 man-hours, and it was loaded onto the machine when Dennis came to work on Monday. This was the sort of job that might have taken the industry months to complete.

Some of the most exciting PDP-1 software was developed for computer graphics. The second PDP-1 was sold to the ITEK Corporation for experiments in electronic drafting. ITEK's engineering staff added a hard disk to the PDP-1, which not only could be used to store programs and drawings, but also served as a display buffer, allowing the creation of a flicker-free display monitor.

The ITEK system, called the Electronic Drafting Machine, could draw straight edges at any angle, and could generate any radius arc by raising a circle on the CRT screen and selecting a portion of it. This was the world's first CAD application, and it attracted immediate interest from the aerospace industry.

After ITEK demonstrated the system's capability by simulating an automated refinery on the CRT, Standard Oil purchased the system to control production processes using visual displays. ITEK also pioneered the commercial I/O idea. Like everyone else, they purchased the PDP-1 for $120,000. A *Time* magazine article in 1962 indicated they were considering selling the modified version for nearly a half-million dollars.

Its high speed and simplified I/O structure made the PDP-1 well suited to emerging laboratory and scientific control applications. A rather unique sequence break system—which I helped design, and which later became a standard for minicomputers—permitted much of the processing associated with I/O devices to be handled within the program, instead of in a separate and expensive processor. Each time an I/O device had information to be transferred to the memory, it caused an interrupt and the processor handled the transfer. In addition, the system's radial design made it easy to connect magnetic tape, displays, printers, and other devices.

Lawrence Livermore Laboratory used the PDP-1 for graphic I/O and to support the processing of their large scientific calculators. Atomic Energy of Canada bought PDP-1s for pulse height analysis and to control experiments with their Van de Graaff generator. The PDP-1 was used in the Mariner space flight project to collect telemeter data being sent back to Earth stations. International Telephone and Telegraph bought more PDP-1s than any other customer, using them to collect, store, and forward Teletype messages—up to then a manual process.

At BBN and at MIT, however, we were primarily interested in human-to-machine, rather than machine-to-machine, interactivity. Marvin Minsky and John McCarthy were two artificial intelligence researchers at MIT who also consulted with BBN on human engineering. McCarthy realized that if substantial research was to be conducted on the man-machine interface, at a time when computer power and memory were still almost unbelievably expensive by today's standards, some way would have to be found for researchers and students to share expensive computing resources. The way all computers run today—paying attention to lots of different tasks, switching from one to another—is an outgrowth of John McCarthy's simple and elegant concept of timesharing.

Dr. McCarthy's original idea of timesharing was dependent on the necessary memory residing with each user, but in the early 1960s memory was still too expensive for that. I had an idea for what might be called "simulated" timesharing: if we could design a high-speed device that "swapped" different users' programs on and off the PDP-1, the machine's high cycle speed could support a significant number of users, while, from each user's standpoint, it appeared he had the system to himself.

Our swapping drum was a great success. In a single rotation, everything from the core could be transferred onto the drum, while everything on the drum was transferred back into core. The drum could do a total swap of memory onto the core in 20 milliseconds. If you typed ten characters a second, there was only a hundred milliseconds' pause between characters. This was the basis of a very responsive timesharing system. Jack Dennis at MIT, who saw timesharing as a way to make his computers available to more students, contributed to the system by designing a debugger called DDT, which kept on debugging no matter what a user program did.

The only problem then was to get our system manufactured. Jack and John McCarthy and I had extensive discussions about this possibility with Ben Gurley of Digital. "Why don't you build this drum," we'd say.

"Why don't you give us an order?" he would answer.

"What? You haven't even said you'd build it."

"Well, we can't without an order."

On and on it went. Finally we decided on a cost for producing the drum. Jack Dennis ran off and phoned the head of his lab at MIT. I called Dr. Licklider. In half an hour we had two purchase order numbers, one from MIT and one from BBN. That's how the timesharing revolution got started.

For years, a hot debate raged over timesharing. Visionary purists like Wesley Clark, who designed the TX-0, TX-2, and LINC computers, deplored the "thrashing competition and waste" of the timesharing approach. Clark rightly pointed out the limitations of timesharing for real-time computing, and interactive computing with complex displays. Clark could see all the way from the TX-2, which was a five-million-dollar personal computer, to the one-thousand-dollar personal computers of today. I and other advocates of timesharing shared this vision, but thought it was important to do something in the meantime. Later, Clark, a superb system designer, grudgingly admitted that "timesharing resulted in a huge and productive impetus to computer science at a critical time." Even in the early '60s he tacitly admitted that

Spacewar!

In the early 1960s, MIT wasn't the only institute of advanced research on the north bank of the Charles River. The augustly named Hingham Institute was, in reality, a dingy tenement on Hingham Street a few blocks from MIT. Home to two programmers, the institute served as a meeting place for assorted students who shared one common trait: a growing addiction to MIT's new PDP-1.

When he wasn't pursuing his avocation, Steve "Slug" Russell assisted John McCarthy's artificial intelligence research on MIT's IBM System 704. But he preferred the PDP-1: "It had a switch. You could turn it on. You got a satisfying clunk. You could type a single character at it and it would type a little message back. It gave you a great feeling of power."

Fueled by this sense of power, which was supplemented by their interest in Japanese monster movies and the pulp science fiction of E.E. "Doc" Smith, Russell and his Hingham Institute associates created the most elaborate computer "hack" of their era: a two-player game called "Spacewar!" played on the PDP-1's CRT screen.

After Slug wrote the main control routine, Shag Graetz, a Hingham fellow, recalls, "it was like Tom Sawyer with the whitewash brush." Unimpressed with Russell's random stars, one hacker wrote a program that put them in their proper constellations (and respective magnitudes, naturally). Another found the whole thing annoyingly non-Newtonian, so he added gravity to the paths of the spaceships and missiles.

Inspired Alliance: Project MAC

According to Marvin Minsky, "It wasn't until about 1970 that the professors could be said to know more than the students about computers." Minsky should know: he was one of the professors.

In the 1960s, Professor Minsky and MIT colleagues such as John McCarthy and Seymour Papert were creating a new field of study called artificial intelligence. To bring their theories of robotics and thought simulation into being, they harnessed the formidable if unorthodox talents of the true experts in interactive computing: the hacker community then growing up around MIT's TX-0 and PDP-1 systems.

When a grant was received from the Defense Department's Advanced Research Projects Agency, a serendipitous alliance was born. The ambiguity of the new program's name neatly expressed its dual focus. Project MAC could mean either Machine Aided Cognition (a synonym for AI) or Multiple Access Computing, a reference to the sophisticated timesharing capabilities being coaxed out of the PDP-1 by Jack Dennis, Ed Fredkin, and others.

With a nod to MIT's officially blessed, IBM-based Compatible Timesharing System (CTSS), the MAC hackers called theirs ITS—the Incompatible Timesharing System. Their most highly publicized demonstration of artificial intelligence came when a program called MacHack defeated the philosopher Hubert Dreyfus, an AI skeptic, in a chess match. The headline in an AI journal read, "A Ten-Year-Old Can't Beat the Machine—Dreyfus." The subhead read, "But the Machine Can Beat Dreyfus."

timesharing was the wave of at least the immediate future by declining to submit a minority report to an MIT Study Committee which recommended campus-wide timesharing: "I knew a steamroller when I saw one and went to the other matters."

The PDP-1 also helped influence the distant future of computing. After leaving BBN, I started a software and consulting company called Information International, which created PDP-1 applications. Ben Gurley left Digital to join this company, which had its offices in the same old woolen mill as Digital. One day we were visited by John Cocke, the now legendary advanced system architect from IBM. John and Ben went over our PDP-1 in great detail, Ben explaining the intricacies of its design.

Like the TX-0 computer, the PDP-1 had a very limited instruction set. It had been expanded somewhat to make the machine more commercially suitable to a range of applications but, at 28 instructions, it was a very simple set.

In the late 1970s, I got a late-night telephone call from John Cocke. (This apparently is his habit, though at the time I thought I was the only one to receive such calls.) John asked me if I remembered the machine Ben had shown him at the Mill in Maynard. I said yes. He said, "I have this idea." He had worked up a design that was based on the PDP-1. It had a very simple instruction set, like the PDP-1. John had made some modifications; he used a 16-bit word instead of an 18-bit word, for instance. Another change he had in mind was the timing cycle: instead of 5 microseconds it would be 5 nanoseconds. At John Cocke's insistence, IBM spent more than a decade constructing the machine he outlined for me on the telephone. They called it the RISC System/6000, and over the past several years, its technology has resulted in increasing computing power a few more orders of magnitude.

For a computer that changed the course of computing history more, arguably, than any other system, the PDP-1 was not a very successful product. Only 49 were built. People were very slow to catch on. The computing establishment continued to create ever more powerful, but no more accessible, batch-processing systems.

Part of the problem was that customers, especially larger customers, were skeptical about buying something as complex as a computer from a company with less than one hundred employees and less than a million dollars in sales. Many doubted that Digital could be a reliable and long-lived computer supplier. Believers in interactivity often had a hard time convincing their organizations that the PDP-1 was worth its extraordinarily inexpensive price. There is a story of one customer with a limited budget who couldn't pay for the whole system, and so was sold a PDP-1 without its modules. On the purchase order it was called a "logic connector." They then bought the modules out of their maintenance budget.

Even within the interactive computing community, decisions were made that postponed full realization of the promise of the PDP-1 for decades. Subsequent timesharing systems didn't support the interaction of timeshared programs the way the PDP-1 did. Other timesharing programs input a whole line of instructions, instead of the character-by-character system we developed for the PDP-1. This made building an effective editor very difficult. Superbly useful graphics features of the PDP-1—the ability to plot XY, for instance—

simply disappeared from later graphics systems. Jack Gilmore has traced the decay of computer graphics in the 1960s and 1970s to the fact that the industry began spreading the idea that huge amounts of memory were required to produce the sort of graphics we were doing on a 4K PDP-1. The motive here was to sell more memory.

The basic problem, of course, was that available technology did not—still has not—fully caught up with the promise of interactive computing. Between our work at BBN, Ivan Sutherland's Sketchpad system (which used the TX-2 system) and the Electronic Drafting Machine, we had much of the graphics that are available today on the Macintosh, and some that aren't, in 1962. But it was 20 years before the cost of hardware was low enough to make these systems feasible as mass products.

Still, in the few years before the PDP-1 was supplanted by more powerful if less elegant machines, the handful of interactive computing converts grew to perhaps a roomful. And what a roomful, with names like Marvin Minsky, Bill Gosper, Gordon Bell, Richard Greenblatt, Stewart Nelson: an honor roll of computing pioneers of the 1960s, 1970s, and 1980s.

In a paper he published in 1960, J.C.R. Licklider referred to a study that estimated that it might take five years to develop meaningful "man-machine symbiosis" (his term for interactive computing) and another 15 to reach true artificial intelligence.

"The fifteen may be ten or five hundred," he wrote, "but those years should be intellectually the most creative and exciting in the history of mankind." Five hundred years is a long time, but one thing is certain: we're a long way from reaching the end of this creative and exciting era. Then again, Jack Gilmore had a saying: "The early Christians get the best lions." They never made a better lion than the PDP-1.

Part II

Managing Growth

Driving Digital's explosive growth throughout the 1960s, 1970s, and 1980s: innovative product engineering, quality manufacturing, and a unique approach to sales and service.

Engineers run diagnostics on a PDP-8

4 From the PDP to the VAX

The year was 1965. Computing came out of the lab and into offices, factories, and new territories everywhere. The combined speed, size, and reasonable cost made Digital's PDP-8 the first successful minicomputer. Before long 50,000 systems—at one-sixth the price of a PDP-1, one-fiftieth the cost of a mainframe—were put to work in business, production, and research.

The PDP-8 realized the dream of putting computers directly in the hands of the people who can use them. In the years since the PDP-8 helped popularize computing, radically condensing the circuitry has made computers ever faster, cheaper, more reliable—and more accessible to more people than ever before.

Without a fundamental vision, adapting constantly changing technology would be a forbidding challenge. But Digital made a bold move for a small company in introducing a "personal" mainframe, months before the breakthrough success of the PDP-8. The PDP-6 was designed to give each user the sense of having a powerful computer to himself, without having to wait for results, a goal consistent with Digital's vision. The market may not have been ready for it, but the PDP-6 was designed as a timesharing machine, and its successors—the DECsystem-10 and DECSYSTEM-20 families—were the choice of the major U.S. computer science centers for artificial intelligence research. The PDP-6 helped generate a new industry of computer timesharing as it led Digital to approach design from a longer-range perspective.

Let's move ahead to 1970. A result of that thinking was compatibility, an important trait that set the PDP-11 apart from the pack. The new architecture was a marvel of disciplined design. All components could be connected directly to the UNIBUS, the first data bus to communicate data without involving the processor. The new machine was 10 inches tall—half the size of the original mock-up—and ready to ship a month ahead of schedule. Six months later, 17 more PDP-11 projects were under way.

Between 1967 and 1977, Digital's revenues tripled, staff ranks swelled by 40 percent, and shipments multiplied by a factor of nine.

Then came VAX, and a new kind of computing.

This was the generation when computing came of age. Knowing how to keep ahead of unprecedented demand, when to cut losses, and when to anticipate change without compromising standards helped Digital weather the growing pains. But it took perspicacity and cooperation, and a catalog of virtues, for Engineering, Manufacturing, and Sales to consistently deliver computers to Digital's growing number of customers.

Specifications
PDP-8

First shipped
April 1965

Word length
12 bits

Speed
1.5-microsecond cycle time

Primary memory
4K 12-bit word core memory

Secondary memory
32K maximum

Instruction set
3-bit op code, 1 indirect bit
8 bits of address
Addressing subdivided into 1 page bit
and 7 bits of absolute address

Input/Output
Teletype (ASR-33) standard
Standard I/O includes paper-tape
reader and punch on ASR-33
DECtape available thereafter

Software
Paper tape, includes symbolic editor,
FORTRAN system, PAL II Assembler,
DDT-8 Dynamic Debugging Tape,
Floating Point System, Symbol Print,
Macro 8 Symbolic Assembler

Architecture
Single accumulator
2's complement arithmetic
All PDP-8 systems parallel,
except the serial PDP-8/S

Power
780 watts

History
Logic modules derived from flip chip series,
developed for general sale by Don White,
Russ Doane . . . Modules developed for the
PDP-8 include the R210 (accumulator),
R211 (PC, MB, MA) and
G808 (power supply control)

Price
$18,000

PDP-5, 1964

Computing in the '60s

On campus at MIT and Stanford, scientists and students were making headway with timesharing and expert systems, and at Bell Labs, UNIX simplified and standardized some of the timesharing and file-sharing features of the Multics operating system that was developed jointly by MIT, GE, and Bell.

Every decrease in the price/performance ratio—a result of the shrinking size and price of semiconductors, and increased speed and reliability—offered the possibility of computing to new users. The U.S. government used computers first to test rockets before launch, provide onboard guidance, and track multiple targets via phased-array radar. Industry soon recognized the gains of making banking more accessible through automated tellers, making airline reservations more convenient over a telephone network, and monitoring freight trains more efficiently via automated databases.

Preparing shipments

LK201 keyboard

". . . in PDP-8 checkout, I'd be called in to help determine what caused the problem. In checkout, the systems sat on a piece of plywood, and I noticed that on each piece of plywood was a serial number. First, I think, I saw the number 22. The next number I noticed was 49, then 87.

Shortly after that I noticed a serial number in the 200s, and it then occurred to me that we were moving a lot of these systems, and things were starting to happen."

— Don White
Joined Digital 1960

1965 *Corporate Profile*

Employees	Revenues	Locations	Highlights
876	$15 million	13 United States 3 Europe 1 Canada 1 Australia	Digital reorganizes by product lines: large computers, small computers, modules, and special products; to better define responsibility and authority throughout the company.

"A far cry from the office machines
of fifty years ago. . . ."
Industry, May 1965

PDP-5

Higher Speeds, Lower Costs, Easier Connections—Birth of the Minicomputer

In 1964, Atomic Energy of Canada Ltd. acquired a PDP-4 as a reactor-control computer system. The need for an elaborate analog monitoring system as a front-end processor led Digital to develop its first 12-bit computer. The PDP-5 was designed to serve the purpose for a variety of process control applications.

The PDP-5 was innovative in replacing the radial structure of earlier designs with an I/O bus. By allowing peripheral equipment to be added incrementally—rather than pre-allocating space, wiring, and cable drivers—the I/O bus design lowered the base cost of the system and simplified the configuring of machines in the field.

After the success of the PDP-5, Digital engineers conceived a new machine of far greater performance. The introduction of "flip chip" logic modules promised substantial speed improvements. New core memory technology reduced cycle time from 6 microseconds in the PDP-5 to 1.5 microseconds in the new machine.

In April 1965 the first PDP-8 was delivered. The concept of minicomputers took hold and the PDP-8 took the lead in a multibillion-dollar industry.

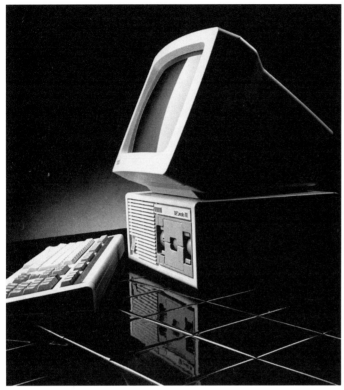

DECmate III, 1984

PDP-8: No Other Computer as Easy to Connect

At $18,000, the PDP-8 was less than half the price and four times the speed of the PDP-5. Flip chip modules enabled a new manufacturing technique called automatic wire-wrapping to make production fast and accurate, and the price low.

Half the size of the PDP-5, the new PDP-8 fitted comfortably in the back of a Volkswagen convertible. More important, no computer at the time was as easy to connect with other systems and machines. This was the minicomputer's most notable advance.

The PDP-8 was at home almost anywhere there was an outlet. It could control other devices or be controlled by them, and it could serve as a component of a larger system. This last option led Original Equipment Manufacturers (OEMs) to repackage the PDP-8 and sell it to customers in need of specialized applications.

In late 1966 the "classic" PDP-8 was followed by the more economical PDP-8/S. The size of a file-cabinet drawer, the S model's cost reduction came from implementing the PDP-8 instruction set serially. Three years later the PDP-8/I was the first Digital computer to use medium-scale integration (MSI) integrated circuits. In 1976, the entire PDP-8 instruction set would be put on a single chip.

12-Bit Family Timeline

1962	Laboratory Instrument Computer (LINC) developed at MIT
1963	PDP-5, Digital's first 12-bit computer
1965	"Classic" PDP-8, world's first mass-produced minicomputer
1966	LINC-8 combines LINC and PDP-8 processors PDP-8/S, serial version of the PDP-8
1967	PDP-8 systems manufactured in Reading, England Annual sales: $38 million
1968	LAB-8, small, general-purpose laboratory package TSS/8 timesharing software PDP-8/I, integrated circuit version of the PDP-8 PDP-8/L
1969	PDP-12, third member of LINC family
1970	PDP-8/E features OMNIBUS synchronous bus for bidirectional communications between system elements TABS-8 newspaper application
1971	PDP-8/M, OEM version of 8/E
1972	PDP-8/F
1974	PDP-8/A miniprocessor PDP-8/A package allows OEMs choice of memory type and quantity
1976	PDP-8/A 600 series WPS-8 word-processing software CMOS-8 chip
1977	VT78, complete PDP-8 system in a terminal, uses the CMOS-8 chip, anticipating the DECmate series WS 102, multiuser WPS
1982	DECmate II word processor
1984	DECmate III

"With the PDP-8, you never had enough memory, so you had to become very proficient at writing your program in as few codes as possible. Memory was expensive, and processors were slow, so every word and every cycle counted. I became good at making things small and fast."

— Richie Lary
Joined Digital 1969

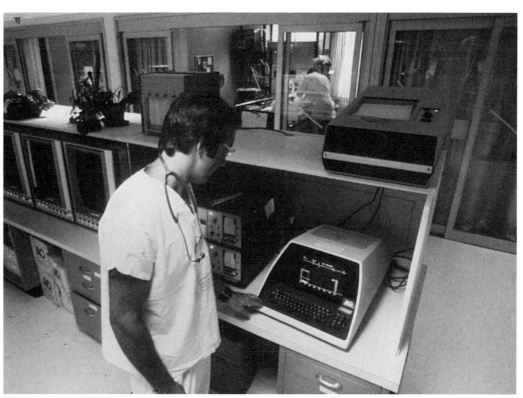

PDP-8 in medical environment

Education application

PDP-8 Applications Multiplied

The PDP-8, like the PDP-5, was designed for task-specific environments—process control and laboratory applications that include controlling pulse height and spectrum analyzers. Over time, the number and variety of applications multiplied to encompass message switching and small-scale general-purpose timesharing. The TSS/8 timesharing system developed at Carnegie Mellon University made multiprogramming—when a computer performs calculations for one program while retrieving data for others—on minicomputers a reality.

The PDP-8 found uses in places undreamed of for computers: chemical plants, newspapers, laboratories, refineries, oceanographic studies, and schools. Its low cost and high speed opened such a wide range of applications that the PDP-8 became the standard for the industry.

Conceived in an era when changing new technology or manufacturing techniques was expensive, its basic architecture has survived the transition to integrated circuits, to medium-scale integrated circuits, and to large-scale integration.

PDP-8 controlling scoreboard at Boston's Fenway Park

Moving Computers out of the Laboratory

The small size and adaptability of the PDP-8 brought computers out of the laboratory and into the office, factory, and field. Sports fans watched sophisticated graphics displays controlled by PDP-8 systems in the digital scoreboards at Boston's Fenway Park. A PDP-8 was used to control the news display seen by millions of visitors to New York's Times Square. The PDP-8 fuelled exports to other countries and found its way into hundreds of new applications.

More than 1,200 "classic" PDP-8 systems were manufactured, and a total of 40,000 PDP-8 systems ultimately produced.

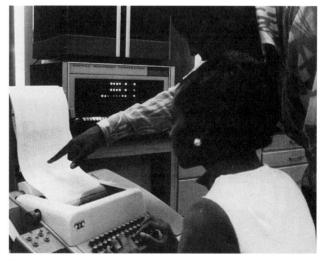
Education application

Specifications
LINC

First shipped
March 1962

Word length
12 bits

Speed
125,000 memory accesses
per second

Primary memory
2048 words of core memory,
8 microseconds

Secondary memory
Tape

Input/Output
Tape, keyboard, oscilloscopes

Arithmetic
1's complement

Number produced
50 (21 by Digital)

Technology
Transistor, using
Digital System Modules

Power
1,000 watts

History
Designed by Wesley Clark
and Charles Molnar,
MIT's Lincoln Laboratory

Price
$43,000

Achievements
First to process data from
laboratory experiments in real time,
accepts both analog and digital inputs
directly, first to process data immediately
and to provide signals to control
experimental equipment

LINC processor cabinet, 1962

LINC: The First Practical, Affordable PC

One machine that had a great influence on the design of Digital's 12-bit computers was the Laboratory Instrument Computer (LINC). This small stored-program computer accepted analog as well as digital input directly from experiments. It processed data immediately and provided signals that could be used to control experimental equipment.

The first version of the LINC, built in 1962 by Wesley Clark and Charles Molnar at MIT's Lincoln Laboratory, was designed to control experiments in the interactive, hands-on environment of biomedical laboratories.

In 1966, Clark refined his design at Digital with Dick Clayton. Combining the LINC with a PDP-8, the LINC-8 executed both instruction sets in parallel, enabling it to operate at five times the speed of the original LINC at a lower cost.

The LINC system Digital manufactured included a sophisticated tape software system and a powerful CRT-based console. Priced at $43,000, the LINC-8 was the first practical, reasonably priced personal computer on the market.

DECtape

LINC Software

On the early PDP machines, modular design ensured many alternatives for interconnecting computer components. By contrast, the LINC design was more restrictive, with a relatively modest primary memory and a single CRT. Limiting the system to a single configuration made it possible to provide a complete computing environment that included software users could easily exchange.

The LINC had its own file system, called LINCtape, the forerunner of the small floppy disk, which only became more widely available almost 10 years later, in 1971. When the system's designer, Tom Stockebrand, came to Digital from Lincoln Laboratory, he made changes to LINCtape, which was renamed DECtape. It was a great improvement over existing tape systems, which often had to be rewound several times and sometimes destroyed data.

"DECtape was wonderful, because all you had to do was take this little spool of tape and stick it on the machine, and lift a little blue button. The DECtape would load itself and the operating system would be copied right off the tape.

"A few years ago I was down in the Mill at a meeting where they . . . announced the end of support for DECtape. The last contract had expired; no more operating systems supported it.

"As I looked around the room I realized that a lot of these people were too young to have ever used any tape system. I just couldn't let it pass. I raised my hand and said 'Wait a minute, I would like to tell you about DECtape and what it meant to me. . . .'"

— **John Hall**
Digital employee

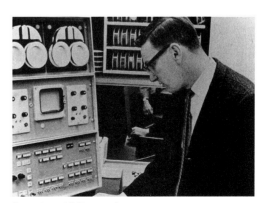

Operator at LINC console

PDP-6

First shipped
June 1964

Word length
36 bits

Speed
.25 MIPS

Memory
18-bit physical address protection
and relocation registers

Instruction set
2's complement

Input/Output
I/O and memory bus

Software
FORTRAN compiler, text editor,
a debuffer (DDT), copy program
called PIP (Peripheral Interchange
Program), assembler

History
Designed for timesharing and
real-time lab use, with straightforward
interfacing capability, served as
PDP-10 production prototype

Price
$120,000–$300,000

PDP-6, 1964

The 36-Bit Family: The Courage to Invest in New Technology

The first deliveries of the computer Digital called its "most dramatic" came even before the PDP-8, in the summer of 1964. The PDP-6 was shipped to MIT's Project MAC (known variously as Multiple Access Computing and Machine Aided Cognition), the University of Western Australia, Brookhaven National Laboratory, and Lawrence Livermore National Laboratory.

PDP-6: A Personal Mainframe

The PDP-6 originally was designed to extend the performance of Digital's 18-bit processor series, but several factors influenced the course of the new design.

First, 36 bits was the standard for scientific computing. This extended word length also accommodated LISP, a new language developed for work in artificial intelligence, still an active subject of university computing research. Finally, competing with IBM mainframes meant producing Digital's own 36-bit machines.

The PDP-6 was designed as a new kind of mainframe, to be used for both timesharing and real-time laboratory applications, with straightforward interfacing capability. It was the

(Seated, left to right) Lydia McKalip, Bill Coburn, Ken Senior, Ken Fitzgerald, Norman Hurst, Harris Hyman. (Standing) Peter Samson, Leo Gossell, Gordon Bell, Alan Kotok, Russ Doane, Bill Kellicker, Bob Reed, George Vogelsang.

first of what might be called a "personal" mainframe. It also was the first commercial computer available with software for timesharing applications.

Although system sales were only 23, the PDP-6 had a much greater influence than its small number would suggest. Most were sold to universities, where a new generation of computer scientists was introduced to the idea of interactive, time-shared computing. Although compatibility was not a specified design goal, the series evolved into five basic designs over 18 years—PDP-6, KA10, KI10, KL10, and DECSYSTEM-20. By January of 1978 more than 700 systems would be installed.

The PDP-10 came next, followed by the DECsystem-10 and DECSYSTEM-20 series: large systems, all designed to give each user the illusion of having his own large computer. They offered economical cost per user via timesharing for commercial, scientific, and communication applications and eliminated the long wait for results associated with batch processing.

"The PDP-6 was a bold move for a small company. University computing centers and research departments wanted this machine for distributed timesharing, and for conventional mainframe computing. These unique features got the attention of leading-edge computer users, giving us early sales against much larger competitors with conventional batch systems.

The 1964 sale to the University of Western Australia was made when Digital had fewer than 1,000 employees. It took courage on the part of the customer and the company to invest in this leading-edge computing technology."

— Ron Smart
Joined Digital 1964

"Digital's large
DECsystem-10 and
DECSYSTEM-20 were
sold worldwide, to
countries including
India, Venezuela,
Finland, Germany,
Ireland, Nigeria, New
Zealand, the USSR.
. . . Major Japanese
companies ordered
about a dozen KL10
systems with TOPS-20
when they began
their 'fifth-generation'
development efforts;
they knew it was **THE**
machine for artificial
intelligence, because
it was used by all the
major U.S. labs."

— **Allan Titcomb**
Joined Digital 1962

Two views of the DECsystem-10

DECSYSTEM-20

Timesharing: A New Industry Built on Large Systems Software

Large systems contributed to the progress of software development by promoting FORTRAN and LISP languages in computing on university campuses and COBOL in business. Because of the many processes and programs required to manage large systems transparently for many users, these systems also demanded a new design discipline of Digital software engineers. Consistent design rules and program compatibility became increasingly important.

To meet the demand, the main software user interface, TOPS-10, included user files and I/O device independence, a command control program, and multiprocessing capabilities. A second user interface, TOPS-20, was based on multiprocessing operating system advances.

The fast program response provided by TOPS-10 real-time facilities, and the system's advanced queuing capabilities made both DECsystem models instrumental in creating a new commercial industry of computer timesharing. More companies began to use large Digital computers to develop specialized applications and manage the entire system, leasing "time" on the computer to their customers.

36-Bit Family Timeline

1964 PDP-6, Digital's first large, 36-bit computer

1966 PDP-10 succeeds PDP-6
Model KA10, first Digital large system in production

1971 First DECsystem-10

1972 DECsystem-10 line offers unrivaled expansion
KI10 model offers high performance in scientific and real-time applications
TOPS-10 operating system

1975 KL10 introduced as two new DECsystem-10 models, 1080 and 1090

1976 DECSYSTEM-20, lowest-priced commercial timesharing system
DECsystem-1088 and DUAL 1080, most powerful Digital systems to date

1977 DECSYSTEM-2050 and full line of peripheral systems
TOPS-20 operating system

1983 Digital stops developing DECsystem-10 and DECSYSTEM-20 systems
Continues support by converting users to VAX-based solutions

PDP-11/45, 1972

Specifications
PDP-11/20

First shipped
Spring 1970

Word length
16 bits

Speed
800 nanoseconds

Primary memory
Magnetic core
(56 Kbytes maximum)

Instruction set
PDP-11

Software
Initially, symbolic editor,
debugger, utilities, PAL

Architecture
UNIBUS

Price
$20,000

Achievements
Became industry standard for
16-bit minicomputers

A New Architecture

The more people used minicomputers, the more uses they found for them. By the mid-1960s, many customers began to outgrow their machines. As the cost of hardware dropped, the costs of developing software and training rose.

Five years after the success of the PDP-8, Digital engineered a new machine with more power at a lower price. The PDP-11 introduced the idea of compatibility as a safeguard against obsolescence and sold close to a million machines.

By 1971, all the power of a CPU could be packed onto a sliver of silicon. In another year, floppy disks offered a cheap, portable alternative to built-in hard disks, parallel processing presented an alternative to von Neumann's original step-by-step scheme, and relational databases showed the potential of electronic libraries—as the video game craze emptied pockets of loose change.

By the mid-1970s, computers in medicine performed CAT scans and were used to confirm diagnoses, Wang sold word processing, and the CRAY-1 was the first successful vector processor.

PDP-11 system manufacture

"Our goal was to have a family of expandable, plug-in processors. I remember making many visits to customers, and hearing them talk about the speed of the instructions, and so on. It impressed the OEM marketplace. That was the marketplace that was buying them, because it had a job to do—go and create applications. Our computers were easier to interface to, easier to develop software on. Our customers were technology-hungry companies."

— PDP-11 Engineer

1970 *Corporate Profile*

Employees
5,800

Revenues
$135 million

Locations
68 around the world

Highlights
Digital stock begins trading on New York Stock Exchange.
New training centers open in Munich and Paris.
More than 8,000 Digital computers installed, 1,800 in Europe.

PDP-11 automates newspaper publishing

LSI-11

The PDP-11 Family

To take advantage of the new hardware technologies, Digital proceeded to build a series of compatible minicomputers to span a wide range of processing power. At the time Digital produced four computer families: 8-, 12-, 16-, and 32-bit computers. They offered a range of performance, but the machines were not yet compatible.

Making hardware compatible would save customers time and money by enabling them to move applications easily to larger—or smaller—machines as their needs changed. Compatibility would eliminate the need to rewrite software and retrain users on new machines, and dramatically reduce the need to invest in new peripheral equipment.

In April 1970, Digital delivered the first PDP-11 system, the PDP-11/20. More than Digital's first 16-bit computer, it was a new idea that guarded against obsolescence, and the start of a family of compatible computers designed for simple, incremental growth in power and performance that the company and Digital customers could build on.

DECwriters in production

A Lasting Success

From 1970 to 1990, Digital built four generations of PDP-11 systems, ranging from a small 4-user system to a large 64-user machine. In 1975, a new generation of hardware technology, Large Scale Integration (LSI), further streamlined the PDP-11 design. The "computer on a board" provided greater performance than the PDP-11/20 and maintained compatibility with the PDP-11 systems that preceded it.

The PDP-11 was an instant success. In its first week of release Digital received 150 orders. Today more than half a million PDP-11 systems are still operating around the world.

The phenomenal popularity and growth of the PDP-11 product line led to a change in Digital's organizational structure. As larger and more complex PDP-11 systems were engineered, Digital reorganized product lines to correspond more closely to specific applications and markets.

Much fanfare attended the design and manufacture of the PDP-11. To escape the fire of PDP-9 wire-wrapping guns, the design team worked below the loading dock of the Mill, coming up regularly for design reviews.

PDP-11 Family Timeline

1970	PDP-11/20, first of the PDP-11 series of compatible systems, first UNIBUS product
1972	PDP-11/05, better price/performance for OEM low-end requirements PDP-11/10, end-user version of 11/05, for data acquisition and industrial control applications PDP-11/45, fastest in its price range, uses three types of primary memory
1973	PDP-11/40, PDP-11/35
1974	PDP-11/04
1975	PDP-11/03, LSI-11, "computer on a board" incorporates Large Scale Integration (LSI) technology PDP-11/70, internal cache-memory design
1976	PDP-11/34, PDP-11/55 PDT-11/150, Programmable Data Terminal, first terminal-based PDP-11 system, based on the LSI-11 board
1977	LSI-11/2: LSI-11 in half the size PDP-11/60, PDP-11/74
1978	PDT-11/110, /130, packaged inside the new VT100 terminal
1979	F-11 chip set MicroPDP-11/23, minicomputer performance and software in micro-sized package, runs RSX-11M operating system PDP-11/44
1981	PDP-11/24, entire computer central processor on single 8 × 10 circuit board GIGI, low-cost graphics generator uses LSI-11 board T-11 chip, first chip-level PDP-11
1982	Professional 300, 325, 350 personal computers, the "Personal PDP-11" J-11, a PDP-11/70 in two microprocessor chips
1983	Micro PDP-11/73
1984	PDP-11/84, Professional 380
1985	MicroPDP-11/83
1986	MicroPDP-11/53
1987	MicroPDP-11/53+
1990	MicroPDP-11/93, MicroPDP-11/94

PDP-11/24, 1981

"**The PDP-11's unified bus architecture (UNIBUS) is 'democratic' in that every part of the computer can be addressed as if it were a location in memory. . . . Switches can be arranged to form matrices permitting communications among several bus structures, constrained only by the imagination of the user. . . ."**

— *Electronics*
February 15, 1973

The Incredible Shrinking Machine

The first working models of the PDP-11/20 used backplane wiring and standard flip chip logic cards. Then, module by module, as the design checked out, bulky assemblies of standard cards were replaced by dedicated printed circuit boards, etched specifically for the new machine.

The computer kept getting smaller and smaller. By the time it was done, the entire PDP-11/20 fitted into a box 10½ inches high—half the size of the original mock-up.

The PDP-11 team of hardware and software engineers, experts in diagnostics, marketing, manufacturing, and field service all helped to champion changes to produce machines that were at once reliable and economical. One example was significantly reducing hardware, assembly, and service costs by putting memory cores down flat on large boards and running wires through in one pass, rather than stacking them in layers and then wiring the layers together.

Another efficiency was giving field service technicians who would install and service the first shipments on-the-job training by helping manufacturing gear up for production.

In all, design to delivery took 13 months—the team beat their own schedule by one month.

PDP-11 components

UNIBUS

The PDP-11 computer family was built around an innovative design called the UNIBUS. Traditionally, the central processor not only processed information, but also continually monitored and controlled all interactions between memory and I/O devices. With the UNIBUS, all components were connected— not to each other, but directly to a single, bidirectional bus. Each device now had its own unique address and interrupt priority. The UNIBUS was the first single data bus to send, receive, or exchange data without processor intervention.

The new design improved performance by off-loading the CPU and simplified system design. It provided a new level of modularity in computers. By defining an interface for each piece of the system, it allowed independent, parallel development of memory, peripheral, and central processor. And because components were connected to the UNIBUS, peripherals, memory, even processors, could be removed and replaced, or added later, without affecting the rest of the system.

In April 1970, when the first two PDP-11/20 systems were delivered to customers, dozens of PDP-11 development projects were under way at Digital. From May to November, 17 new products were introduced, and PDP-11 options developed at such a pace that it was not unusual for price lists to be out of date by the time they were printed.

PDP-11 systems on factory floor

PDP-11 telephone switchboard application

Refining PDP-11 Software

The first PDP-11/20 systems were shipped with either 4K or 8K words of core memory, rudimentary paper-tape software, a Teletype, a paper-tape reader, and punch.

The original software consisted of a few paper-tape utilities: an assembler, a loader, an editor, and a simple operating executive. In the fall of 1970, DOS (Disk Operating System) was released, which offered alternatives to paper tape, including DECtape, a fixed head disk, or a removable disk. Since prototypes of the new PDP-11 were not yet available, programmers used a simulator on a PDP-10 to waste no time capitalizing on the new technology.

After DOS, which was designed for general-purpose use, came the introduction of operating systems that were optimized for certain applications: RSX-11D and RSX-11M for real-time applications, RSTS and RSTS/E for timesharing, and RT-11 for real-time applications such as monitoring and control.

PDP-11 education application

New Markets for PDP-11 Applications

The PDP-11 did not replace the PDP-8, as some had forecast, but it did open new markets and new applications.

Its modular design made it possible to configure the best system for the cost, performance, and reliability customers needed, both by interconnection and, when necessary, by adding new components.

The first PDP-11 systems were sold to technical customers. But as the software became richer and the range of computers and options multiplied, a variety of "packaged" systems expanded their appeal to commercial customers.

PDP-11 Software Timeline

1970 RSTS-11, timesharing operating system

1971 MUMPS-15
DOS-11

1972 MUMPS-11
Typeset-11, timesharing application for typesetting

1973 RSX-11D, real-time system for online data acquisition, monitoring, and control
RSTS/E, timesharing operating system for education and computation center environments
FORTRAN-11

1974 RSX-11M, real-time operating system for data acquisition and control
RT-11
IAS, Interactive Application System

1978 DSM-11

1979 RSX-11M-PLUS

1982 MicroPower/Pascal

PDP-11 system

Specifications

VAX-11/780

First shipped
1978

Word length
32 bits

Speed
1 VAX MIPS

Memory
4K MOS RAM chips, originally limited
to 1 megabyte total physical memory
Original memory cycle time:
1,200 nanoseconds

Instruction set
243 different instructions on several
basic data types: 8-, 16-, and 32-bit integers,
32- and 64-bit floating point,
packed decimal, and unpacked
numeric strings up to 31 decimal digits,
character string (up to 65,535 bytes),
variable-length bit fields up to
32 bits aligned on any bit position,
and queues

Input/Output
UNIBUS or MASSBUS disks and
tapes typically, 1–2 tape drives
and 2–6 disks configured
RPO5, RKO7, and TE16 most common

Software
VAX VMS Version 1, intended
as the all-purpose operating system
for the VAX family,
FORTRAN-77, COBOL, BLISS-32,
and VAX-DECnet optional
layered products

Architecture
Enhanced PDP-11 architecture to
increase virtual address space
from 16 to 32 bits, doubling
general registers from 8 to 16

History
VAX-11/780s were sold until 1988

Price
$120,000–$160,000

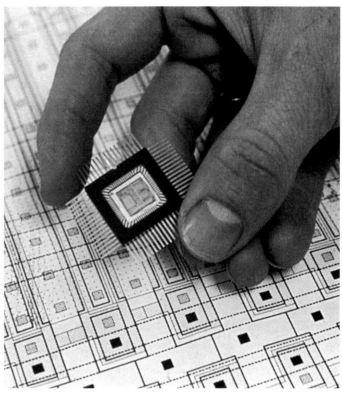

VAX system chip

Enter the VAX

The VAX changed Digital's approach to architecture and became a standard of comparison for a new breed of super-minicomputers. At the same time, the PC industry was launched by the Apple II, which could be hooked up to any color television. The first desktop computer from Tandy laid the groundwork for a global PC market.

WordStar and VisiCalc provided popular word-processing and spreadsheet programs that personal computers could run. In 1981 IBM introduced its first PC. Running MS-DOS as its operating system ensured the future of Microsoft. Soon Lotus 1-2-3 combined VisiCalc's spreadsheet capability with graphics and data retrieval.

DECtalk converted text to speech, and Apple's Macintosh made a success of the mouse as interface, which was developed some years earlier for the short-lived Lisa.

Apollo's first workstation gave engineers and designers enormous computing power at a fraction of the cost of powerful processors. Programs such as PageMaker promoted desktop publishing, compact disks economized optical storage, and precautions were on the rise against computer viruses.

"To deal with complexity
and changing technology,
it's necessary to break
a system down into lots
of pieces and establish
stable, well-defined
interfaces between those
pieces. This approach is
known as an architecture.
There are good and poor
choices of architecture.
A good one will be long-
lived, and will make it
easy to manage com-
plexity and deal with
change."

— Bill Strecker

"It seems programs
always grow to match
or exceed the amount
of memory available."

— Richie Lary

Engineering lab

1977 *Corporate Profile*

Employees	Revenues	Locations	Highlights
36,000	More than $1 billion	100 United States 53 Europe 28 General International Area	PDP-11/70, 1,000 in operation. LA36 DECwriter, 50,000 sold. First computerized remote diagnosis in the industry: Colorado Springs, Colorado; Basingstoke, England; Valbonne, France.

"The best of what we've learned about interactive computers in our first 20 years has gone into this machine. We have spent more than 300 man-years of intensive engineering effort in its development, and during that time I have sensed more excitement and enthusiasm among the developers of VAX than I remember seeing at any other time in Digital's short history."

— Ken Olsen
October 25, 1977

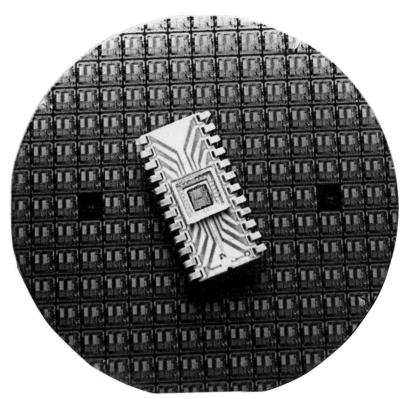

MicroVAX chip and wafer

A New Kind of Computing

By 1975, Digital had reached a crossroads. The need for a new kind of computing became increasingly evident. Not only did customers need more power and memory, but they needed computers at minicomputer prices that would work compatibly with the growing PDP-11 family of processors, peripherals, and software.

A New Economy of Design

Extending the PDP-11 architecture was becoming awkward. A 16-bit computer can address 2^{16} or about 65,000 different locations. But as larger programs were developed, it became harder to fit them into that number of locations. Extending the architecture to 32 bits, a matter of simple multiplication, would supply that power. Deciding on a name for the new machine was the final step.

The acronym VAX—Virtual Address eXtension—reflects the increase in the system's memory capability over the PDP-11. With twice the address space, the VAX can address 2^{32} or roughly 4 billion locations. With virtual address extension, memory space no longer had to be in the system's internal memory all at once. Instead, the whole program sits on a disk, and the operating system moves pieces in and out

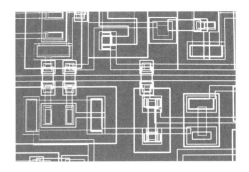

VAXstation 2000

VAX programming

of internal memory as needed. This was important for the first VAX systems because they had very little internal memory.

Compatibility emerged as a dominant theme from the earliest days of the VAX. Compatibility was in keeping with Digital's original vision: making investments last by ensuring that systems are efficient, easy, and economical to use and maintain. The VAX A team developed the Virtual Address eXtension architecture to ensure its compatibility with the PDP-11. It was important for customers to adjust easily to using the new systems. The VAX B team reviewed this architecture and still is responsible today for maintaining the compatibility that makes a VAX a VAX.

"In the early 1980s we ran into trouble. We were designing computers so complex, our engineering processes couldn't keep up with them. We discovered we had to use the latest VAX to simulate the new one we were building. Building VAXes on VAXes—our first computers became tools for building the next generation of VAXes."

— Bill Strecker
Joined Digital 1972

Examining a disk under development

"VAX was the project
name, but it was never
meant to be the product
name. When it came
time to choose a name,
we thought PDP-what?
Then some marketing
specialist said there are
really two attributes that
are really important in a
name, if you want it to
be memorable. One is
that it be short and
pronounceable and the
other that it have an *X*
in it, because *X*s are
pretty rare letters, so
they catch your eye.
According to that theory,
we had the best name
sitting right in front
of us: VAX."

— **Peter Conklin**
Joined Digital 1969

The VAX Family

In the original VAX strategy, the VAX-11/780 was the top of the line, followed by lower-cost and lower-performance models, the VAX-11/750 and the VAX-11/730. In 1979, a new high-end system was conceived, code-named Venus.

Introduced in 1984, the VAX 8600 was the first of this new generation. Smaller systems made VAX VMS power more available and affordable by taking advantage of new technologies, such as Large Scale Integration (LSI), which gave the VAX-11/750 60 percent of the power of a VAX-11/780.

In the first VAX multiprocessor—the VAX-11/782, with two CPUs and shared memory—the primary processor conducted all the I/O and scheduled work for both processors, while the other provided additional power. Although its 8 megabytes of memory tended to overload the primary processor and limited the job size and efficiency of time-sharing, it enhanced performance considerably and was an important first step in multiprocessing. Processing interaction was transparent to the user, as in VAX 8000 and 6000 series systems to come. And the second processor was available as an upgrade to the original VAX, the 11/780.

VAX programming

Reducing the size of the VAX-11/700 series led to some practical firsts that meant a lot to users. The VAX-11/730 was the first VAX to fit in a single cabinet, and the VAX-11/725 was the first deskside VAX model.

Many other high-end, low-end, and midrange systems were to follow, including the desktop MicroVAX II, several models based on the new high-speed VAXBI bus—the interconnective heart of the VAX 8000 series—and the powerful VAX 9000 mainframe.

Even these large VAX systems do not test the limit of VAX power. By clustering as many as 32 large VAX systems, they can be linked to form a single, tremendously powerful computing resource, one that is unique to the industry. As the DECUS saying goes, "Old VAXes never die. They just get clustered."

The heart of MicroVAX systems is the "VAX-on-a-Chip," with 125,000 transistors and the functional power of 3,200 conventional chip sets. The chip was the first newly developed integrated circuit to be protected by the U.S. Copyright Office. The Semiconductor Protection Act of 1984 protects the mask work, the pattern of materials that make up the layers of the chip, from unauthorized copying.

"A good architecture allows you to add to it. If the foundation is sound enough and if the process disciplined enough, an architecture is almost infinitely extendable."

— Bill Heffner
Joined Digital 1975

Left to right, Bill Strecker, Bob Glorioso, and Ollie Stone

"Software development is very creative, very individual. We want to give the engineers the freedom to work independently, to work together, and to do the things they want to do."

— Bill Heffner

VAX systems

The Goal: Building the Most Flexible System Possible

The aim of the first VAX designers was to build the most flexible system possible. They designed a modular, "layered" architecture, with each layer corresponding to some level of the computer's operation. A similar approach was followed in developing the VMS operating system.

Specifications for the interface between hardware and software had to be so precise that hardware engineers building a VAX system of any size at any time in the future would be able to design "up" to the software specification.

In the same way, software engineers, working on an application at any point in the future would be able to design "down" to the hardware specification, confident that their program would run on any present and future VAX machine. The ultimate test was whether any piece of VAX software program would work, without change, on any piece of VAX hardware.

The VAX system was one of the first computers designed from the ground up by both hardware and software engineers. As a result, VMS is easy to program since languages and tools for developing software applications are fully integrated.

VAX Family Timeline

1975	Digital's 32-bit system first proposed	**1987**	VAX 8978, with up to 50 times the power of VAX-11/780
1976	VAX program office established		VAX 8974
	Starlet (VMS) project begins		100,000 VAX computers shipped
1977	Digital's first 32-bit computer, the VAX-11/780		VAXstation 2000
1979	Venus, VAX 8600 project begins		MicroVAX 2000

1975 Digital's 32-bit system first proposed

1976 VAX program office established
Starlet (VMS) project begins

1977 Digital's first 32-bit computer, the VAX-11/780

1979 Venus, VAX 8600 project begins

1980 VAX-11/750, the industry's first 32-bit minicomputer, uses Large Scale Integration (LSI) technology
First use of gate arrays in major system

1981 Gemini/Nautilus (VAXBI) project begins
VAX-11/782, first dual-processor VAX

1982 VAX-11/730, first single-cabinet VAX

1983 VAXcluster systems, loosely linked multiprocessing concept
MicroVAX I, VAX-11/725

1984 VAX-11/785, most powerful VAX to date
25,000 VAX computers shipped
VAX 8600, first new-generation VAX, Digital's highest-performance system to date
VAXstation I

1985 MicroVAX II, industry's most powerful superminicomputer, and VAXstation II extend VAX power to single-chip personal-size systems.
VAX 8650
VAXstation 500

1986 VAXBI-based systems: 8200, 8300, 8800
VAX 8800, most powerful Digital system to date
Digital's first ECL multiprocessor
VAXmate
VAXstation II/GPX
VAX 8500, VAX 8550, VAX 8700

1987 VAX 8978, with up to 50 times the power of VAX-11/780
VAX 8974
100,000 VAX computers shipped
VAXstation 2000
MicroVAX 2000
VAX 8250
VAX 8350
VAX 8530
MicroVAX 3500/3600
VAXstation 3200/3500

1988 VAX 8840, first 4-processor VAX runs symmetric multiprocessing (SMP).
VAX 6200 series: VAX 6210, VAX 6220, VAX 6230, VAX 6240—first small system to run SMP.

1989 VAXstation 3100
MicroVAX 3800/3900
MicroVAX 3100
VAX 6000, -200, -300, -400 series
VAX 9000 series

1990 MicroVAX 3100e
VAXstation 3100-76
VAX 4000-300
VAX 6000, -400 and -500 series
VAXft Model 310, fault-tolerant VAX
VAX 9000 series expands by 10 servers

1991 Four new VAXft models extend high availability.
VAX 4000 triples previous model's performance.
VAX 6000 Model 600 doubles previous model's performance.
15,000 VAX 6000 systems sold.

Engineers review program on paper tape

5

Doing the Right Thing

"In 1971 we had just introduced the first PDP-11, the PDP-11/20, but it was a giant machine and Gordon Bell's analysis showed that it was too complicated and wouldn't compete with Data General's new Nova. We needed to put out a new low-end machine fast, and we'd been working on a 16-bit PDP-8. Gordon was on leave of absence at Carnegie Mellon, but he'd come up to the Mill on weekends. One weekend, my boss couldn't make it and he needed someone to go to the meeting so I went.

"In the middle of the night before the meeting, we sat down with the PDP-11 user manual and came up with this idea that the PDP-11 could be microprogrammed, which was a very new technology at the time, so we figured we could build a complete low-end PDP-11 as cheaply as we were building this PDP-8 machine. The next day I proposed that and Gordon said, 'Then build it—it's obvious.' So we sketched out a paper machine, the PDP-11/05, and announced it within a couple of weeks—those were the days when you introduced things and built them later. But, we were supposed to go to this trade conference two months later with the real machine, and we had no way of making it. It was just impossible. We tried to lay it out and it just couldn't be built. Everything that could go wrong went wrong. The design was so complex that the printed circuit board people didn't even want to help us, or be assocated with us, so we had to make our own boards. These were wild times.

"One day, some guy showed up in the lobby of the Mill. He shouted, 'I can sell you a 1K PROM for $5.' I said, 'Come on! Let's go!' I took him up, and said, 'What the hell are you talking about?' He told me that they had developed a PROM [Programmable Read Only Memory] that could be programmed with microcode using a blaster. They didn't know exactly how it worked, but they could build a few.

"The conference was on a Monday, and all the stuff came in the week before. One of the greater comedies of errors was that all the electrical power in the Mill was scheduled to be turned off that weekend for maintenance. Roger Cady, the PDP-11 group manager, got a giant extension cord and ran it to Building 5, powered up our area and we kept going. The last step was to dump the writable control store into the PROM. Right as we were doing it, some turkey walked up to the PDP-10 where we were doing all the programming, and turned the switch off! The programmer who was working on the project just got up and left. I came up with this idea of how to dump the ROM [Read Only Memory] out of a programmable box, and we eventually got everything together the night before we went to Las Vegas to the show. I said, 'Let's turn it on and if it runs for 15 seconds, we'll ship it.' I turned it on, it ran for 15 seconds, we put it in a box, we all went home and got one hour's sleep.

"I think of Digital as being this giant herd of engineers running around looking for an opportunity to make money."

— Tom Stockebrand

"The culture has always been engineering-oriented. It runs on technical peer evaluation, and many managers have technical backgrounds. They respect directness and straightforwardness; excessive diplomacy gets in the way."

— Bob Taylor

"To some extent, engineers have always been king of the hill at DEC. Ken was a circuit designer, so he loved and appreciated what circuit designers and other engineers did. But more important, the engineers had a jargon that others didn't share. And the customers, at first, were engineers, too, so we could talk to them. We understood each other's engineering jargon."

— Russ Doane

The next morning we bought a seat on the airplane for it, took it to Las Vegas, plugged it in, and the damn thing ran for a week. In fact, some of the other machines that had been better engineered didn't work there because the power was bad. In those days, we had so many problems that the only way to make things work was to engineer things way over the limits.

"The 11/05 was a roaring success. We came home and started working to put it into production. They said, 'We're going to move manufacturing to Puerto Rico.' I said, 'That's pretty funny, ha-ha.' They said, 'Everything is stable now.' I said, 'Right, how can it be stable if we can't even test one yet?' We had no understanding of what was happening across all the different processes, it was just a midnight prototype, how can you transfer its manufacturing to Puerto Rico? So they said, 'OK, we'll just send the whole engineering crew to Puerto Rico.' They sent us there for about 90 days. Eventually we got the PDP-11/05 line up and running, and we sold a whole bunch of them."

— Steve Teicher

Proposing and Doing

Digital is an engineering company, first and foremost. Its founders were engineers, its managers are mostly engineers, and one out of every two professionals is an engineer. Digital's products sell less on price than on their engineering excellence. An engineering ethic saturates the entire operations of the company.

"There are certain generating principles at Digital," says Russ Doane. "The first one is to 'Do the right thing.' Another is that 'He who proposes, does.' Another one, although not really formalized, is to foster competition internally to keep people and groups slightly off-balance, so that they have to think individually."

Engineering is all about creating new and better things to meet practical ends. "When you engineer something, you're always stretching to create something that's never been done before," says Gordon Bell. "As a result, a project's always going to be in some kind of trouble."

How do you structure a company to continuously come up with new products in a changing high-tech environment? Traditionally, you use a command-and-control hierarchy in which top marketing management dictates new product directions. At Digital, that process is virtually reversed.

"Ideas bubble up from the bottom and find their ways into products," says Wayne Parker. "Freedom and creativity go hand in hand. You think up an idea, propose it, and all of a sudden—it's yours. Good luck!"

"We always tried to make DEC engineering highly entrepreneurial," says Gordon Bell. "I coined the slogan 'He who proposes, does' to make engineers totally responsible for what they did. We always gave engineers a lot more responsibility than they had control or ability to execute things. Otherwise, you'd have tremendous finger pointing going on."

The ethic of proposing and doing created a self-regulating mechanism for developing and managing engineering projects. "In engineering, you're expected to execute what you propose—so if you can't execute it yourself then you're not about to commit to it," says Stan Pearson. Proposers need to form ad hoc project groups, find their own resources, and get "buy-in" from other groups upon which their projects depend. Engineers need to be both entrepreneurial and responsible for what they committed to—and this required a certain cultural shift for many new-hires.

In Digital's tremendous growth years, from 1959 to about 1983 (through which the company grew by an average of 35 percent per year), Digital tapped the best and brightest talent from the top engineering research labs and schools. "We were lucky in that we attracted more than our fair share of really good, very creative engineers," says Gordon Bell. Those that were offered jobs found the atmosphere akin to engineering heaven. "The environment we tried to create was very open and supportive," says Bell. "Everyone was on a first-name basis, there were no time clocks, and dress was informal and casual. A lot of other engineering organizations had hierarchies, called people Mr. and Mrs., wore suits and left at five o'clock. [Ours] wasn't a university environment—they can often be very, very uptight and closed. The goal was an absolutely open and free exchange of information so that everybody was free to propose, criticize, and review, and ultimately do what they thought they should do—the 'right' thing."

"The idea of doing the right thing came from Ken," says Bob Reed. "It was a combination of the Yankee ethic and the engineering ethic. If you do the right thing, you'll be rewarded; do it wrong and you'll be scolded; but initiate nothing at all and you'll be fired. Ken always talked to managers about treating your employees like your own family. When family members are engineers, you want to encourage them to come up with ideas on their own and guide them, as appropriate, on that path."

Engineers love a creative environment, but primarily they love to make things. They want to be on the cutting edge of technology and to work on hard problems with the best people in their field. But they also want their work to be appreciated and used, to make a contribution to the world. So many engineers migrated to Digital from research environments and government labs. "In a government lab, nobody ever buys or uses your stuff," says Tom Stockebrand, who, like Ken and many other early engineers, came to Digital from MIT's Lincoln Lab. "You get so frustrated because your work never gets out. Working at DEC gives you the opportunity to get your ideas into production and do something for the world." Other malcontents from top technology research and development organizations worldwide came to Digital for the same reasons. For example, many of the leading engineers of the Xerox PARC research group—those folks who in the '70s first developed today's crucial computing technologies such as window user interfaces, client/server computing, Ethernet, and multiprocessing—came to Digital in the early '80s for "the fun of being able to get real products out into the market," as their manager, Bob Taylor, puts it.

"Although Digital is a very large company, it operates in a beneficial way like a small company," says Bob Taylor. "If you want to make something happen at Digital, you find out the people that agree with you who are strong technically, and you can usually make it happen. That's both a blessing and a curse. When I first joined the company and was exploring and trying to learn what was going on, I found seven different display controller projects scattered through engineering and no one of the seven knew about the other six. You

Space, Atmosphere

"What impressed me about Ken and the general engineering atmosphere at DEC was they give you a job to do and then give you a lot of space to do it in. They didn't prescribe here is how you should do the job, they let you find your own way to do it."

— Barbera Stephenson

"The atmosphere encourages people to try to do things even if they're not funded or approved. There's a lot of controlled leaks around the bureaucracy. Any engineer, with enough will, can get almost anything into development."

— Russ Doane

can say that's wasteful, and yes, it is, but look at the alternatives. You could have some czar or committee deciding, sitting and making judgments that sometimes cut out the wheat as well as chaff, which would be much worse."

High-Quality Products

The ethic of proposing and doing the "right thing" resulted in high-quality products. "Quality was always number one at DEC," says Barbera Stephenson. "It was very exciting for an engineer. You always felt that what you are doing is important and that people cared about it being done and being done well. You spent whatever time you had to to get it right." Success depended on extraordinary personal commitments, often creating high levels of personal stress. "The atmosphere has always been that of small groups of engineers with extremely high energy, working hard and aggressively for long, long hours—always on the edge of burnout," says Jesse Lipcon. "That can be both positive and negative."

Another constant challenge was in understanding what, exactly, was the "right thing" to do. For example, when engineers are responsible for defining products and product quality, there is a tendency toward overrunning budgets and slipping schedules. "As an engineer, you can figure that you're only going to be working on an average of 6 to 10 major projects in your entire career," says Tom Stockebrand. "So it behooves you, no matter how late or how much over budget a project is, that it be top quality because you're going to be measured only a small number of times."

The ethic has resulted in a perception that Digital engineering tends to "over-engineer" products—creating extremely elegant product designs, and making sure that they would work theoretically even in the worst case. "DEC sometimes can be very conservative in hardware design," says Gordon Bell. Many of the PDP computers of the early 1960s kept running at customer sites into the 1980s, turned off not because of system failures but because of new cost-efficiencies. Newer large computers were designed with extraordinary redundancies, especially in power supply systems. Some members of Digital's original PC line were even over-engineered to the extent that they could perform satisfactorily in outside environments ranging from the Arctic to South American rain forests—not a plus in a typical office environment. "On the other hand," says Allan Kent, "I've never heard a customer complain about a product being too well-engineered."

Looking Out for the Customer

From the very beginning, the "right thing" to do was to do what was best for the customer, and being very close to customers was a key element of Digital's success. In the early days, virtually every system sold had to be custom-configured and often custom-designed, and the engineers designing the systems spent considerable time at customer sites, understanding the customer's requirements and designing solutions. "We didn't separate ourselves from the customers," says Russ Doane. "Our strength was in being customer-driven, not market-driven. When you're customer-driven it means that there's a specific human being that you've hung around with where they work, while they work, and you have a profound knowledge of how they work. We could smell the warm armpits."

Many an engineer's first weeks of employment at Digital were spent not in internal training programs but with customers. "Two weeks after I was hired, three of us spent a few days down in New Jersey touring pharmaceutical companies," says Cathy Learoyd. "You often worked right at the customer site. We spoke the same language as customers because we were engineers and the customers were engineers too. Going down into those laboratory environments and seeing the mass spectrometers and blood analyzers and learning about the process of collecting and analyzing data for 10 years to prove a drug is valid, you could see what kind of a contribution you could make, and what you needed to do to meet their needs."

Managers sent new-hires directly to trade shows or regional meetings of DECUS, the Digital Equipment Computer Users Society. "When we hired new kids, we'd send them right to DECUS," says Bill Heffner. "They'd see who the customers were. Then we'd make them give a presentation at the next DECUS. They'd have to get up in front of their users and get yelled at and shouted at, and they would come back with a much more realistic viewpoint of the world than the computer science viewpoint they learned in college."

"DECUS gave us a self-correcting process for meeting customer requirements," says Stan Pearson. "If you let the customer down or didn't meet a schedule, you were nose to nose with them. Having a customer show you their disappointment was really hard on people, because you were talking to the actual person you let down. The engineers would feel terrible. But then they'd come back with a list of customer needs, and really fight to get them implemented in projects."

New products came directly out of the ethic of proposing and doing. Engineers took their understandings of customer requirements, blended with their understandings of technology and product directions, to propose, develop, and test new products out in the marketplace. "The first versions of products don't always meet customers' needs all that well," says Lynn Berg. "Our crystal balls aren't perfect. That's what DECUS is all about—showing customers first versions of products or new product ideas, making lists of what changes they'd like to see, and helping us to decide when we'll fix all those things. In fact, most new products come from engineers saying, 'This looks neat, let's try it.' Sometimes, that's as good a place to start as any—then you can get some customer feedback and start to amend your original ideas around that."

Soldering Transistors Together

At first, Digital found its niche in designing modules for laboratory and research engineers. "When we started, there were all these transistors becoming available," says Russ Doane. "Anyone could have soldered them together themselves, and, in fact, that's what our customers had been doing. The trick was to find applications for circuits using these transistors that nobody else had found, and that's what we did." Doane says that the art at that time was in designing circuits; Ken was a circuit designer, and understood that niche better than anybody.

First Woman Engineer

"I was the first woman engineer at Digital—in fact, I was the first woman engineer that most people at that time had ever met.

"Ken came down to MIT one day to interview EE candidates. The list gave just last names, and there was a mixup in rooms. I was walking back and forth and  he was walking back and forth. Fortunately, he was bolder, and asked if my name was Stephenson. He invited me to the plant and offered me a job as an applications engineer.

"At first, I fielded module configuration requests. Customers would call for an applications engineer. They'd say, 'I want to speak with an engineer' and I'd say, 'I'm an engineer' and they'd say, 'No, I want to speak with a real engineer.' I developed this patter: 'Well, tell me about the application you have in mind. We have three lines of modules ranging from 5 to 10 megacycles and if you're going to use one as a front end, you'll want a higher frequency than in your later stages, but maybe you'll need to mix and match them, depending on different signal processing input and output characteristics . . .' The line would go dead, and I'd hear 'Hey Joe, guess what, I've got a . . . woman . . . engineer on the phone.'"

— Barbera Stephenson

"We started Digital with some interesting ideas," says Ken Olsen. "We were absolutely the fastest computer company only once in our life—when we opened our doors. We started Digital with a set of circuits and a concept for making computer systems based on these circuits that would be very fast, much faster than anyone else's. The laboratory customers bought all these little pieces from us—modules, connectors, sockets, cables, piddly little mechanical things—and they'd put them together and they worked. We worried about the customer, we worried about every little detail the customer needed, and we changed the computer industry."

"In 1960," says Barbera Stephenson, "these digital modules were completely new, even to Ph.D.'s, because nobody was teaching digital circuits or logic courses in college yet. To use them, people had to interface, hook up, and program them themselves—which meant we had to teach them to do it themselves. Ken came up with this idea of creating a lot of little application data sheets and incorporating them into a Digital Logic Handbook that would explain how to do it. I took on the job as one of my first projects and wrote the first logic handbook, as well as the next four versions of it. It worked both as a textbook and as a promotional tool, and they were incredibly popular. We sent them to every customer and handed them out like hotcakes at trade shows. We did print runs of 25,000—amazing for such an esoteric subject."

Many customers started by ordering single modules for specific laboratory tasks, but soon found ways of growing their logic applications by adding more modules and connecting them in innovative ways. "Engineering customers built subassemblies of our modules that started to take on the characteristics of computer systems," says Russ Doane. "A whole lot of the electronics applied to physics, psychology, and manufacturing in the 1960s depended on the wide variety of these Digital products. I personally designed about 150 distinct modules." Handbooks offered about 500 of them and they were extremely profitable for a couple of decades. Digital built pre-computer systems for many modules, and in the 1960s they were important to business. Many were memory testing systems, which evolved many years later into the PDP-5 and PDP-8. But the most important modules were some logic modules that Ken decided to make—the ones eventually used to make the PDP-1. It was a clever strategy, because when he finally got the encouragement to go into computers from Digital's somewhat reluctant AR&D investors, he was already well prepared. Modules were for many years Digital's bread and butter, but computers had been a gleam in Ken's eye right from the start.

Connecting Modules into Systems

With success and a steady revenue stream from modules, Digital was able to enter the computer business. Just as modules could be created by soldering standard transistors together, a complete computer system could be created by connecting the company's modules. Again, the enabling art was in circuit design, but also, Digital engineers' experience in using modules for customer applications provided the critical expertise necessary for systems engineering. No other company in the world was in a better position to take module technology and engineer low-cost computer systems.

Still, the American Research & Development investors balked at getting into the computer business, which up to that time had meant extraordinary investments, for machines costing millions of dollars, with little promise of profitability. It was a risky proposition, to be sure. Digital engineering consisted of a staff of 10 people—not the hundreds of engineers working on computers at IBM, UNIVAC, and other ventures—and those 10 engineers had to keep busy working on module circuit designs. Ken's solution was to call the project the PDP-1, a Program Data Processor, not a "computer." "But of course it was a computer," says Gordon Bell. "The PDP-1 was really the first viable commercial computer application of transistor technology."

Ben Gurley headed up the PDP-1 engineering effort, and Dick Best remained in charge of the module design business. "But each engineer had their fingers in both computer and module design," says Bob Reed. "It was who you worked with, not who you worked for. We were all working on modules, but Ben or Gordon would always be coming up to you to say, 'Look, I need some help on this widget for the PDP-1,' and you'd just do it."

Everyone could monitor the PDP-1's progress daily. Jack Gilmore remembers that, "In the fall of 1960, Ken set up a room with a window right by the entrance way, so that everyone coming to work could see the PDP-1 being put together." The first PDP-1 was given free of charge to MIT. "That was a strange bit of reasoning," says Bob Reed, "but it worked. It gave us a test bed for finding bugs, and since we weren't planning on developing or selling any software with the PDP-1, it was a way to get some basic software developed. And of course, it gave us some credibility that we had a real product." The strategy worked: orders for the PDP-1 started coming in.

"Those were the days when you first offered something for sale, and then if someone ordered one, you designed and made it," says Gordon Bell. "Every PDP-1 order was custom-designed and full of custom-built options. For example, one of our earliest customers, Lawrence Livermore Lab, ordered a system with virtually every option we could think of—IBM and UNIVAC tape-drive interfaces, punch card interfaces, even a 5-inch scope with 4096×4096 resolution that's still nearly unrivaled today in its precision. We were lucky we didn't have more orders for such exotic equipment. And we were lucky to get an early order of 20 or so PDP-1s from ITT because they were all configured the same. That introduced the idea of a standard system. If that hadn't happened, I don't think we would have survived in the computer business."

Engineers had extremely tight relationships with customers. "We knew mostly all of our customers from previous module applications, and we were expected to sell," says Bob Reed. "We took the orders, customized the machines, delivered them, fixed them, and stayed there until they worked. I was amazed at how much give and take there was. Usually the systems didn't work at all right off the bat, but customers were roll-up-your-sleeves types and were willing to work together with you to make them work. They put up with a lot, but they knew that they had a machine that was comparatively very inexpensive, interactive, approachable and had a lot of potential in their application." Allan Kent, then a PDP-1 customer at Raytheon, remembers how Digital's top A/D module engineer, Barbera Stephenson, was constantly on site for application development. "One of the key skills you needed to

Tell Me, Little Lady . . .

"Since I had so much interaction with customers, I was on the committee that decided on new product ideas, and it was the exact same situation. Visitors would think I was a secretary at the meetings, there to take notes or get coffee. Once I said something technical, their mouths would fall open.

"We had a lot of fun at trade shows. People would assume I was a model. I remember one guy who lifted up one of the modules and said, 'Tell me, little lady, what kind of capacitor is this?' I said, 'That's not a capacitor at all, it's a pulse transformer.' He said, 'What are you, an engineer or something?' I said yes, and he went running away. Ten minutes later he came back with his buddies and said, 'Say something in Engineerese.' I consented, and gave each of them a handbook with some descriptions I wrote up, to help them understand how to use these modules. I'd say, 'I have the patent on the design of these A/D modules.' It was hilarious, you should have seen their faces."

— Barbera Stephenson

HELP

"At first, we had no idea how to build complex computer systems. Our approach was basically to plug it in and see if it smoked. We spent endless hours trying to make the early machines work—engineers were in the Mill seven days a week until 2:00 A.M. I remember calling Gordon many a night, and he'd come down in his bathrobe and pajamas with his toolkit under his arm and try to get things to work.

"We made the classic mistake of trying to design complex hardware and complex software at the same time, so you couldn't debug anything. Every night something different had been changed—but you wouldn't know exactly what. So I came up with this idea of typing 'HELP' when you first logged in, and you could see what changes had been made. That evolved into the first interactive 'help' program, and now they're standard on any computer system."

— Larry Portner

succeed as a Digital engineer," Stephenson says, "was to learn how to climb up over the stockroom wire fence at night to pull out a spare part that a customer needed immediately."

New Product Ideas

With the success of the PDP-1, new product ideas came fast and furious out of engineering. "The PDP-1 was an 18-bit machine, and in those days the word size of a computer was not something that people had settled on yet," says Alan Kotok. "Sixteen-bit and 32-bit computers hadn't taken over the world, and we hadn't yet figured out that you could get better performance more easily by pushing the technology, rather than changing the architecture. So when customers started asking for more power, it seemed to be obvious that they needed larger bit-size machines."

"The PDP-2 was a mythical machine number, reserved in case we wanted a 24-bit computer," says Gordon Bell. "It was never defined on paper. The PDP-3, a 36-bit computer, was defined and one of our customers actually built one using Digital modules. We almost got an order for a PDP-3 from the Air Force, but Harlan Anderson and I persuaded them to take two PDP-1s—two 18-bit machines instead of one 36-bit machine."

Need for Smaller Machines

At the same time, the need for smaller, less complex, and less powerful computer systems was being understood. "The PDP-4 18-bit computer was at first custom-designed for Foxboro Corporation and started us in a new line of business for real-time control," says Gordon Bell. "Because we didn't understand the cost or value of software, and we didn't develop any, the PDP-4 turned out to be a business mistake. Fortunately, it led to the PDP-5, which in turn led to the PDP-8 and the start of the minicomputer industry."

But in 1962, the real glamour seemed to be in developing ever larger and powerful computers to compete with the reigning behemoths of IBM and UNIVAC, at a fraction of their system costs. Alan Kotok remembers that "Gordon came running into the lab one day in 1962, as he was wont to do, and said, 'Time to build a big computer, guys!' MIT was looking for a large time-sharing system and Gordon felt that there was no reason that we shouldn't build one for them. So we started designing what would become the PDP-6."

"By time-slicing a computer among many users, we provided each user with what appeared to be their own large computer," says Gordon Bell. "The idea of timesharing came from two PDP-1 customers—Bolt Beranek and Newman, and MIT. We designed the PDP-6 from scratch to be the first commercially available timesharing system ever offered, so that everybody could have their own piece of a large computer for interactive personal computing."

"Technically," says Alan Kotok, "it seemed that a 36-bit architecture was the way to go. We wanted to directly address a lot of memory, and MIT at that time was rather enamored of this programming language that John McCarthy had just developed, called LISP. The structure of LISP required two pointers, and so we decided that the word size needed to be 36-bits to handle it. Also, because memory was at a premium, we discovered that having an architecture composed of a large repertory of instructions could increase system performance.

We wanted to have very powerful instructions where in one instruction you could cause a whole sequence of events that seemed useful to occur. So we came up with this scheme of using 365 different instructions for the PDP-6. It was the original CISC (Complex Instruction Set Computer) machine. Nowadays, with memory so cheap, RISC (Reduced Instruction Set Computer) machines are more efficient, but in those days of expensive memories, the PDP-6 architecture was the most elegant thing that anybody had ever seen. It seemed to strike the fancy of every computer hacker who came in contact with it."

"Unfortunately, our ability to design and build something of the size and complexity of the PDP-6 was somewhat lacking," says Alan Kotok. "We built a few and sold a few, but none of them ever worked right. There were a lot of flaky electrical signal problems—a static discharge from the line printer would crash the system, the memory would die, things like that. It was hard to get up and running for more than a few hours or so. It was a great embarrassment."

Kotok says that Ken called the PDP-6 group together in the cafeteria of the Mill one day and said, "Well, at Digital everyone gets a chance to make a mistake and you people have made yours. I always knew that big computers were a bad idea. So you really have to be thinking about doing something else."

Eventually, the PDP-6 group recovered from their original failure, and began redesigning a "smaller" large computer system, based on the PDP-6 architecture, that resulted in the PDP-10 product family. "The PDP-10 was basically the PDP-6 done right," says Larry Portner. The PDP-10 used new circuit modules to more than triple performance, and a new wire-wrapped backplane design for much higher system reliability. "The PDP-10 ran a lot faster and essentially it worked all the time," says Alan Kotok. "The PDP-10 got to be known as the machine to have in the computer community, especially at universities. The price was reasonable, and you got a lot of machine for the money. The architecture and the huge instruction set were viewed as being very elegant. There was also no competition in the realm of high-performance interactive systems—IBM's batch-mode systems were always viewed with great disdain in universities."

Enabling Technology

Meanwhile, throughout the PDP-6/10 development effort, a number of technology innovations started emerging to increase the viability of the less-glamorous small computer efforts. First was the development of an inexpensive data storage medium—DECtape—that allowed a computer to be used interactively. "Fixed disk storage systems had been around for some years," says Tom Stockebrand, "but they were incredibly expensive. Tape storage had also been around for years and was pretty cheap—but you couldn't use it interactively because you always had to write new data at the end of the tape, so it would take forever to find any specific data you were looking for. We came up with this idea at Lincoln Lab of making sectors on the tape—just like today's diskettes—that gave you random access to data, so you could use DECtape as a fast, interactive I/O storage system. DECtape really changed computing styles, because for the first time, you could make a small, interactive computer that was really inexpensive."

Failure and Success

"The PDP-6 project was way too big for the company at the time. It ate up all of our resources for three years, and to make it a business success would simply require more cash than the company could generate from profits. We had bitten off much more than we could chew. In retrospect, its failure was the main impetus behind the creation of small computers and multiple product lines, which would allow people to choose sides and be responsible for the success of one or another computer."

— Gordon Bell

Designing

"I had worked on the LINCtape for three years at Lincoln Lab, and when I came to Digital I was sick of doing tapes. DEC promised me I wouldn't have to work on them anymore, and I started working on some interesting subsystem designs. But there was a project going on to turn the LINCtape into a product—DECtape—and it wasn't going well. The engineer would keep coming up and asking me, 'What should I do?' Then one day I ran into Ken walking down the aisle. I don't know what happened, Ken is so smooth, but within 30 seconds I was saying, 'Oh, darn, it's so simple, it shouldn't take any time at all, I'll do it.' I learned very quickly what older engineers already knew: never make promises like that to Ken."

— Tom Stockebrand

A second enabling technology was the beginning of integrated circuits, which allowed complete circuits of transistors and interconnections to be shrunk down onto a silicon chip and mass-produced. Starting in 1963, Digital invested heavily in one of the first IC technologies, called "thick film ICs." "Basically, the technique was to put a bunch of very small components in some conductive gloop and melt them in the oven," says Tom Stockebrand. "Then you flipped them over and bonded them to the printed circuit board. Ken labeled the gadgets 'flip chips' and we set up a production line with a bunch of ovens and some 30 people on the top floor of Building 4 in the Mill. Unfortunately, the yields were terrible and after a year we called it quits because the flip chips were simply too expensive to produce, and we moved on to newer IC technologies. We continued to call the new module products 'flip chips' even though they used real ICs. But Ken came around three years later, and told us, 'Don't feel bad. We got into and out of that technology way before our competitors did, and now they're all wasting millions of dollars on it and we're way ahead of them.'"

A third enabling technology was the idea of creating very small computers designed with minimal instruction sets. "When we saw what our PDP-4 customers were doing," says Gordon Bell, "we came upon the idea of the PDP-5, a really fast and inexpensive general-purpose computer that could be embedded in larger systems to do process monitoring and data collection. The PDP-5 was further refined into a design for the PDP-8, the first real mini-computer. The PDP-8 was exactly half the cost of the nearest competitive system, and it was half the size of the PDP-5—you could put it in the back of a Volkswagen, as we showed in our ads. But it wasn't a component—it was a complete computer system that sold for $18,000, and it sold like hotcakes."

"The PDP-8 design was the most simple and trivial way you could possibly compute," says Russ Doane. "It wasn't what we call low-end today, it was bottom-end, designed to be as cheap as the dickens. Back then, to introduce computing to people who couldn't afford it before, it had to be absolutely bottom-end. The PDP-8 used only eight instructions, unlike the 365 instructions used for the PDP-6, so it was truly the world's first RISC (Reduced Instruction Set Computer) machine. It was developed by only two engineers, and made out of the standard flip chip modules we had hanging around."

"When the PDP-8 was announced, it blew the company wide open," says Bob Reed. "At first, we were planning on making a few of these things on speculation. But then the orders started coming in by the thousands. The original machine, the 'classic' PDP-8, was the Model-T of computing—a totally standard, minimal system, but one that anybody could afford. Its success really changed the engineering mind-set of the company."

A Brilliant Organizational Concept

With the success of the different PDP computing platforms, Digital reorganized in 1964 into product lines, pushing responsibility for developing and nurturing products onto the shoulders of product line managers. "The original product lines were essentially marketing groups with their own separate engineering groups," says Jesse Lipcon. Some were organized along technology: a modules group, an 18-bit systems (PDP-1) group, a 12-bit group (PDP-5/PDP-8), a

36-bit group (PDP-6/PDP-10), and so forth. Others were organized along customer application lines: laboratory data processing, manufacturing and distribution, academic computing, and so forth.

"The idea was to delegate profit and loss responsibility to product line managers, who could be responsive to different niche-market customer needs," says Gordon Bell. "It put responsibility to maintain commitments and revenue along divisional lines, as opposed to the functional organization Digital had at that time. It was a brilliant organizational concept, and because each product line was essentially at cross-purposes with each other, it created a new kind of entrepreneurial spirit."

Engineering projects thus became funded by product line management, "who could develop and acquire anything to meet customer requirements and be responsive to local market opportunities," says Larry Portner. As a result, the development of software and peripheral systems took on an expanded role, because product lines weren't just selling CPUs—they were selling customer solutions.

Software Comes from Heaven

Early software development efforts were minimal. "DEC for many years was strictly a hardware company," says Larry Portner, "and software was viewed as a necessary evil. Software budgets were initially zip, and we didn't sell software as products. Until the mid-1970s, new CPU projects happened without a software plan, and hardware engineers just threw the new machines over the wall to software engineering, where somebody would scramble like hell to put together some software to make it work. We'd put whatever we developed into the DECUS library so customers could get hold of it. I used to complain to Ken and he'd say, 'Hey, you do the hardware and the software is free—software comes from heaven.'"

Basically, software at that time did come from heaven. Originally, customers wrote their own software, using the instruction sets of each PDP system. Most freely shared their programs with other users through the DECUS program library, so that programmers didn't always have to totally reinvent the wheel—and that, in turn, helped to foster the use of more computers by more users. Universities were an especially fertile source of programs for the DECUS library. "Digital gave away its first systems free, or at least at sharp discounts, to universities," says Richie Lary. "These were actually seeds that they planted, because, in a few years, they'd reap both software for the DECUS library and people who could develop software for them."

Software developed by Digital for early machines was seldom more than an assembler, a compiler (usually FORTRAN), and a debugger. All were developed as afterthoughts to the PDP CPU development. "It used to be really hard to make good, clever, cheap computer hardware," says Russ Doane, "so that's where we put our development dollars. Of course, today it's the software that sells the machines." That trend began around 1970, "when competition, in the form of 16-bit systems from Data General, started to come in and customers started realizing the value of software as a differentiator," says Larry Portner. "Morale in software engineering at that point was pretty low. We were all feeling like second-class citizens, because the fruit of our labor had no relevance internally in the company—because software wasn't a product. A product

It's the Output That Counts

"One of the first PDP-8s came to Brooklyn Polytechnic, where a bunch of us would spend all of our time programming it, to the exclusion of everything else, and to the extent that some of us didn't graduate. So, naturally, we wound up at Digital, working on PDP-8 software. We put in 100-hour weeks because, to a certain extent, there was nothing we would rather be doing.

"At the time, there wasn't an operating system for the PDP-8. We had picked up something called the 'Cooley Programming System' from the University of Michigan and I modified it for the PDP-8. But when I got the sources, I found that it used too much memory and was otherwise horrible. Its user interface was designed like an IBM 360 and was incompatible with everything else. Our manager understood and for six months would say, 'Yes, we're making some slight modifications to the Cooley system,' but that was an out-and-out lie, because we threw it out completely, and started building a single-user system that would make the PDP-8 look just like a PDP-10. By that time, we were developing our code on the PDP-10 and were rather enamored of it. It was a neat machine.

"Finally, we got this operating system finished and our manager said, 'Here's the modified Cooley Operating System, how do you like it?' Of course it looked just like a PDP-10, and everybody loved it. We called it PS/8, the Programming System 8, and it was the first software product that we had ever shipped and actually charged for. But in reality, it was a midnight hack, and really set a good tone for us in working at Digital. The message we got was that it's the output that counts, not the process."

— Richie Lary

was something that you shipped, you invoiced for, that brought in money. So we put together something called the Software Product Proposal to unbundle software and charge for it. We spent almost a year selling that to the company."

"There were huge product line manager meetings," Portner says, "where people stood up on their chairs and screamed a lot and said, 'It's immoral to charge for software. Software is supposed to be free, it has no intrinsic value.' Despite the fact that it had high development costs, the simple fact that software had virtually no manufacturing cost made it zero value. But finally the economics and the concept of charging based on value, rather than cost, set in and we charged full speed ahead into software development."

David Stone was one of hundreds of software developers that Digital hired in 1970. "I responded to this *New York Times* ad entitled, 'Portner's Complaint,' in which Larry lamented the problem of ever getting all the programmers he needed in his operating systems engineering group. Our main focus was on developing operating systems that could meet different customer and product line needs," Stone says.

Software engineering technology was becoming much better understood, says Stone, along with the idea that you could do many things more easily in software than you could do in hardware alone. This led to the idea of creating multiple operating systems for general-purpose computers. "From a design perspective," Stone says, "you can design an operating system in one of three ways. First, you can focus on doing batch processing, the classic IBM way, where you optimize the use of the computing hardware at the expense of the users. Second, you can focus on timesharing, where each user gets a slice of time and you optimize on the perception of the user; that's what the PDP-10 operating system did. And third, you can focus on real-time performance, which means the highest priority gets all the resources; that's what the PDP-8 operating system did, and what the new PDP-11 was designed to do." But you could also mix and match these three characteristics into specialty operating systems that could run on different general-purpose computer hardware. For example, real-time and batch capabilities were added to the PDP-10, and most important, each product group could develop customized operating systems for the PDP-11 to meet the needs of customers in its target markets.

The PDP-11 was designed to be a long-lived family of compatible and low-cost, general-purpose hardware systems. Product lines seized the opportunity to create specialized PDP-11 operating system software to meet their customers' unique needs. After the original DOS, a general-purpose operating system, came the RSX-11D and RSX-11M real-time operating systems; RSTS and RSTS/E for timesharing; RT-11, a fast, single-user, real-time operating system similar to OS-8, and a whole host of others—14 different operating systems in all.

A Handful of People in a Corner of the Mill: Creating the PDP-11

The year was 1969, the 12-bit PDP-8 was the minicomputer, and Digital was the PDP-8 company. But several firms had already introduced low-cost 16-bit machines, and customers were anxiously awaiting Digital's answer to the competition. Internally, there was an understandable resistance to a product that might displace PDP-8 business.

A follow-on to the PDP-8 had been discussed for several years. In fact, two projects had been started. The first was abandoned because it failed to meet cost goals. The second, code-named DCM (Desk Computing Machine), had run into design problems. Two CPUs—one 8-bit and one 16-bit—had been partially designed. A memory system was ready for release, software was under way, and packaging had been designed. But the processor design was not crystallizing. Benchmarks were run and instructions added, and one change led to another and another, with no end in sight.

Roger Cady took over the DCM project in the beginning of 1969, along with a handful of people in a corner of the Mill—just one project among many that were then in development. "Hal McFarland, one of Gordon Bell's students at CMU, had proposed a completely different architecture for the instruction set processor," says Cady. "Time-to-market was so important that it seemed to be way too late to make such a wholesale change. On the other hand, the architecture we had was not working out. We wanted an architecture that would last. So in the course of about a week, we decided to discard about a year's worth of work."

The decision was made to switch to an entirely new 16-bit architecture that simplified programming and would take full advantage of a common data bus, the UNIBUS. Work then proceeded at a frenzied pace to get a machine ready for market. Cady renamed it the PDP-11. Digital was coming from behind, and the pressure was on.

Within 12 months' time, the team, never numbering more than a couple dozen, brought the first PDP-11 from concept to delivery. "There was a great deal of informality, and little stratification of effort," says Bob Puffer. "Managers were designing, technicians were designing, designers were managing, and everybody was expediting. Jobs were parceled out to people who had time. Relatively little was systematized or written down. Much happened verbally in face-to-face conversations—people walked around with engineering note-books under their arms, had impromptu meetings in hallways, jotted down notes, and went off to make things happen." According to Roger Cady, "Only one person on the team was doing anything close to the job he was trained to do—Bob Hamel had previously done some memory design."

Gordon Bell advocated the use of a single bus architecture as opposed to the separate bus structures that had been used in all previous computers. This concept, embodied in the PDP-11's UNIBUS, provided an unexpected bonus for the design team. It gave interface specifications for each piece of the system. This meant that memory, peripheral, and central processor development could all proceed independently and in parallel. "That enabled us to go faster to design system units modularly and expand as we went along," says Cady.

Digital had previously designed computers using backplane wiring and standard flip chip logic cards. The PDP-11 group used that technique to build the first working modules. Then, module by module, as the design checked out, bulky assemblies of those standard cards were replaced with dedicated printed circuit boards etched specifically for the PDP-11. "Engineers wrote their own component specifications," Cady recalls. "Drafting, printed circuit layout, the board shop, and other support operations were all near at hand in the Mill so it was relatively easy to get things done and make changes." The computer kept getting smaller and smaller. By the time it was done, the entire PDP-11/20 fit into a box 10½ inches high—about half the size of the original mock-up.

"We didn't have much experience," says Cady, "but we were energetic, enthusiastic, and too dumb to know what we were doing couldn't be done. So we did it anyway. Our goals were always to build a family of compatible computers and establish an architecture that would last a long time, lowering the costs of computing and giving priority to making them easy to use. The fact that it let us grow at the rate of 80 percent a year and catch up with the competition, that was just gravy."

Original sales of PDP-11s were mostly to highly technical customers and OEMs. Then, as the Digital-supplied software tools grew richer, and more and more applications were developed for the PDP-11 by third parties, the PDP-11 became a huge success and started to gather most of the company's attention and development budgets—much to the frustration of the other product line engineering groups.

Internal Rivalry

"The start-up of the PDP-11 caused a lot of internal rivalry with the PDP-10 group," says Bob Stewart. "There were a lot of snide cracks made back and forth. The -10 group felt that the -11 group didn't pay enough attention to details, didn't do a thorough job on technology, had a machine that was too small for any practical purpose, and so on. And the -11 group felt that the -10 group wasted money, built gigantic boxes that didn't go any faster than the -11s, and so on." Part of the rivalry came from the basic technical design dichotomies inherent in the instruction sets of the different machines. "The instruction set for the -11 was certainly radically different: in retrospect, one might even say downright weird," says Stewart. The instruction set "purists" in the PDP-8 group, who had created the ultimate simple machine, didn't like the -11 very much either. "We thought they were bent on making everything as complicated as possible rather than as simple as possible," says Richie Lary. "There was a lot of sniping at the -11 group going on because they were trying to do a lot of things the hard way."

While there had always been rivalries among the product lines, the PDP-11 seemed to bring matters to a head. "The markets and customers had always been almost totally separate up until then," says Allan Kent. "The -8 group at the low end, the -10 group at the high end, the different laboratory modules and PDP-15 systems and so forth. But the -11 family started to overlap each of the other groups' turf."

"A certain amount of rivalry was healthy," says Stan Pearson, "because when you compete against yourself you get better. But it started to get out of control." With overlapping businesses, it became more difficult to know what the "right thing" was to propose and do. There were basic conflicts between doing what was right for the customer, right for Digital, or right for one's product line management. "Digital had really come to look like four completely different business fiefdoms with four completely different sets of platforms—PDP-8, PDP-10, PDP-11, and PDP-15," says David Stone. There were many redundancies in designing elements that could have been shared. "We used common modules and common cabinets," says Allan Kent. "We shared manufacturing and different floors in the Mill. But there was no commonality between designs, and little interaction between product engineering."

"When I came back from Carnegie Mellon in 1972," says Gordon Bell, "engineering resources were few and they were owned by the product lines. I was playing vice president of Engineering, but I had no resources. But by then it seemed to me that the original entrepreneurialism had become fake. Each product line was simply building new follow-on machines that would simply compete with each other and not our competitors. There was a lot of conflict and waste—we were supporting 14 different operating systems, and there were 17 different projects going on to develop terminals. And a lot of the product line engineering projects were simply ill-conceived. Many were attempts to increase margins, or do product differentiation between groups where no differentiation was needed. They were even using operating systems to segment their markets. So, in February of 1974, I basically proposed to centralize Engineering and have every engineer report to me."

Making the Most of Resources

The creation of Central Engineering allowed Digital to make the most of its technology investments and scarce engineering resources. It resulted in immediate economies of scale, for example, by consolidating engineering projects for peripheral systems into common lines of terminals, printers, disks, and so forth that could be used by each computer platform. But it especially positioned the company for efficient growth in the future. "The industry was just poised for the explosive growth that new technologies like large-scale integrated circuits and networking would bring," says Stan Pearson. "These technologies required much higher resource investments and longer-term commitments. The reorganization happened just at the right time to let us make those large-scale investments effectively."

Under the reorganization, product lines became focused on customer applications, not on base computing platforms. While product lines retained small engineering appendages, their product design, engineering, and planning functions were negotiated and integrated through Central Engineering.

"When Central Engineering got going," says Bell, "we needed enormous new methods. You could say we were intuitive on one side, but we measured every damn thing and ran the whole place on semi-log graphs! We planned for everything to increase exponentially—our systems performance, our product output, our revenues and growth and space requirements—everything. To do that, our planning had to become much more formalized. We developed all kinds of mechanisms for making a good coupling between Engineering and Marketing. Products got proposed to the Marketing Committee, where strategies were determined for various price bands, market uses, and new investments. Every engineering group had a board of directors composed of all the marketing groups, which forced people to analyze their proposals from all angles. All of this was aimed at the budget allocation process, and allowing each group to understand what they were really doing. It was really just enforced self-management."

Communicating

"The move to Central Engineering didn't make much of a difference to most individual engineers. It was a big deal for managers, who tend to think a lot about careers and so forth, but engineers tend to think only about the product or project they're working on. Things were a lot more project-oriented than group-oriented back then, and there was a strong network among engineers, with all the engineering groups working together in different parts of the Mill. When a project was about to finish, we'd just talk to our buddies and find out what new things were starting up, the word would spread, and soon you'd find a new project to work on.

"That worked really well until we started moving engineers out of the Mill. As groups split up and moved to remote locations, it became less practical to trade people from one group to another, both because of the geography and because the informal network didn't work as well. So things gradually became more group-oriented. When the PDP-10 group moved out to Marlboro, that took them out of any contact with the rest of the world. We all worked for the same company, and every so often we'd attempt some meetings and so on, but it only increased the rivalry between the groups.

"Of course, things came full circle again later on, when the engineering data communications network got going. By then, most engineering groups had been squeezed out of the Mill, but it didn't matter any more because with electronic mail and notes files, you could communicate sometimes more easily with an engineer in Marlboro, say, than with one at the far end of the Mill."

— Bob Stewart

Some of the methods installed by Central Engineering formalized engineering procedures, product planning, and accountability. A whole series of engineering standards, both technical and procedural, were codified to describe the company's combined knowledge of engineering processes and product quality requirements. A phase review process was instituted, in which projects were reviewed by engineering and product line managers before proceeding into development, announcement, and manufacturing production. Plans were communicated through a series of color-coded documents. There was a red book that described each project, a yellow book that showed the schedules and dependencies, a beige book that outlined the budgets and funding that was used as a negotiating tool, and several others.

"Basically, the new Central Engineering processes were just a formalization of the ethic, 'He who proposes, does,'" says Stan Pearson. They created checks and balances for a certain level of quality control and sanity checking, and they worked quite well at first. They provided the glue for different groups to work together successfully, for the good of the company. Eventually they started to degenerate, as all good bureaucratic processes do, and began to get in the way. The phase review document grew from a single page into a huge notebook. Engineering standards grew to be thousands and thousands of pages long. The color strategy books started filling with fluff and disinformation. But, as usual, when processes at Digital start to crack under their own weight, the first principle of "doing the right thing" would kick in again and everybody would just ignore them to get things done.

Tom's Terrific Terminal and The Toilet Paper Printer

With the success of Digital's multiple computer lines in the early 1970s, a key thrust was to expand into peripheral systems: terminals, printers, disk drives, and so forth. For example, one strategic and eventually very profitable challenge was to improve the ways people interacted with computers—specifically, to create a better terminal. Most users used either Teletypes or expensive third-party terminals to communicate with their Digital CPUs. Product lines had created interfaces for different kinds of terminals, but Digital's first terminal product, called the VT05, was competitively too expensive and, although well-designed, not a hot seller.

Tom Stockebrand formed a group of 20 people to build the next-generation terminal product. "We had ambitions to create a video terminal that would be super low cost, with super functionality, and just take over the world," says Tryggve Fossum. "Stockebrand is an incredible person who really encourages people to be creative and to do innovative and countercultural things. He let us come up with dozens of wildly interesting features to put into this thing. At that time, television sets were coming down in price, and the technology was well understood, so we set about merging TV sets, computers, mass storage, terminals, and printers in one single product. Some of the features we dreamt about are now featured in PCs, but not always in the form we envisioned.

"We called it 'Tom's Terrific Terminal.' First of all, it would be able to work with any different Digital computer or competitor's computer. In those days, there were dozens of changing terminal protocols and no standards. This one would have a microprocessor built-in to do the conversions, and use an idea—borrowed from Teletype—called XON/XOFF to accept any different screen character size or line format, so each screen of information wouldn't go scrolling past you, which was a problem at high transfer rates. Second, it was going to have full-vector graphics so you could do pictures as well as words. Third, it was going to have a cheap printer built right into the back. We came up with this elaborate little scheme of using a helical scan facsimile device that would take what was on the screen, and using the same screen electronics, scan it across this small roll of paper. That became known as 'The Toilet Paper Printer.'

"One version was going to have a PDP-8 built into this slot in the back, along with a cassette tape drive that could be used like DECtape. The cost goal was $600. Even in 1971, that was dirt cheap for what would have been the first personal computer." As it turned out, the ideas behind Tom's Terrific Terminal were a bit ahead of their time. "For a while, we were optimistic that we could do these things, or at least a lot of them," says Stockebrand. "But we were under a lot of pressure to get a product out. So we did some advanced development, and then we went to meetings and compromised, and scaled back a bit and went to meetings and compromised and scaled back a bit, and did that again and again and again. Finally, we came out with something called the VT50. Ken introduced it at a sales meeting, saying it was the ugliest thing he'd ever seen, and actually it was way too big since it had all this room for all these options we never made, and after nine months it hadn't sold worth beans so we all got reassigned."

"In retrospect," says Tryggve Fossum, "the features on the VT50 seem laughable today. It used only UPPERCASE characters, there were only 12 lines on the screen, there was no numeric keyboard, there was no PDP-8 or printer or graphics options available, and it did look cheap with all this space inside, collecting dust. The VT52 included the printer, which, in spite of its problems, did well in Japan because of its ability to print Kanji characters easily. But we quickly came up with another version of the VT50, called the VT52, which was competitive for some time and we sold lots of them."

In spite of its traumatic birth, Tom's Terrific Terminal eventually led to one of Digital's largest engineering successes, the VT100 terminal. "The VT50 series got us into the terminals business," says Russ Doane. "There were expensive and unmanufacturable aspects of the design, but through it all we learned how to work with Manufacturing to produce high-volume products." A lot of what Digital does today was learned from the VT52. The difficulty was that it had never been done before. The VT100 was a solid step forward from the VT52. It was manufactured and sold by the millions. It was the industry's best-selling terminal of all time.

The experience with the VT52/100 was the archetype for Digital's ventures into the printer and disk drive marketplaces. At first, printers, disk drives, and other peripheral units were outsourced from third-party suppliers, Digital Engineering created interfaces to them, and they were imprinted with the Digital label. As the company began to venture into engineering and later manufacturing its own peripherals, most early models were far from marketplace successes. But over the long run, the experience gained and continual process refinements led to successful and competitive products.

Killing Projects

"I'm probably the greatest computer genocide guy going. That's kind of a paradox. It's one of the most brutal things you can do to an engineer: kill their project. But the worst thing for an engineer is to face the market and have a product fail in the marketplace. So what's the kindest thing to do, and what's the most profitable? Take your losses early."

— Gordon Bell

"If you can kill off your own project, you're a hero. If your boss kills it, you're a failure. But viewed from above, either case is exactly the same. It's hard, because it's human nature to fall in love with the things you're designing, but Ken always used to say, 'No one will fail in this company who raises their hand and says they screwed up.' The only ones who really fail are the ones that know they've screwed up and keep it a secret. Ken always did a good job of eventually rewarding honest failures. People who failed honestly were those who were doing new things for you."

— Tom Stockebrand

"You don't often see the 97 failures out of 100 attempts that go on in engineering. But the freedom to fail was essential to the atmosphere that made those three successes possible. However, when you do fail, you do have to take the consequences when you're responsible. I failed miserably on one project, where I wasted two years trying to develop an NC controller for the PDP-8, and had to work like crazy for another two years to overcome the stigma."

— Russ Doane

Push the Technology

"We had a conscious strategy that basically said push the technology hard. Listen to customers, try to understand what they want, and then do it, be responsive. But compete with the other minicomputer companies by constantly expanding the playing field. When everyone else could do processors, then start building printers and terminals. When competitors could do them, then start building mass storage devices. When everybody caught up again, start interconnecting, and when everybody else can interconnect, start providing software and services and so forth, always trying to maximize our internal efforts, our strengths and capacity and financial clout."

— Larry Portner

Meaningful Compatibility

The Central Engineering review processes ensured that peripherals were designed to be compatible across the different and otherwise incompatible product platforms. But to achieve any meaningful level of compatibility required common communications products and networking software. A communications products group was started in the PDP-11 engineering group, says its early manager, Tom Stockebrand, "to figure out how you could hook up two computers over a telephone wire so that they could beep back and forth." This led to the development of dozens of communications board options for the PDP-11, each designed to meet different communications interfacing and protocol format requirements—sync and bi-sync, single and multiplexed lines, based on different international standards, laboratory standards, IBM and other industry standards, Digital standards, and on and on. Each board module had to have software drivers developed for each of the PDP-11 operating systems. The result was a crazy mishmash of communications hardware and software options—40 pages worth in the price list. It was daunting even for engineers to understand, not to mention other people who had to sell, configure, support, and use them.

"DECnet was developed to solve the problems of the different operating systems not talking with each other," says Larry Portner. The goal was to create a single, comprehensive networking protocol, such as IBM had just announced with its SNA, but one that would be modeled on peer-to-peer communications among different intelligent devices, just like the Defense Department's ARPANET. The beginnings of DECnet were not auspicious. "Stu Wecker, the original architect for DECnet, designed it with a real-time operating system in mind," says Tony Lauck. "When the first version was implemented on RSX it ran pretty well for starters. But when people tried to implement it on other PDP-11 and PDP-10 operating systems, there were some serious worries that their buffers would runneth over. There was a tremendous hue and cry, and all these implementors from different groups claimed you couldn't build DECnet, which, of course, they couldn't, and refused to implement it." The problem was elevated to Central Engineering, and further development was put on hold. "DECnet Phase I was really a mess," says Larry Portner. "Ken came up to me at the time and asked if we should kill it. That was tempting, but then we looked at the options and decided no, we didn't have any choice but to make it work."

Portner created a task force in 1975 to try to fix DECnet. "There were about a dozen people from different groups on the committee, and each brought in a big pile of the specifications they wanted implemented," says Tony Lauck. "Basically, they were not going to be allowed out of the room until they came to an agreement. The DECnet group had hired a bunch of people from IBM to fix the problem, and they were proposing to make it incredibly complicated, just like SNA. Stu Wecker, of course, disagreed vehemently and was excluded from the task force, but every night after the committee met he'd work with certain committee members to try to undo what they had done that day. At the end, the group kludged together some very complicated protocols, but luckily Larry Portner, instead of freezing the specs, handed them to me to create an architecture group and manage a final review committee, to make sure this was going to be a workable system. And, of course, we disagreed with much of what the original committee had done. So in the best DEC tradition, while creating the impression that the specs were frozen and we were just fixing some bugs, we surreptitiously went around changing many things, simplifying the protocols as much as we could get away with."

As DECnet was eventually implemented successfully across all of Digital's product platforms, it became the first glue that could tie together different systems. As engineers started experimenting with using the network, they started to understand the benefits of networking and of creating compatible systems that could use it more effectively. "By understanding that a network could be involved in practical computing solutions," says Lynn Berg, "we launched ourselves way ahead of the market in understanding the technologies, and the benefits of compatibility."

DECnet was a natural follow-on to the timesharing environments of the 1970s, and a precursor of today's advanced networking. "In timesharing," says Bill Demmer, "we developed systems that could provide various services to users who connected to those systems. The design often focused on maximizing the number of users the system could support. In today's client/server model—where the client requests the work, and the server does it—the balance of computing shifts to the desktop. The focus is on maximizing the services provided to the client.

"Over time," Demmer continues, "users began to realize that not all of the functions they wanted were immediately available from their timesharing system. They wanted access to data lying elsewhere in a corporate database or access to some computing resource that wasn't directly attached to their system. Digital and the industry started to work on that problem. In the 1980s, as a leader in peer-to-peer networking, Digital created a large, complex network of systems that would allow users to gain access to remotely located data or other computing resources.

"Today, we have advanced the state of the art of networking to the point where our customers have very complicated multivendor network environments. Each department in an enterprise might have a separate and different set of computing resources for its own use. In addition, individuals in these departments have a variety of personal computers which may be tied together in various local area networks. With client/server computing we want to take all the functionality that exists anywhere in that multiple vendor, complex, network structure and make it available to any user. And we want to do that in a way that feels no more complicated than timesharing."

Common Vision

"The key to compatibility is architecture," says Mahendra Patel. "The most important contribution of developing an architecture was to provide a common vision between different engineering and marketing groups. When you create an architecture, you have a vehicle through which you can negotiate technical goals and business goals to converge." Gordon Bell, Digital's original systems architect, says that at first, there was no notion of architecture. "It was all in one person's head. But as systems became more complex, we had to learn to write down the entire specifications to show how different system

Architects as Gods

"There's a reason that DECnet Phase III was very simple. There were only three architects, one of whom was in town one day a week. Each Wednesday, we'd spend the morning designing, and keep on designing things of increasing complexity up until noon. Then we'd go out to lunch at the pub across the street from the Mill. We'd have a few beers and we'd come back, look at the blackboard, and be completely puzzled by all the stuff we had designed. It would be way too complex, and we'd spend most of the afternoon simplifying things. In the end, we came up with something that all of us could understand even when we were not quite sober, and as a result, anyone else could understand.

"I was amazed at how much power we had then as architects at DEC. I had come from being a product manager, where you were responsible and you had no authority. When we got jobs as architects, we just puttered about as usual, trying to do a decent job, but I found out later that many of the engineers who implemented our specifications thought of the architects as gods. They wouldn't give us a lot of grief, they'd just humbly consent and implement the stuff we designed and make it work."

— Tony Lauck

elements would work with other ones. Primarily, architecture is the ability to take complex problems and structure them down into smaller problems in a simple, tasteful, and elegant way."

"Gordon's architectural model was a layered approach," says Larry Portner. "It's what we called the Onion Skin model. If you define standardized interfaces at each layer, then you can have development go on in parallel, and if you design those interfaces right, then new and old products at each layer will work together."

Originally, Digital architectures were developed to allow different portions of a new CPU to be developed in parallel. One group could work on the arithmetic processor, another on the memory, and so forth. In the mid-1960s, architectures started expanding in scope to include peripheral interfaces, the internal bus structure, and software. "An architectural approach was key to achieving software compatibility," says David Stone. "At first we set about defining the obvious kinds of interfaces. We standardized on language compilers and file systems. Then we started to combine the command languages for the PDP-8, PDP-11, PDP-10, and PDP-15. To do that, we locked the best and brightest people from each of the groups in a room until they came up with DCL, the Digital Command Language. That was just another architectural layer. As we added more and more layers, we started calling it "middleware," and middleware is today one of Digital's greatest strengths. Back then the middleware functionality was glommed together into each operating system, but we started pulling them out and defining different layers. Our ideas of defining different layers through architecture, in fact, is what made today's client/server computing style possible."

Architecture: A Simple Vision

"Digital has always been great at architecture," says Dick Rubinstein, "and it's the way we defined architecture that made us great. Architecture isn't just an interface or an instruction set, and it's not a product in the price book—it's really a simple vision of what a computer or a system means to an end user. It gives users a framework to solve their own problems." The PDP-1 architecture meant that the user had an entire, interactive computer to himself. The PDP-10 architecture allowed users to timeshare, equally and interactively, the power of a big computer. The PDP-8 architecture offered affordability. The architecture of the PDP-11 and the UNIBUS meant that boards from other vendors could be purchased and plugged in to build a complete system, an open systems architecture. With the VAX, the architecture was the simple, powerful, and radical idea of compatibility and scalability over time—old programs could run forever, on different small, medium, and very large VAX machines, without having to be rewritten.

The VAX started out not as a vision, but rather as a Central Engineering advanced-development hardware project to create a follow-on machine to the PDP-11. "I happened to walk into Gordon's office one day when what was foremost in his mind was the need to get more than 16 bits of addressing in a computer," says Richie Lary. "So I got drafted into the 'VAXA,' or VAX architecture group committee, which Gordon chartered to come up with an architecture to replace the PDP-11. There were six of us, and we met daily, usually all day long, for three months. At the beginning there were a lot of very unfocused discussions, and we'd call in people, both customers and internal people from product groups, and grill them on what they expected out of a follow-on PDP-11. Ultimately we came up with a couple of schemes to do simple, compatible extensions to the PDP-11, but we didn't like any of them. Finally we decided that there wasn't any free lunch—that became our committee motto—and that we would have to start absolutely from scratch. We said, we won't be absolutely compatible with the PDP-11, but we'd be culturally compatible and treat data formats the same way and have the same flavor of programming and so forth."

The VAXA group considered multiple alternatives, ranging from a RISC-type architecture to a PDP-10 type architecture, but found none of them compelling. "Then one day," says Lary, "Bill Strecker, who was one of the six core members of the group, came in with this beautiful and nearly completely thought-out scheme that he had come up with on his own. We diddled around with it, but basically, that was the VAX architecture you see today. We proposed it, and for the next two years people developed a crash project to implement it as the VAX-11/780."

Development of the VAX Strategy

At the time, though, the VAX project was just another machine, one out of many being proposed and developed by the different engineering groups; what really made the VAX successful was the development of something called the VAX strategy. "Ken kept pushing us to come up with some kind of coherent strategy for a change," says Stan Pearson, who ran the Engineering strategy committee. "And there were three separate, inconsistent views. The CPU people said that the CPU was the dominating factor and therefore everything should revolve around that. The peripherals people argued that peripherals should be optimized across different platforms, because they were rapidly becoming 50 percent of all system costs. The software people said that since you could do anything in software, the hardware wasn't important at all. There was lots of frustration and angry meetings, and nobody would back off, and in fact you could make legitimate arguments for any of the three perspectives. It came down to everyone looking to Gordon, and putting more and more pressure on him to decide. Finally, he came in one day and said, 'I'm going off to Tahiti for three weeks and when I come back I'll write down all of the strategy myself.'"

"The VAX strategy came solely out of my head in Tahiti in the summer of 1978," says Bell. "It was the idea of a three-level hierarchy: big machines in the data centers, midsize machines in the departments, and single-user machines on the desktop. Each machine was a VAX, and could run exactly the same software as any of the others. They would range from a VAX on a chip to the highest-performance computers that could be built. They would be totally binary compatible and have networking built in. A user could choose to use a single machine or to distribute work across other machines. The strategy also specified compatibility with other DEC computers and intercommunication with other standards and products."

Pot Stirring

"I met a guy recently from IBM who said, 'God, when you came out with the VAX and the one architecture, we knew we were dead, we didn't know what to do.' I said, 'Of course! It was designed to drive you guys crazy!' I got a kick out of that."

— Gordon Bell

"Gordon's pot-stirring and architecting on the backs of envelopes and injecting crazy new ideas into the system and poking holes in everybody's basic assumptions was essential to the health of the company back then. After he left in 1982, it was no longer possible for any one person to take on that role in Engineering."

— Dick Rubinstein

"Gordon is a real idea-generator and a volatile person. He would literally hop up on tables and scream and jump up and down, and people would tend to cower, but it was just his way of expressing himself. He threw out lots and lots of ideas and really expected people to say, 'No, Gordon, that's the stupidest thing I've ever heard.' You'd have to do that, and then he'd stop and think about it and say, 'Oh yeah, you're right,' and go on to the next thing. In the early days, I always thought the most important part of my job was to try to filter out Gordon's bad ideas before they went too far, which I did. But I don't know, maybe I shouldn't have done that, who knows where they would have led."

— Alan Kotok

The VAX strategy also was a radical marketing ploy in that it squarely addressed user demands for compatibility. It specifically exploited the fact that most other computer manufacturers had a menagerie of product lines and operating systems designed to segment the user base. Of course, Digital was also one of those companies; to follow through on the promise, Digital would have to consolidate its efforts and reinvent itself. Says Bell, "The VAX strategy was so simple, everyone could understand it—engineers, customers, sales reps, the press, even product line marketing groups. The strategy was something that I personally drove night and day until the Board approved it six months later, and then I drove it for another four years to try and get buy-in from all the product line marketing groups. And it caused enormous stress between Marketing and Engineering. The VAX strategy was the ultimate nail in the coffin of any business group oriented around a computer."

Stan Pearson remembers the difficulty in getting the VAX strategy accepted by all the different engineering groups that needed to implement it. "Gordon had to go around and sell it, and that was hard," Pearson says. "To succeed, he had to convince most of the engineering groups to completely reverse their directions, and there was naturally a huge amount of push back. In essence, they were being asked to sacrifice being on the leading edge for compatibility. Some of the human dynamics were: Who's going to lead the effort, product line marketing or engineering? Who's going to make the strategy? Who's going to eat the costs? Who's going to have to shut down existing incompatible product families and make good on the implied customer commitments? In the end, it was Gordon's personal power and the respect that everyone in Engineering had for him that finally drove the strategy through, but it took years to sort out and took its toll on everyone, most especially on Gordon himself. When he had his heart attack in 1982 and decided to leave the company, it was an apt metaphor that we all learned from: no one person could possibly do that again."

Pumping Code

While virtually every engineering group in the company had a critical role to perform in implementing the VAX strategy, probably the most important task was in creating the VMS operating system and supporting software products.

"Up through the PDP-11s, you could develop the hardware first and then get around to developing software later," says Bill Heffner. "But a VAX wasn't a VAX until it ran VMS. The VAX hardware without VMS would have been nothing, so we had to develop the software in parallel with the hardware and meet tight schedules. Today, you try to separate the software from the hardware, but back then it made sense to totally integrate the software and the hardware into one system. I had the advantage of having been a customer before I came to Digital in 1975. I knew the problems customers had, and the major one was to achieve compatibility between systems. Departments want to talk together with one another, and users want to talk to one another and share the same information. It's that simple. You don't want to recode and redo your programs all the time. So we set out to achieve two goals: one, you will never have to recompile your programs again, and two, all our systems will be able to talk with one another. We believed that if you did those two things, customers would flock to your door."

"Actually, we looked strongly at UNIX to see whether that should be the base for our operating system, but we rejected it," says Heffner. "At that time, it wasn't sound enough, it was a computer developer's toy, and in many ways it still is. We also looked at basing VMS on our other 12 incompatible operating systems, and that was not an easy decision to make. But in the end, the first customer we tried to satisfy was the technical customer, the FORTRAN user using RSX on a PDP-11, our largest installed base. So we made VMS upwardly compatible with RSX, and the first version of VMS had only one compiler, a FORTRAN compiler. We wanted that compiler to be the absolute leading FORTRAN compiler in the industry, so that if you talked to any FORTRAN programmer walking down the street and asked them what system would you prefer to use, they'd say, why, VAX VMS. Later, we put our energies into developing compilers for COBOL and BASIC and Pascal, and so forth, and into developing applications like VAXmail and WPS and ALL-IN-1, and so forth, but that FORTRAN was our first priority."

"It worked out that there were about a million lines of code in each new version of VMS," says Heffner. "The first version was about a million lines of code, and by the time we got to Version 5, there were 5 million lines of code. We're talking about a really heavy-duty operating system here, with more functionality than the world at that time had ever known. The biggest problem was to figure out how to make sure all of the new changes would work together with each other. Dave Cutler came up with this idea of base levels. Every two weeks we rebuilt the system whether you thought you needed it or not. We had a red week and a green week. In the red week, the system was locked. The green week you could put in your changes. Each week corresponded to a different base level, and that gave us the structure to do base-level testing. We'd do internal testing on that basis, and the joke used to be, well, it's not significantly slower than the last version."

The Intangibles of Developing Software

Managing software development is challenging. "Software engineering is an intellectual property business," says Bill Heffner. "It's very intangible because it's all up here in your head. It doesn't come in or go out of the loading dock — it walks in and out of the front door at all hours of the night and day. It's a strange business, full of strange people. As a manager, you need to provide a supportive environment, both physical and cultural."

The VMS development group started out working alongside the VAX hardware group in an old shopping center in Tewksbury, Massachusetts. "I think of DEC as a giant hermit crab that kept taking over disused shells of buildings and filling them with steelcase partitions," says Dick Rubinstein. "DEC hardware engineers have always taken a perverse delight in putting up with conditions that nobody else would," says Bob Stewart. "You couldn't hire a lot of people who were used to working in places like California because they just wouldn't work in the environment we had here. So the people we did tend to attract were pretty dedicated, but other than that, I can't think of any

Chaos Management

"Some business school guys came around once and looked at our organization and called it Matrix Management, but they were wrong. That's an old idea. In Engineering, we were far more evolved than that. In reality, it was Chaos Management. Ken's strategy was to make sure that new ideas kept spewing into the system and then wait for them to formulate, and eventually the truth would come out. His role was to make sure that the battles were equal. There were always open communications and no secrets, at least not for long, which always prevented localized chaos from turning into anarchy."

— Tom Stockebrand

"When I started at DEC, chaos was the order of the day, and that was a really new culture for me. Everybody was pulling in different directions and contradicting each other as often as they could. It was maddening, having come from a traditional engineering environment where everything was really what it seemed to be. It took me a year to find out that in fact, this was planned mania. That's how we wanted it. And there were clearly a lot of beneficial side effects."

— Mahendra Patel

Ladder Rungs

"One of the major reasons I joined Digital was that it had a technical career ladder. You could keep being promoted up through the engineering ranks, up to being a senior corporate consulting engineer, which was like being close to God. Very few companies have a technical ladder. At Digital, you could choose either the technical ladder or the managerial ladder, and that was really the biggest strength in attracting engineers to work on VMS.

"The whole role of management was to create the environment so that the technical guys could do their job. When I got here, nobody wanted to be a supervisor. There's this macho thing among Digital engineers that says you're nothing if you're not on the technical side. I tried to change that, and so did a lot of other good engineering managers.

"It's actually harder to find technically competent software development managers than it is to find technically competent individual contributors. When you're on the leading edge, your managers had better know what it's all about technically. College teaches you to be a good designer, but they don't teach you to be a good craftsman, have a concept of schedules, be a team player, to develop relationships with customers, or to keep your fingers off the specs, because developers will always want to add a bit more. We'd assign new kids to a senior person who would look after them, like an apprentice. Managing a good software engineer is like raising a kid—you want them to get into a little bit of trouble, but you don't let them burn down the house."

— Bill Heffner

obvious benefit." Engineers tended to complain a lot about the Mill, but as self-styled "Mill rats" they were always somewhat endeared to it. The Tewksbury facility, however, was a facility that was strongly and universally disliked.

The VMS software engineers, in particular, had difficulties in adjusting to the Tewksbury environment. As the group grew, it had the option of moving to a new facility on Spit Brook Road in Nashua, New Hampshire. "We jumped at the chance," says Bill Heffner. "Right from the start we were able to design it to be a good place to do software engineering. First of all, that meant making it quiet, because noise drives developers crazy. We banned copier machines, printers, and typewriters in the office spaces—secretaries didn't much like that, but of course it forced them to use word processing and do things online, which was a plus. We banned bells on telephones—the telephone company wouldn't give us phones without bells so some of the EEs, who in college seemed to have majored in upsetting the phone company, went around and removed the bells. We gave everybody equal office space. We had more consulting engineers per square foot than anywhere in DEC. We had contests to name all the conference rooms after computer scientists. But best of all, we chose the cafeteria vendor on the basis of what vendor could provide the best ice cream break at 2 in the afternoon, which became somewhat of a tradition."

One of the things that made VMS successful was that it was used by the corporation as it was being developed. "Everybody had to use VMS to develop VMS," says Heffner. "People had to drink their own bathwater, so if there was a bug or a lousy design, peer pressure would cause it to get fixed pretty quickly. Of course, you never know what you have in software until you have someone besides the developer try and use it, so the fact that other groups were also using it across the company provided an excellent feedback mechanism."

Moving Out of Maynard

As the company grew, engineering groups started moving out of the Maynard area to take advantage of engineering talent and resources in other areas of the country and the world. "Every few years, Digital would go through these periodic fits, worrying about using up all the available labor pool in Massachusetts," says Richie Lary. "Which, in fact, we were doing. So group managers would start to propose and get approval for setting up remote engineering groups in faraway places."

One reason remote engineering groups were set up was to attract new hotshot engineering talent. "For example, Barry Rubenstein proposed to move the Storage Systems engineering group out to Colorado Springs," says Lary, "because there was a feeling that you could attract people from California to move to Colorado but not to Massachusetts. But a lot of Massachusetts people, like me, said, 'Ooooh, Colorado—mountains, low humidity,' and decided to move. That created a bit of tension with Central Engineering, who felt that we were skimming top people away. It also made it more difficult to coordinate joint engineering design efforts between Colorado and Massachusetts. But when electronic mail and the engineering network got put in place, that made it possible for isolated groups to work together and to do remote engineering successfully."

Other remote engineering groups were formed simply "to get away from the politics in the Mill," says Lary, "or to work on systems and advanced development efforts that weren't mainstream." Tom Stockebrand, for example, started up a terminals engineering group in Albuquerque, and advanced development groups were set up in Seattle, the Silicon Valley, and multiple other locations, to take advantage of local talent and to have a certain amount of freedom that a large physical distance from headquarters would evoke. "That's a tight line to walk," says Tom Stockebrand. "Distance from Maynard gives you a certain amount of freedom in developing new, even radically new things, but it also gives you less influence in making them successful than if you were sitting through hundreds of meetings where the decisions get made. You'd still have to spend a few days a month back east to be able to have the necessary influence."

Geographical Efficiencies

Other remote engineering groups were formed for geographical efficiencies. As local Software Services groups began to do more and more customer-related engineering projects, decentralized engineering groups formed across the United States, and eventually worldwide, to support customer and industry-specific development projects.

International engineering groups evolved in the same way, with country-specific and large regional engineering centers evolving to support European and GIA (General International Area) engineering needs. As these centers grew, they supported and evolved Central Engineering's strategies in potent and unforeseen ways. "For example, you need to define things much more precisely in Europe and GIA, simply because of language barriers and geographical distances," says David Stone. "You can't just bring people to a lot of meetings and hash things out like you do in Massachusetts. You have to set out very clear goals, strategies, and architectures to make sure that development projects will be in sync or else they won't. That kind of discipline is something that we're learning to address to make isolated and even local engineering groups in the States more effective."

Midnight Projects

Digital engineering has always excelled at creating products that are useful to engineers themselves. "We do a much better job at creating technologies that we use ourselves—operating systems, programming tools, electronic mail, and so forth," says Lynn Berg. "We're better at being market-driven when we're the market. Our most important innovations traditionally are those that solve our own pragmatic needs. To a large extent, in fact, consolidating our efforts behind the single, compatible VAX VMS product family was for the benefit of our own engineers. We couldn't support all of those operating systems any more. We started with our own internal need for compatibility, and luckily customers had that same problem, too."

Many new software products were originally created as "midnight projects" that engineers would create because they seemed useful. "VAXmail, for example, which today no engineer can do without, was never invested in by the company," says Dick Rubinstein. "VAXmail was done as a midnight project, like dozens and dozens of other applications. That's how you got things launched here in the late '70s. Then we'd just start giving these things away to customers, unsupported, through the DECUS library, or just embed them in VMS or other products as part of the system."

"If you could come up with a midnight hack and sneak a project through the system, it was blessed," says Larry Portner. "There was even a certain premium associated with sneaking it through. That's always been a major source of new and innovative ideas. But we wouldn't always turn them into proper products, and we started seeing how something we called the Support Monster would sneak up and get us. One day we extrapolated and came up with the conclusion that the cost of supporting all of these initially unsupported hacks was going to exceed all of our revenues in three years' time. To head off the Support Monster, we decided we had to change the way we addressed software quality, that we would have to start treating software development as a discipline, not just an art form."

The problem in both funded products and in midnight hacks at the time was that they were too often incompatible in some ways with other VAX VMS software products. Much more discipline was required to complete the vision of compatibility, and Central Engineering took on that management role. This led to changes and more formalized processes in project management, and again, a certain perception that Central Engineering over-engineered products. But the price to be paid for compatibility created friction in field sales and engineering groups. "Customers would ask to use some of our internal unsupported products, or wonder when a new product we were developing would be available," says Lynn Berg. "The answer was always that Engineering was working on a product that is beautifully architected, elegantly integrated with all of the other products, and at least two years away."

As more and more support engineers were hired in field office locations, and not part of Central Engineering, the field engineers started developing, sometimes informally, customized applications that would meet customers' needs and their own. "The engineers in Central Engineering would get very offended by the inelegant way that some of the things were cobbled together in the field," says Berg, "but, in fact, some of the most interesting and useful solutions have originated with local people working directly with customers. The classic example, of course, is ALL-IN-1."

The Charlotte Package: The Creation of ALL-IN-1

"In 1977 I was a field software specialist, and we would work with 10 to 20 customers in a given day," says Skip Walter. "For each customer contact we'd have to fill out a stupid time reporting form that cost $1, took 10 minutes to fill out, and took someone else even longer to process. It was a nuisance, because we were out there using Digital systems to automate these kinds of applications for customers every day. But, like the shoemaker's kids, we had a silly manual system.

"After one staff meeting, John Churin, another software specialist, and I went into a room and started drawing madly on the white boards, trying to find a better way. We approached it at first as a paperwork automation problem, then started adding wish lists of functions we'd like to include. John had an incredible ability to look at specific problems and see how to make general-purpose solutions that could integrate different applications, and we realized that all the components we needed for a first-class Office of the Future system already existed inside the company. Three days later, we had designed what would become ALL-IN-1. All it would take was SMOP, a Small Matter of Programming. And somebody to fund it.

"We were excited about what we came up with because we figured, if we at Digital had this problem, odds were that customers did, too. In fact, we had recently received Requests for Proposals (RFPs) from five different customers in the Charlotte district for variants of an Office of the Future system. One customer had IBM develop a spec; when we saw it, we asked for another day to deliver our proposal. We spent eight hours putting together a beautiful 50-page, customized document with charts, using a word processor and a letter-quality printer for one customer. We returned the next day. The guy was amazed. He said it was six months' worth of work, and issued us a purchase order, on the spot, to do a functional spec. Back at the office, the sales reps were amazed—a purchase order for a piece of paper? Not even for a piece of hardware? What's going on? That was their first realization of how valuable consulting and meeting customer application needs could be.

"The spec we developed for R.J. Reynolds was a generic design and didn't include a piece of hardware. But the one thing we could guarantee was that it would be buildable. They gave us the go-ahead to develop the next level of detail.

"At that time, we didn't know what hardware we would use. John Churin came from a DECsystem-10 background, I came from a PDP-11 background, and we had just introduced the VAX. We decided to base it on the VAX, since neither of us knew anything about the VAX and it would be a fair learning experience. That was a very lucky decision.

"Another customer, Milliken, was enamored with an installed office system from Datapoint, but also invited us to bid. We learned that the ability to customize was key to meeting each company's varied needs. What the customers wanted in an office system wasn't just word processing and mail. They wanted an integrated environment in which they could mix and match custom applications and give that power to the end user.

"The R.J. Reynolds and Milliken experiences gave us a demo to propose Office of the Future solutions to DuPont, Western Electric, and the U.S. Army at Fort Jackson. DuPont proposed we turn our single-user demo into a multi-user system that could be run across the network; they liked the system so much that they considered turning it into a corporate standard."

Implementing the Demo

"After spending a year and a half trying to convince people that we had the answer to 90 percent of the world's problems, DuPont gave us our chance to actually implement our demo in a real, live environment," continues Walter. "We were finally going to get real revenue for our software product. We hired an additional programmer and made the first version of what would become ALL-IN-1, funded solely by those first five customer RFP contracts out of the Charlotte office. We were able to do it without a dollar of investment from

Venus and a Complexity Barrier

"I was asked to take on the Venus [VAX 8600] program management in 1981. It seemed that the probability of it succeeding was close to zero. The program had been in trouble for so long that the engineers had just become demoralized and disempowered.

"The basic problem was that the designers had been under such pressure to produce that they were sending out chip designs to fabrication before they had been debugged. Each time they'd get the chips back there were errors, and it would take forever to debug them, and they'd send off a new hurried design and the same thing would happen again and again. We had hit what's known as the complexity barrier, where the amount of complexity in the chips was far more than any one person could keep in their head or manage.

"So we decided to use simulation to get the design down before going off to do the chips. That was the first project on which we used simulation as a serious tool. We developed a whole bunch of simulation tools and ran them on a simulation environment composed of DECSYSTEM-20s and VAX-11/780s! Making them communicate was a nightmare.

"The core CPU team for the VAX 8600 worked almost two years, nights, and weekends, 18 hours a day. We created a supportive environment. We know that when you design things you're going to design some good stuff and some bad stuff. We rewarded people for finding the most bugs, and we changed the culture from turnaround time to correctness and discipline, which they weren't used to. And ultimately they succeeded. We got our priorities straight and the product out, and it was very successful."

— Bob Glorioso

DEC. We designed it to be a customizable, applications integration environment, a generic solution to real customer problems. The difference was that we envisioned a general-purpose product as opposed to the typical software services thing where you just create a specialized application for a specific customer's needs. We saw the general case from day one.

"I'll never try to name a product again. The grief you get for coming up with a name is not worth the pain. At first we nicknamed the thing 'OA,' for Office Automation, but everybody and their brother was using that.

"ALL-IN-1 was a good name, but the problem was that nobody could figure out exactly what it was. The whole point, of course, was that it was a totally customizable integration environment. You could integrate all sorts of applications with it, like word processing and MAIL and calendars and databases and all your homegrown applications, but by itself ALL-IN-1 was just the flow control mechanism and menu system. You couldn't do anything with it without adding applications. So if you wanted word processing, you had to order the ALL-IN-1 word processor, if you wanted a spreadsheet you had to order the ALL-IN-1 spreadsheet, and so forth. This totally confused customers, sales reps, and internal marketing people alike. Worse, it made customers angry. Luckily, the office automation analysts and consultants understood what we had done, and recommended ALL-IN-1 above everything else because of its customizability. 'DEC's got it right,' they said. 'None of us has the same office. We all want a system that we can customize, and integrate all the applications we need to use in our own special work situation.' On that simple premise, which was in fact the original founding concept we had come up with in 1977, ALL-IN-1 went on to automate 7 million desktops around the world."

Making Things Better

The 1980s were a time of refinement, consolidation, and extension of the VAX strategy. "In the 1980s, as throughout the industry at large, people primarily just developed and polished and commercialized and honed the ideas of the 1970s," says Butler Lampson. "PCs, workstations, networking, office architectures, and distributed processing were all invented in the '70s. The challenge of the '80s was to develop more and more complex systems that would allow these ideas to work on a larger scale, and be reliable, predictable, and affordable. With the VAX and VMS being so successful, we didn't have to do anything too different—we just worked on making it better."

Building on existing successes was a large part of the equation. "We often take for granted that when we come out with a major advance in computing, we make it out of existing products rather than having to develop something totally new from the technology up," says Bill Demmer. "The VAXstation II was built around the same MicroVAX chip as our MicroVAX II product. In other words, we leverage our basic systems development and our basic processor development into a range of products and functionalities."

Hardware packaging was one area in which economies of scale could be realized. Using the same monitors, keyboards, system boxes, and so forth, for different products helped to avoid duplication of design and create a strong company identity for Digital's products. "Ken was chief packaging engineer," says Cathy Learoyd. "He was marvelous about understanding that the look and the feel of the terminals' and PCs' physical boxes were the image the corporation projected to the end user. He worried that the new monitors under design looked too clunky. He went down to the Lechmere store to look at TV sets and find out how TV manufacturers had solved the problem of looking too boxy. He came up with the 'shrink-wrapped' design look you still see in our terminals today. He was always asking me to invite him down to the labs where the new terminals were being developed so he could play with our toys."

A fascinating example of cross-functional "design by committee" at Digital, says Mahendra Patel, was the development of the new LK201 keyboard. "We had maybe 50 different terminal and workstation and PC projects going on, and they were all proposing to design their own keyboards. I took on the job of trying to integrate all these diverse views. Everyone thought that they knew best. There were all kinds of arguments about what function keys ought to be included, what the layout of the keyboard should be, what the software usage of the keyboard was going to be for the different groups, and how Manufacturing was going to be able to make it at a reasonable cost. Lots of groups tried to secede and go back to making their own designs and ignore the realities of manufacturing and distributing and inventorying and training people to use and fix these things in all of the hundreds of different districts around the world. The problem was that we had suddenly become a very large global company, and people were only just beginning to learn what it took to create standardized systems in high volume, and to go about designing products to do that more rationally."

Separating the Issues

The key to the success of the keyboard was separating the issues of hardware and software, and delegating final design responsibility to a combined team of Human Factors and Manufacturing engineers. "By creating programmable function keys," says Patel, "we could give each group the flexibility to customize the keyboard to a particular application. That allowed the Industrial Design and Manufacturing engineers to design the keyboard itself so that it would be easy and functional to use, appropriate for different countries and applications, and could be manufactured successfully."

Similar lessons came from Digital's venture into personal computers. "The PC effort was an unmitigated disaster," says Gordon Bell. "We made so many stupid decisions." While well-engineered, each of the three PC lines was designed by committees and singularly unfit for the new, high-volume standardized personal computing market that seemed to grow up overnight. But the experience provided Engineering with a wealth of knowledge that would prove invaluable in further commodity market ventures. "It was painful, but we were forced to reevaluate what the real contribution was we could make to computing," says Russ Doane. "We learned that if you want to make a contribution, you have to understand what it is the customer really wants. At the same time, you can't be doing what everybody else is doing because what contribution is there in that? We guessed wrong about what customers wanted in a PC. We had gotten too far away from the customer. We started to understand that we can't keep trusting the intuition of engineers sitting around in the

No Design by Committee

"Design and engineering are fundamentally two different things. Design is a matter of figuring out what to build, and engineering is a matter of figuring out how to build it. An engineer is somebody who can build for a dollar what any fool can build for 10, but it presumes that you know what it is you're supposed to build.

"When our customers were all engineers and engineers worked closely with customers, it used to be that engineering really was able to design what our customers wanted. But that's not necessarily true when your customers are accountants or secretaries or small business people.

"It took us until the mid-1980s to figure out that design, especially in software, should be done by designers, not engineers, and that requirements should come from customers and marketing, not engineers. And to figure out that designs should be proposed, many of them if necessary, but not negotiated. Requirements should be negotiated, and committees should make yes or no decisions about requirements and designs. But never, ever, should products be designed by committees."

— Dick Rubinstein

Mill, and that we'd better find out what it is the customer really wants before we start designing products to meet those needs."

Forging the Family Jewels

At the same time the company was learning to be more customer-driven, Engineering was ironically becoming even more technology-driven due to the increasing importance of semiconductor design to the process of designing computers. "In the old days," says Tryggve Fossum, "you could sketch out a circuit design yourself by hand, go upstairs in the Mill to the acid baths and etch the board, and assemble your prototype using the wire-wrap machine and a handful of standard components out of catalogs. You could make an entire board by yourself in a day or two and get instant gratification. You'd see the results quickly, so you could afford to design things to a certain extent by trial and error. That sort of encouraged you to try out a lot of designs and ideas and midnight prototypes without necessarily telling anyone what you were trying out. Nowadays you don't even do breadboards or prototypes, you spend a lot of time doing software simulation, and there's a lot of pressure to get the design right the first time. "

"Today, a chip still often takes months or years to design," says Cathy Learoyd. "Making changes, in 1980, was at minimum a $10,000, six-week process. The design can no longer be an individual effort; it's a team effort, and an indispensable team member is the computer-aided design and simulation software, without which designing chips of today's complexity would be unthinkable."

Digital's first ventures into large-scale integrated circuit chips were the LSI-11, F-11, T-11, and J-11 projects, all PDP-11 microprocessors. At first, Digital developed the designs in-house, and sent them out for fabrication to third-party production shops. "Working with semiconductor technology was incredible; even working with it every day you just couldn't believe it was real," says Cathy Learoyd. "The T-11 was like solving an immense jigsaw puzzle of circuits of 12,000 transistors, which is nothing today, on a chip of silicon that was only a quarter-inch on a side. It required a different way of thinking about design. To create a board, you'd first lay out the components and then design the connections, the wiring, on the board; if there was a problem, it was fairly easy to change the wiring. With a chip you have to think the opposite way; you first have to figure out the wiring, the topology, and then design the components or cells within the budgeted area required by the topology. And when there was a problem, especially because the circuits were extremely dense, you were always looking for ways to find more space, so you looked for solutions that eliminated transistors with minimal wiring changes."

"Our chips are our family jewels," says Wayne Parker. "In 1980, Digital started to get serious about developing its own semiconductor facility. Basically, we needed to protect our proprietary chip designs and tools and algorithms and processes and directions, and so forth. It's a huge and continual investment to get into chip manufacturing, but when you work with outside vendors you give them an insight into what you're doing, and soon your competitors learn about it and you lose your added-value. We could see that it was going to be absolutely critical for our future success as a computer manufacturer to do our own fabrication." A chip fabrication plant was set up in the new facility in Hudson, Massachusetts, and top design and fabrication engineers were brought in to staff up the new semiconductor engineering group. "We were pushing the limits of technology, going to CMOS designs very quickly," says Wayne Parker. "We took a lot of risks, but it kept us ahead of the competitors."

First designs fabricated in-house were for low-volume semiconductors, such as bus controllers, communications controllers, and graphics chips. Eventually, schemes were proposed to put the entire VAX on a chip.

MicroVAX II: Creating a VAX-on-a-Chip . . .

"In 1981, microprocessors were these toys that you'd use for subsystems or PCs," recalls Bob Supnik. "They didn't have any relevance to complex processors like the VAX. The state of technology wouldn't allow you to put a whole VAX on a single chip, and we weren't planning to do so. Then two things happened. First, a chip maker, Zilog, approached us with this revolutionary suggestion—you could put the entire VAX on one chip if you just emulated some of the more complex instructions in software. That opened up our eyes. And second, we tried to interest the larger microprocessor manufacturers in licensing the VAX architecture, but they all refused. They all said that their own proprietary architectures were too important to give up.

"So I started drawing sketches of a single-chip architecture and researching VAX microcode to figure out whether we could put a VAX on a chip ourselves. Chip vendors started coming in to propose some very complex and expensive designs that would take years to do. I proposed we do it internally, with our own chip process technology, CAD technology, and advanced design team. It could have gone the other way, but I committed to an insane implementation schedule and we got the funding. We proposed a 15-month schedule for developing the world's first 32-bit microprocessor chip, not only because that would coincide with our manager Jeff Kalb's birthday, but also because that was the timeframe the competition, Intel and Motorola, was promising. In the end, we were three months late, but they were years late.

"In August 1984, we had finished the design and were running VMS. But coincidentally, the official interest in our project within Digital had gone to zero. The marketing analysis showed that there was no customer interest in a small VAX. But by then Jesse Lipcon and his renegade team in the PDP-11 systems group in the Mill had gotten hold of it, and the rest is history. Jesse's MicroVAX II system became the most successful start-up business that's ever been seen in Digital."

. . . and Putting It on a Bus

"Once Supnik had developed the vision of a single-chip VAX," says Jesse Lipcon, "and in typical Digital fashion had tired of negotiating with the chip vendors and said, 'To hell with it, I'll do the chip myself,' the Engineering Committee spent a year debating—what are we going to do with this chip?

"The official corporate strategy was to put it on the new BI bus, in a system called Aurora, which was to be a five-year development project. In the PDP-11 engineering group, we thought that was just plain stupid. We were used to cranking out low-end PDP-11 systems, using F-11 and J-11 microprocessor

An Engineer's Dream

"When we were working on the BI bus chip, there came a point just before we had figured out the final logic schematics, where I actually had a dream in which I saw the chip as a floor plan in three dimensions, and I saw what we had to do. A light came on, and I said, if I just do this little thing it would work. I finished the design and when the plot came out it was pretty amazing, just as I had visualized it. You can't put everything into algorithms and CAD systems. Chip design is a real art, and everybody thinks of it differently. I don't actually see electrons spinning around but I do see a mind's eye view of how all the devices and connections work and what you need to do to accomplish what you want it to do."

— Wayne Parker

chips, in a year or two. We based them on the Q-bus, which had thousands of third-party boards and peripheral interfaces. So we proposed putting the VAX chip on a Q-bus to leverage off the half-million PDP-11 Q-bus systems that were out there. That seemed the obvious thing to do, especially since there weren't any BI bus systems even in existence at that time.

"We were way out of the mainstream, hidden in a corner of the Mill in Building 5, and the Engineering Committee said, 'Hey, that's pretty funny, these crazy PDP-11 guys want to take this toy 16-bit-wide bus and try to put together an actual VAX with it.' They rolled their eyes and kind of humored us for a while, but didn't at all take the idea seriously.

"So Mike Gutman, our group manager, and I figured that if a Q-bus VAX was to be done, we were the only ones to do it. We never brought forward a formal proposal to the Executive Committee or anything, we just did it, guerrilla-engineering style. The only way to bring the MicroVAX to market quickly was to put together a very, very lean, mean team. So I got together another half-dozen engineers and managed it as a project, with everybody working long, hard hours together. The project just gathered momentum and nobody said stop—until it was too late to stop it. We announced it and it just took off.

"In its first year, the MicroVAX II brought in $800 million in revenue. And of course the Aurora BI system never happened; it was so far behind and expensive and never fit. In retrospect, it was fortunate that nobody took our little PDP-11 guerrilla-engineering effort too seriously. We had great fun, and most important, it altered Digital's view about how computers needed to be built in the future."

CAD, simulation, and modeling systems replaced the Mylar and component catalogs of the circuit designer's trade. Digital developed many of its own design and simulation tools, replete with proprietary algorithms and running on huge banks of VAX systems.

With a dependence on Engineering's developing expertise in semiconductors, schedules for many central processing units dependent on the advanced microprocessor chips in fabrication slipped, as chip delivery schedules slipped, often by a year or two. "We were taking a lot of risks, and taking cracks at what hadn't ever been done before," says Wayne Parker. "When you're doing something that complex and that new, especially in the semiconductor realm, there's always a high probability that you're going to face some problems you've never seen before. We just couldn't predict the amount of time it would often take."

But through Digital's growing expertise in semiconductor and system design, investment throughout the 1980s, and increased project management experience, project slippage has decreased. "Our chip design and fabrication capabilities are now perhaps our biggest competitive advantage," says Jesse Lipcon. "We're in the top tiers of semiconductor manufacturers today, and we're now in the fourth generation of technology in developing VAX micro-processors. The sophistication nowadays of our simulation tools is giving us unheard-of results. We can crank out incredibly complex VLSI chips and systems that work perfectly right on the first pass, so we're now exceeding our time-to-market goals by months and months. We no longer have to debug chips, and we get VMS up and running on the first pass. Now, we're in a fabulous position for the future. Our semiconductor fabrication expertise is going to give us a huge jump on competitors through the 1990s."

"The engineering breakthrough in CMOS technology in Hudson allows us to triple the raw performance of our VAX processors across the whole line," says Bill Demmer. "What's significant is the performance advancements in combination with the expanded capabilities of our NAS software, which will help customers navigate the maze of standards and build truly open systems that bridge multiple platforms easily through standardized interfaces. Now our customers can concentrate on their destination rather than directions on how to get there."

Rewards for Engineers:
An Inner Light, and a Higher Challenge to Meet

"Engineers love elegance," says Russ Doane. "They want to find a solution that gives them an inner glow." Such are the rewards of being an engineer. You want to create things, you want to do the right thing and you want to fulfill customer's needs so they'll go out and buy and use and profit from your designs.

"I remember one day making a creative insight to a big design problem that had been bugging me for months," says Cathy Learoyd. "I wandered around the Mill for three days feeling higher than the ceiling. That's when it's so exciting being an engineer."

"Time and again," says Russ Doane, "you take on a problem that is hard, really hard. You're doing the right thing in taking the problem on but you don't have the vaguest idea how you're going to solve it. Then one day you come up with a simple solution, totally obvious in retrospect. It's a great feeling, and it gives you the energy to go do the next hard thing."

"For completing really difficult or seemingly impossible long-term projects," says Bob Glorioso, "there are occasional congratulatory dinners and plaques for the wall and things like that, even a stock option from time to time, but basically, the way Digital rewards engineering success is to give you a next project to work on, one that's much, much harder than the last. That's the ethic. You don't get an office with a window, you don't get a huge financial windfall, but you do get an incredible amount of peer respect that makes you feel really, really good."

"Some of the reward you get comes from visiting customer sites," says Cathy Learoyd, "so you can see exactly how what you've designed is being used. I remember seeing one system in action at a hospital, and it was very gratifying. You can see the indirect results of your efforts and understand that we really are changing the way the world thinks, and you really feel that you're personally involved."

"When I came to DEC," says Tom Stockebrand, "it was like, wow, not only do you get to do something that could benefit mankind, but you could get paid to do it! The company's entire reason for being seems based on giving engineers the power to satisfy their internal cravings for creating interesting toys and making them available for people who might want them."

"Digital's contribution to computing," says Jesse Lipcon, "is figuring out how to do things that are really complex. It's the fact that we can create and manage complex things that other people can't do."

"Ken has always guided us to ask, 'What contributions can we make?' " says Russ Doane. "Often, that's taking on the really complex problems."

"Would I do it again? Absolutely," says Gordon Bell. "Any engineer you could ask would say that. We've all accomplished an enormous amount at DEC."

"The engineering culture is keeping the company going," says Bob Reed. "We always do a lot of beefing, but I have faith. We're engineers, and we're going to keep doing smart things."

6

Coping with Growth

Manufacturing at Digital

*Edited by Bob Lindgren
and Bob Lynch*

"The way it worked, when I was hired in 1966, was to run new people through the whole manufacturing process real fast and then give them a machine to make on their own. The PDP-8 was the hot new product, and my first machine was the PDP-8 number 68. I personally built that machine all by myself, every wire and every component, all the way through from assembly to final test.

"The assembly line itself was a bunch of steel rollers running in this big horseshoe in Building 5 of the Mill. At the beginning of the rollers, you would assemble the metal frame with the power supply and make sure the power supply was good. In the next section, you'd use a processor that was known to be good and check out memory modules. To check out each module you'd have to load in these paper tapes that went 'tica, tica, tica,' for about five hours. Then in the next section you'd use those proven memory modules to check out processor modules and find some good ones. It was all manual—insert modules, solder wires, load tapes, then make it go 'tica, tica, tica' for hours and hours.

"Next, the machine would go to the option line—we called it the Optionary—and you'd assemble and check out all of the options the customer ordered. Then you would roll the thing into this wooden heat chamber, one per machine, and you'd crank up the heat until the metal was feeling really warm. Very scientific. You'd run all of the diagnostic tests again, tica, tica, tica, in the heat tent for hours on end. A lot of time you were doing the heat diagnostics on nights and weekends, and there was a benefit to that. Since there was no place to cook your dinner, we used to put lasagna, franks, and anything you could get your hands on into the heaters, right on top of the systems, to warm them up.

"After the heat chamber, you'd roll out the system for a final acceptance test. That was also kind of fun because you ran every diagnostic test over and over, along with some mechanical tests, and the strangest things would pop up. There was a vibration test, in which you poked a 6-inch nylon rod over all the modules at different angles and shook them around. We'd slam the doors shut and sometimes parts would fall off the boards and the machine would start smoking. Anything that passed slamming was a real good machine.

"The typical cycle time for building a machine from start to finish was about a week; that is, if you didn't have any big problems. The options were often very hand-tailored-type things, very temperamental. You'd plug in the modules, hope that they were good, and then turn the machine on. And it never ran. I never saw anything that ran on turn-on in those days. So then

System module manufacturing at the Mill

you'd go through a very manual debugging process. Every manufacturing tech had his own little set of toggling routines—there were these little bat handles on the PDP-8s and you'd toggle them back and forth—that was how programming was done, you didn't use terminals back then. People could toggle these things back and forth at amazing speeds; I held a record for toggling one diagnostic for years.

"One of the biggest problems I had was with this one machine that wouldn't run, and then it would, and then it wouldn't run and then it would. It was driving me nuts. Finally, I found that it literally had a bug in it—one of our friendly Mill spiders had built a nest right on the clock timing circuit, and the clock was drifting in and out. I found out that the Mill was a regular spider heaven, and spiders would constantly get into options at night when you went home. Weekends in particular—when we came in on Monday morning, we learned to vacuum off all the modules just to make sure nothing was living on them.

"People on the lines would shift back and forth between tasks, whenever people needed help. It was like a big family environment. Virtually everybody knew Ken and he would wander around on the lines and ask, 'What are you working on? How's it going?' and people would say what was on their minds and things would get resolved. It was very, very easygoing, but tremendously exciting at the same time."

— Lou Klotz

Sheet Metal, Copper, Plastics, and Sand

At the end of the day, engineers can say they've designed something, sales reps can say they've sold something, services people can say they've solved some customer problem, and marketing and administrative managers can say that their blood pressure has skyrocketed. But only the people in manufacturing can say that they've made something.

Making things is the heart of Digital's business, and the craftspeople who make Digital's products have a perspective that is different—even radically different—than other Digital employees. Manufacturing at Digital, as in many other companies, is a world unto itself. People in manufacturing don't deal primarily in words or sketches or concepts, they deal in three-dimensional deliverables. Their major concerns are singularly focused: either a product ships today, or it doesn't.

It is not easy to ship products consistently when everything is in constant turmoil. The nature of Digital's business requires a very fast production ramp-up for a steady stream of new engineering designs. Each design uses new components and requires new manufacturing techniques. To be competitive, designs, components, and processes stretch the limits of technology, so problems are inherent—and rampant.

Like many small job shops that have started up in the electronics industry, Digital manufacturing faced constant challenges to sustaining and surviving growth. "If we were performing right now the way we were performing in 1970, we wouldn't be in business today," says Bill Hanson. "Look at our delivery performance, look at our costs, look at our quality: they weren't great back

"My first impression was that Digital was unsophisticated in terms of manufacturing. But what became apparent was that they were very sophisticated by being unique and different in valuing people. There was a spirit and a sense of 'teamness,' a terrific sense of pride, and people were caught up in the growth—50 percent a year."

— Bill Hanson

"Some people thought that our flexibility stemmed from a lack of planning, but actually it was a well-thought-out strategy. We had learned early that no manufacturing line or plant ends up building the products they were originally chartered to build, and people wouldn't end up doing the job they were originally hired to do."

— Dave Knoll

"Ken always said, 'We're not trying to grow, we're trying to do a quality job.' Half of our success and growth came from that simple cultural value."

— Peter Kaufmann

We Hired . . .

". . . people with fire. People's potential and drive were the most important qualities. We made sure that three people interviewed every candidate and that all three people agreed before we took them on."

— Stan Olsen

". . . small company people who were flexible and could see the interrelationship between engineering, marketing, and manufacturing."

— Peter Kaufmann

". . . more for the fit of the person with the culture than just for their skill."

— Kay Tighe

". . . people without boundaries—your job was what you wanted to make it."

— Cy Kendrick

then. But we were all young and caught up with the idea that there wasn't anything we couldn't do. It's not necessarily that we were that good, but we weren't bad enough to make any big mistakes. Did we miss shipment dates? You bet your life. But we had a set of unique products, customers were demanding those products, and we just had to learn how to make them. We might have stumbled a bit now and then, but we'd just get right up and keep going, a little bit wiser than before."

To a large extent, manufacturing at Digital has been a 30-year learning experience in what it means to balance three interdependent, ever-changing forces: high levels of volume production, new high-technologies (in both products and manufacturing processes), and new concepts of quality based on changing customer requirements.

In retrospect, the way Digital learned to respond to these changes was uniquely successful. No other manufacturer in the computer industry—or in any industry—has grown revenues from zero to $13 billion in 30 years. "People from Honeywell and other places would come in and try to tell us how unsophisticated we were," says Bill Hanson, "and we'd say, 'Wait a minute, don't mess with us. We're winning here now. We must be doing something right.'" Arrogance? Yes. But also, real, world-class manufacturing expertise.

How do you satisfy a skyrocketing demand for products that sometimes doubles or triples in the space of a year? Digital primarily chose to make versus buy, to invest in people and production capabilities rather than to farm out manufacturing to subcontractors.

In the 1960s and 1970s, the issue was always too little capacity, and the solution was more people and plants. "Our plans were to increase people, floor space, and equipment investments by roughly 50 percent a year," says Peter Kaufmann. "We hired people who were bright, flexible, and understood movement and change. We also wanted to keep the plant size small, compared to other businesses. When we ran out of space and had to expand out of the Mill, we moved into small towns where we could stay in tune with the community and not get too big in any one place."

Since products and manufacturing processes changed so quickly, the most important resource was people. Transferring expertise, culture, and values to new plants was a primary consideration. "We recognized that we had something going that was very important," says Bill Hanson. "We started up new plants with teams from existing operations to bring that culture along into the new plants."

By 1980 there were 26 plants and 30,000 people in manufacturing. Projections indicated that another 20 plants and 100,000 people might be needed over the next decade. But the combined impact of the semiconductor revolution, automation, and new quality processes changed the equation dramatically.

The issue of the 1980s turned out to be overcapacity in people and plants. As single chips replaced large cabinets of system modules, Digital's new product designs required far higher capital investments in semiconductor and automated manufacturing processes, and far fewer people in assembly. "There was a major change in the industry," says Ken Olsen. "The electronics business will never have the large number of people it used to have."

By investing in new, quality methodologies, each component and system manufactured no longer needed to undergo rigorous testing and reworking; system components could be safely sent to customers and assembled on-site. And by concurrently linking design and manufacturing processes, time-to-market for new products plummeted, further reducing the need for manufacturing staff. "We recognized the power of having an integrated chip design and process technology game plan," says Jim Cudmore. "We have seen the time for delivery of a new system from engineering drop from years to months. The impact on manufacturing has been enormous."

"Today, we're evolving from an organization that transforms material into one that transforms information," says Lou Gaviglia. "Our real value-added now is in taking customer needs, transforming them electronically, and delivering customized solutions that may come from many production vendors back to the customer. Staying ahead of the technology curve is the name of the game, and we're in the best position to do that—because computer manufacturing today is all based on the technology and expertise we ourselves have developed over the last 30 years."

Early Module Manufacturing

The first products manufactured were laboratory modules. The process consisted of etching simple printed circuit boards, stuffing them with off-the-shelf components such as transistors and diodes, and soldering the components to the boards. The boards then were assembled into aluminum boxes, and each was tested and shipped. While this process was constantly enhanced, refined, automated, and made more complex for new laboratory and computer systems module designs, it would prove to be the basis for Digital's manufacturing operations over the next 20 years.

Originally, the design engineers worked with draftsmen to lay out their circuits on Mylar. "We did the photography in my basement at home," says Ken Olsen. "We printed the circuits in the Mill with real silk, on wooden frames, and etched them in big aquarium tanks we bought from the five-and-ten. We frequently spilled the etch solution onto the furniture store below—I think we bought the same set of furniture several times."

"In the module assembly operation, Gloria's Girls would use hand drills to make holes in the printed circuit boards, one at a time," says Cy Kendrick. "Then they would bend the wires on the components individually to fit the holes, attach them to the boards, and run them over a bucket of molten solder. As time went on, these things started to get automated. For example, Ken would come into the assembly area every night as soon as it closed to play and muck around. One night he invented a little gadget that would bend several components at once into the proper shape, just by pulling a lever. That was a big deal at the time. Eventually, we got into automatic etching machines, drilling machines, and that type of thing, and Ken was always involved in them; he would keep his eye on a lot of the production procedures and came forward with ideas."

Automation tools were internally grown at first; there was little money to spend and considerable internal expertise to draw on. Not that the home-grown tools were always successful: "I had designed a bar device to help put

Gloria's Girls

In 1957 the Maynard unemployment office sent over a young woman, Gloria Porrazzo, who was hired as an assembler and was quickly promoted to the leader of the module assembly group.

At that time, most manufacturing operations were done by engineers and technicians, virtually all male. "We found that technically competent men weren't necessarily the best people to do quality assembly work," says Jack Smith. "In fact, we found that they were the worst people to do it. They didn't have the dexterity to do it well. We found that women, who at that time were a very underutilized resource, did it best."

Porrazzo hired and managed more than 300 module-assembly production workers, nearly all female. They were known throughout the Mill as "Gloria's Girls," and made all of Digital's early products. "I treated them hard, but fair," Porrazzo says. "In module assembly, you progressed according to your ability. If you didn't have an ounce of sense you would never have lasted. Myself, I never asked what to do, I just did it. Sometimes I felt like the only businesswoman in the world."

Porrazzo set company policies before such things as job descriptions existed. She taught the company how to develop work classifications, chose team leaders on the strength of their ability to deal with people, hired minority workers, and championed maternity leave by letting her people stay on the payroll when they left to have babies.

Ken Olsen would sponsor regular afternoon teas with Porrazzo and her 15 group leaders. "It was Ken's way of keeping his hand in," says Porrazzo, "saying what he expected of us, learning, and sharing ideas."

Technical Work

"The difference between manufacturing and engineering was invisible at first. You worked wherever there was a need for you. Everybody pitched in and did whatever had to be done. I was hired as a technician and expected to do technical work. I don't know if you'd classify painting system modules or sweeping the floors as technical work, but I spent a lot of time doing each of them."

— Jack Smith

connectors on," says Ron Cajolet. "One day Gloria called me up to the assembly floor. She said 'We don't quite understand how this works; could you just show us?' And the operator, supervisor, and production manager all stood around while I tried to show them. I struggled and got red in the face, but there was enough variation in the pins and the holes I'd specified on the bar that there was no way that anybody could put those pins through. They were all snickering behind my back, and that was my first lesson in manufacturing process engineering at Digital: if you were involved in design, then you had the responsibility to make sure that manufacturing had a way of producing it. I went downstairs and fixed the thing right away."

Testing each module was a necessary step of the process. "Ken had this theory that the best way to make inexpensive modules was to use reject parts," says Jim Cudmore. "At that time, transistor companies were struggling to make components up to their advertised specs, and we could get ones that met the minimum set of specs we needed quite cheaply. That meant that designers had to be particularly clever in dealing with the uncertainties of the performance of these transistors. But it also meant that we had to test each and every one, not just every batch." Testing every incoming component and outgoing system would also become a standard Digital practice for the next 20 years.

Assembling Modules into Computer Systems

Manufacturing the PDP-1 involved assembling different collections of standard Digital modules into backplane connectors, which were mounted in three large cabinet bays. The backplanes were wired together manually and connected to the power supply in the bottom of one of the cabinets. Different peripherals, such as a CRT, printer, tape, and storage systems, were purchased from vendors to meet the system configuration ordered by the customer. The peripherals were plugged in, and the system was run through rigorous testing.

"To make a PDP-1, an engineer and a technician would get together, put a customer's name on the cabinet, and just start wiring it up," says Ron Cajolet. "That's the way we built computers for the next five years. There was no real process. Everything was just hand assembled. Most of the work in those days was in problem solving, once you turned the system on."

"In terms of configurations, most of the PDP-1s were pretty much the same," says Jack Smith. "But each one took a lot of time. There were about 5,000 wires to install. You'd sit there with this wiring diagram and just put in one after the other. Then an inspector would check the work against the same diagram, and after inspection, the person who wired the rack would solder the wires."

After 50 or so PDP-1s had been made, PDP-4, PDP-5, and PDP-6 systems were all manufactured using the same process. The PDP-5 was the first system to be manufactured in significant volume—about 1,000 were eventually produced. New processes began to be developed to achieve better efficiency.

"We went through a major evolution in manufacturing at that time," says Jack Smith. "There was a strong belief across the industry back then that the only people who could put together computers were technicians and engineers. But the only thing complex about making a computer was getting the wires going to the right places. You didn't have to understand how a computer worked to do that. So instead of using highly technical people, we had Gloria's girls manage this. They had all of the assembly skills necessary. With that step, we had to start hiring lots of people, mostly women, to do the wiring because there were an awful lot of points to connect. And that meant we started getting into a formal organization, with emphasis on managing the people doing that work."

As a result, manufacturing split into two groups—the module manufactuing group (which came to be known as Volume Manufacturing) and the Systems Manufacturing group (which later would be called Final Assembly and Test, or FA&T). This organizational split would continue for 15 years, with the addition of a third manufacturing group, Peripherals Manufacturing, in the early 1970s.

The two groups had a vendor/customer relationship. Systems Manufacturing ordered modules from Volume Manufacturing. At first, Volume Manufacturing's other customers—the people buying Digital's laboratory modules—were perceived to be more important since they were generating almost all of Digital's revenues. There was some tension involved in allocating modules, which were constantly backlogged and in high demand. But, eventually, PDP-5 sales took off. Systems Manufacturing became Volume's largest customer and more profitable for Digital, so priorities were reversed.

The Mini Arrives: Making PDP-8s

The PDP-8 went into production in 1966. It was the first of the "mini-computers" and because of its low price, the volume of sales was expected to exceed any system Digital had produced to date. Little did manufacturing know how successful it actually would be. Over the next 10 years, PDP-8 systems were made and sold by the tens of thousands. The PDP-8 changed the way the world thought about computers and changed the way they were made. New manufacturing processes, automation technologies, and organizational structures were developed to try to meet the high-volume manufacturing requirements of the PDP-8.

"To get the right costs, we started to think about developing assembly lines," says Jim Cudmore. "Stan Olsen had visited a meat-packing plant and saw how they hung carcasses from hooks attached to pulleys that ran on an overhead track. That was the model we used. PDP-8s were hung from two hooks that were on wheels in an overhead tubular rack. They were moved from station to station for assembly and testing. That was a major conceptual breakthrough—it was the first time computer systems were put together on assembly-line conveyors."

The largest manufacturing cost in the past had been in manually wiring the backplanes of each system. To automate that, the company invested in new automatic wire-wrapping machines, each costing half a million dollars. A single operator could wire a backplane in a couple of hours—a job that previously would have taken days or weeks. "They were expensive and absolutely huge machines, but they turned out to be very cost-effective investments," says Ron Cajolet. "They allowed the backplanes to be wired very quickly, precisely, and automatically."

Little Kids on the Block

"The culture in the early years was very much: hey, we're the little kids on the block, we've got to show people we're good. We're a team. We like each other. We're a quality outfit and we like what we're doing. We're informal. Do things simple, ask simple questions, get simple answers. Keep arguing with everybody—conflict creates goodness. Don't be bureaucratic. Do whatever needs to be done. We were just a bunch of young kids that were having fun working together."

— Ed Schwartz

The largest testing cost in the past was in tracing bad wires. "If something didn't work, chances were that it was wired wrong or the connection was faulty," says Ron Cajolet. "Then you had to go hunt and peck for it. The wiring was so thick in some cases that you couldn't even see down to the pins and figure out what was connected to where. We came up with this automatic tester where we could scan through all the wires, match it up with the wiring list, and find the problem automatically."

While Systems Manufacturing capabilities increased, the operation was totally dependent on having sufficient modules available from Volume Manufacturing. "I was hired to solve what was called the 'module problem' — we could never make enough modules, and they were chronically in short supply," says Peter Kaufmann. "Part of the problem was in getting parts. The logistics operation was primitive—always acting in reactionary mode. We put in place a central planning operation for the first time to do proactive planning. We started to develop systems for doing forecasts, doing materials control, trying to understand that cycle and get the logistics under control. The other part of the module problem was in our manufacturing process. We set up a new module line and invested in a lot of new automation technologies to be able to produce modules faster and more cost-effectively."

On the module line, new insertion machines were developed in-house to automatically insert components into modules and reduce assembly time. New etching and soldering processes were developed to give higher yields in the circuit board manufacturing process, and the board shop eventually moved to wave-soldering technology. Automatic test systems were home-grown to test different types of modules more efficiently. "We were constantly being driven by Engineering to develop new manufacturing techniques, because available manufacturing technologies were never sufficient for their new designs," says Ron Cajolet. "So we were always operating on the edge of current technology. You couldn't buy the kind of automation we needed because it wasn't even available on the market. We had to develop most every new manufacturing process ourselves."

"The most encompassing technology transition I had seen at Digital came about with the PDP-8/I," says Dave Knoll. "It required new testing and handling equipment for the new integrated circuits, a new 288-pin backplane connector, new wire-wrapping machines and wiring testers, a change in circuit boards to double-sided, and the first use of plated-through-hole technology. Each of these technologies had the potential of being a 'show stopper,' and each nearly was until a number of tough problems were solved."

While previous circuit board designs from Engineering involved a relatively low density of components, the PDP-8/I module designs involved large-scale integrated circuits and high component densities, shrinking the size and the cost of the system. "The designers kept trying to fit more and more on each board, but the high-density boards caused a lot of problems in manufacturing," says Ron Cajolet. "One reason was that when you put a lot of components on a board, you need more connections on the edge of the circuit board. The first PDP-8s used a standard 144-pin connector. With high-density modules, we needed a 288-pin connector. There was no such thing on the market, so we had to design our own connector. Another problem was that the signal lines on the circuit board needed to be shrunk to .03 inch, which required major process improvements in board manufacturing. Eventually, we came up with guidelines so that engineers would understand just what could be manufactured successfully and what couldn't."

Yet another problem was that the wire-wrap machines couldn't handle the high-density designs. "They had real tight tolerances, and too many pins would be out of line for you to use the machines automatically," says Ron Cajolet. "Tom Stockebrand designed a system that would give the pin coordinates to the operators one at a time, so they could still wire-up the backplane in a semi-automated way."

But the biggest change in manufacturing came with the advent of integrated circuits, which could put the capability of an entire board, or even multiple boards, on a single chip.

Digital's first attempt at integrated circuits, the original "flip chips," never made it out of the engineering prototype stage. "They were hybrid circuits, called 'strates,' and Tom Stockebrand had developed a series of automatic silkscreening machines and transfer mechanisms for manufacturing them," says Dave Knoll. "I was amazed at how a small company tackled huge projects like trying to get into the IC components business. But once we got the flip chip manufacturing process ironed out, it turned out that it just wasn't cost-effective. You could buy the ICs cheaper on the market."

The first LSI chip used was in the PDP-8/I. "That was a major breakthrough that affected manufacturing people in an incredible way," says Peter Kaufmann. "Instead of stuffing transistors and diodes and circuits on boards, suddenly the whole thing was on a single silicon chip." Subsequently, the flip chip LSI modules' style of packaging was used to include more and more components and lasted through third-generation chip technology and into fourth-generation VLSI.

The manufacturing technologies pioneered on the PDP-8 enabled the system price to drop from $18,000 to less than $4,000 and proved invaluable for a quick manufacturing ramp-up of new PDP-10, PDP-11, and PDP-15 systems. But by 1970, Manufacturing had to greatly expand to make these systems, and the Mill had physically run out of space. All the parking lots were overflowing every morning even before everybody had arrived. Something had to be done. It was time for someone to go.

Outgrowing the Mill

From 1970 to 1975, Digital Manufacturing spread out from the Mill into 18 new facilities located in six countries worldwide, effectively increasing production space by a factor of 30 and production workers by a factor of 10.

The first operation to move out of the Mill was the one that had the most people and needed the most space—the Systems Manufacturing operation, newly dubbed Final Assembly and Test (or FA&T). In 1970, most of FA&T moved into a large facility in Westminster, Massachusetts, and overflowed into another plant in Westfield, Massachusetts. In 1971, FA&T for PDP-8 and PDP-11 systems expanded into Galway, Ireland, to support the European marketplace. In 1973, FA&T for small PDP-8 and PDP-11 systems expanded into Aguadilla, Puerto Rico; for PDP-11s, to Kanata, Canada; and

Hero to Dink

"We were very much shipment-driven, and that was the energy behind the company. The people in the beginning of the food chain didn't have the glory of making the shipments, and they were the fall guys if shipments weren't made. I started working in module manufacturing, and remember one Friday afternoon being told, this is super, you did a great job! Then the following Monday morning I was getting chewed out because there weren't enough modules . . . what had happened was we had finished one quarter and started the next! In the space of an hour at work, I had gone from being a hero to being a dink! The total measurement mentality was to work a quarter at a time."

— Bill Hanson

An Ideal Neighbor . . .

"Digital really was the ideal manufacturing company, and communities welcomed us wherever we went. We were clean. We paid well. We had a good name. We generated traffic, but as long as we weren't too close to residential areas that wasn't a problem. In fact, we often took over existing buildings, so there was no negative impact at all."

— Ed Schwartz

for large PDP-10 systems, to Marlboro, Massachusetts. Additional capacity was provided in 1975 in Ayr, Scotland, and in a huge plant in Salem, New Hampshire.

Several existing module-manufacturing operations remained in the Mill, but module PC board, component assembly, and power-supply production shops also were set up alongside the FA&T plants in Westminster, Massachusetts; Puerto Rico; and Ireland.

Some new facilities were acquired along with new business operations. In 1970, Digital acquired Data Memory, a producer of magnetic plated disks, in Mountain View, California. In 1972, Digital purchased RCA's memory business, acquiring a facility in Natick, Massachusetts, for memory module, disk head, and tape head production, and a facility in Taiwan employing 300 people stringing core memory stacks. And in 1975, Digital acquired a semiconductor manufacturing operation from Mostek in Worcester, Massachusetts.

Other facilities were opened to support the production of specialized products. In 1972, metal shops and component fabrication moved to Westfield, as did terminal, printer, and disk production. In that same year, a facility in Springfield, Massachusetts, was opened for specialty products, including cables, power supplies, peripherals, and subassemblies. Backplane wire-wrapping operations and logic-panel manufacturing were expanded in a Kanata, Ontario, plant in Canada. In 1975, another core memory stringing facility was opened in Hong Kong, and another terminal and printer plant was opened in Phoenix, Arizona. Another two dozen manufacturing facilities would be opened over the next decade.

Each new plant had an interesting tale to tell.

Starting Up Plants

"When we started up new plants, we wanted to bring our old culture along," says Bill Hanson. "We thought it was important, especially in manufacturing operations, to retain some consistency between plants in culture and processes and operating methods. To do that, we picked start-up teams from the best of our existing operations, so that new plants would understand Digital's values, its culture, and how it operated."

"Going from a single plant to a multiplant operation involved basic communications challenges," says Peter Kaufmann. "Instead of going upstairs to talk with a guy, you'd start to depend on the phone. If you don't know that person, know what they look like and what their environment looked like, you're not going to be able to communicate that well. If they come from another culture or speak English as a second language, you've got even more opportunities to mis-communicate. We spent a lot of money in travel, and encouraged people to travel a lot back and forth to different plants to have face-to-face meetings, to try to prevent and overcome these kinds of communications problems."

The manufacturing staff in Maynard spread out across the world to shepherd the newly hired into Digital society. In picking locations, Digital consistently selected areas that were apart from major industrial centers, with the intent of establishing a new culture that would be an integral part of the local culture.

"The model we used for growth was simple," says Dave Knoll. "Go only where we were wanted and where there was an abundant labor supply. Geographically, find the political center of the area and go as far away from it as you can. We'd want the site to have at least a hundred acres so we'd have room to breathe."

For the most part, plants were started up in small, blue-collar American towns: the same culture as in Maynard. At first, there were questions about whether the Digital values would blend with uniquely different social cultures: inner-city cultures or, of course, European, Caribbean, and Far Eastern cultures. Each of these cultures presented interesting challenges, but cultural integration was easier and caused far fewer problems than anticipated.

"In each new plant, we'd spend the first year carefully growing to about 150 people," says Knoll. "The overriding task of start-up was installing the culture and bringing people into the Digital family. We would spend a good amount of time doing things that said we care about people, relationships, trust, and that Digital is different. New employees often wondered why there wasn't more emphasis on product output in the first year, but we thought it was more important to install a people-oriented manufacturing culture first. We would hire a local personnel manager—without a doubt our key hire. The other key hire was the plant manager, and we learned very fast what to look for. The ones that succeeded were all 'people persons,' not necessarily a more experienced or professional candidate with a perfect resume."

Plant Portrait: San German, Puerto Rico

The facility in San German, Puerto Rico, was Digital's first major manufacturing plant outside of Maynard. It began limited operations in 1969 with 29 people producing PDP-8 subassemblies. San German grew over the next decade to include a sister plant in nearby Aguadilla, with a total of 2,000 employees producing complete PDP-8 and PDP-11 computers as well as high volumes of modules and power supplies. For a time, it represented more than 25 percent of Digital's manufacturing capabilities.

As Digital considered expanding out of the Mill, Puerto Rico presented a potentially ideal environment for low-cost manufacturing. There was a large and competent labor pool, a compatible local culture with a strong work ethic, and significant tax benefits for manufacturing investments.

"I went to Puerto Rico to check out the opportunity," says Peter Kaufmann. "The industrial people showed me the industrial parks and then I went on my own, driving back and forth from one end of Puerto Rico to the other to explore and get the feeling of it. I didn't want to be where it was heavily industrialized, I wanted to be out a little further so we would be on our own and create the kind of environment we wanted. I got to San German on the west side of the island, and it seemed to be perfect. I remember having mixed feelings—is it worth it to destroy this field and, potentially, this nice culture to put a computer plant here? I hoped and believed that we could add more than we took away and in retrospect, I think we did."

The San German facility was constructed in less than a year, and a core staff of local people was hired and trained by a revolving start-up team of selected manufacturing people from Maynard. "When the plant started up, we sent

. . . Even in Your Own Back Yard

"We honestly believed we were going to be in a place forever. We honestly believed we were going to add value to the community, blend in with it, and that we would be good for the community. And at the same time, we received a lot of support from the communities we went into.

"For example, we found an ideal piece of land in Phoenix for a new plant, but at that time it was zoned residential. The local residents helped us get it rezoned industrial. The planning commissioner said, 'We've never had a situation like this—there were no adversaries.' The plant fit right in, and the residents' kids to this day play on the lawn. We wanted to make sure that all of our plant sites blended in that well with the community."

— Bill Hanson

kits of product components down to them for assembly—they acted as a sub-contracting vendor," says Bill Hanson. "But with the success of their operation and our increasing product demand, we decided to grow San German to a complete standalone operation, making everything from modules to complete systems, and let them buy their own parts and do all their own work."

"We added a circuit board shop that had all sorts of advanced technologies, including our first multilayer boards," says Ron Cajolet. "We evolved to building 5,000 modules a day, balancing demand between the 300 types of modules that we were making. The forecasts were very variable, so we had to be very flexible and loose on the production line, expecting lots of changes all the time. We ended up developing a lot of sophisticated new processes and automated equipment. To meet the local environmental laws, for example, we had to introduce some new waste-effluent collection and cleansing processes that were developed specifically for this operation."

"San German was a golden opportunity to try to advance manufacturing processes," says Lou Klotz. "It was a new building full of new people who weren't pretrained in existing procedures. For example, one of the most significant new technologies we piloted there was called the Automatic Processor Tester. The APT system would automatically download all the diagnostics to each machine to be tested, so people wouldn't have to load in the test procedures manually for each machine. We set up hundreds of cable drops to the plant floor to connect systems in Final Assembly and Test. It was very successful, and the technology was transferred back to the States and other operations worldwide as a standard operating procedure."

To develop a complete, standalone manufacturing operation, a sister plant was opened in Aguadilla—also on the western end of the island, about forty miles north of San German—to concentrate on assembling the modules into small PDP-8 and PDP-11 systems.

"The goal was to get the whole operation run by people from the island," says Cajolet. "And that was achieved. But we needed time to introduce people to each other and establish some common bonds and be comfortable trading information back and forth. We made modules for every plant in Digital, so we had customers everywhere. To effect product and process changes, we also had to interact closely with Engineering and Sales back in Maynard, which resulted in some communications difficulties. It used to be that you could resolve things by going downstairs in the Mill, but in San German, phone calls could take hours to get through, and you couldn't share or discuss things that efficiently over the phone. So it usually meant hopping on a plane and days of delays. As a result, we had to start formalizing things like product and process documentation, to get things written down and distributed across sites."

There also was a language barrier to deal with. The plant was run in Spanish, but management was done in English. The engineers and administrators all had a good grasp of English, but there were very subtle language and cultural differences that caused miscommunication. "There are a lot of meanings that don't get translated with words," says Ron Cajolet. "The plant manager warned me that I'd find that all the people I would deal with speak English very well, they'll say they understand everything you say, but half the time they'll walk away and you'll find out later that there was some miscommunication.

You had to spend a whole lot more time in communicating and confirming that the meaning of what you said and what you heard was what was intended."

"One of the nicest surprises was that the work ethic was so strong," says Ron Cajolet. "The culture of the community was very family-oriented and it carried over to their work. They organized teams in the production departments and they had distinct uniforms for each team. So if you were part of a team that built a certain kind of module, you wanted to be identified with that team so you could brag as a team that you made something happen. There was very high morale and it was an exciting place to work."

Digital supported a number of community activities, including the local hospital and the local university. "We introduced computer courses and supplied computer equipment to the schools," says Cajolet, "and assisted in technical instruction to help develop the kind of engineering talent appropriate to the work we were doing. The result was that, over time, a strong engineering and technical talent pool was created, and other companies started opening facilities in the same area to draw on it."

Plant Portrait: Springfield, Massachusetts

Digital's seventh manufacturing plant opened in Springfield in 1972 with 11 employees assembling power supplies and cables for various storage-systems products. Ten years later, the plant employed 840 people, had a $14 million payroll, and was the sole volume supplier of Digital's most advanced disk drive, floppy diskette, and tape storage systems. The plant had spread over three locations within the outskirts of a predominantly black inner-city area, with the work force racially mixed at every level.

"We've built a lot of traditions in this plant and in this community," says Henry Burnett. "We began by taking a shot at inner-city employment, and we did labor-intensive work that did not require a great deal of training or education. Today we operate a state-of-the-art manufacturing facility, building some of the industry's most advanced products, using sophisticated tools and work systems. And we do all that with the same work force that Digital first came here to hire. Our commitment to inner-city employment has never changed."

Over the years, the Springfield plant became both a business and a social success, confirming to Digital that doing business in the inner city can be profitable. That outcome, however, was less than certain at first. Educating and selling management on the venture was difficult, reflecting the business climate (recession) and social climate (residual bias against minorities) of the early 1970s.

The opening of the plant was spearheaded by Peter Kaufmann and Leroy Saylor. They wanted to get Digital involved in urban ventures that could provide minorities with training and the opportunity to develop and advance to positions at all levels of the company. At the same time, they recognized that an inner-city plant would need to be equally competitive with other plants and not just an experiment in social responsibility.

"I had been trying to get a plant proposal together for the Boston inner city, but the political climate there was difficult," says Kaufmann. "Leroy came up with a proposal for Springfield, which was a smaller and more manageable

Something Special

"I had some problems, quite frankly, when I first saw the physical surroundings of the plant. But when I saw the enthusiasm and started listening to the people, what became clear to me was that Digital had something rather special in Springfield. They shared with me some intimate conversations about their hopes and aspirations, and I was just absolutely convinced that was something I wanted to be a part of.

"Springfield was unique because it was so much a part of the community. The moment I was announced as plant manager, the Chamber came and said, we expect you to be a member of the Board of Directors. The symphony folks came and said, we sure would love to have you sit on the Board of the Symphony. The public television people came and said, we sure would like you to be active with us, would you be a Board member? People were seriously interested in having the plant represented at the policy-making levels of all the various community-based activities, because they were seeing Digital as a major force in that community."

— Ron Payne

Value in Diversity

"We had a lot of visits from notables and groups wanting to find out what we were doing. We'd always try to accommodate them. One day a busload of visitors from China arrived. It became apparent rather quickly that they needed a translator for the technical language that was necessary. In a few minutes we had called up one of our employees who was Chinese, and, after determining that the dialects were the same, we had someone who could interpret for them.

"These kinds of cultural incidents happened every day in Springfield, and invariably we would have a solution for them because of the diversity of our work force. We had 39 nations represented in the plant, with all their flags up in the cafeteria. With that diversity of people, we had an attitude that we had the capability of doing almost anything. We were close with each other, and there was an application of using those differences every day."

— Henry Burnett

community. We found a place in the Armory, walked the streets, and got to know all the leaders of the black community. We talked and made proposals, and nobody quite believed that we'd go in there, but we just went and did it. We went in with a profit motive and a lot of assembly work to get done; over five or six years, we got 400 people off the welfare rolls, and it really worked."

Springfield, the second-largest city in the state, was the hub of western Massachusetts and had an inner city that was struggling. It was particularly hard hit by the business recession in the early 1970s, with major employers closing down operations. A unique site was selected for the proposed plant—a cluster of buildings that were part of the historic Springfield Armory, built in 1774 to manufacture arms for the Continental Army and closed by the Pentagon in the late 1960s. A variety of community and social services groups supported Digital's drawing on the underutilized and underdeveloped labor market in the immediate community.

The first few start-up years of the Springfield plant were rough, largely because of a strategy to develop human resources from the community, not to import expertise from other Digital facilities. Management skills were home-grown; training the predominantly unskilled work force in high-quality, high-tech assembly operations progressed slowly; and the usual logistics problems of meeting Digital's wildly fluctuating production forecasts took their toll. Meeting production schedules and financial projections was difficult at first, like most start-up plants, but since Springfield was a special case and a social experiment in the minds of some, it was subject to intense and somewhat prejudiced scrutiny. "We thought it was a business decision from the outset, but we weren't naive enough not to recognize that there would be social issues and doubt, internally and externally, as to how seriously committed Digital was," says Saylor.

The plant's big break came in 1976, when logistics came under control and it won a competitive bid for manufacturing many of Digital's tape and floppy disk drives—its first chartered responsibility for manufacturing complete end-products. A support engineering group was brought in to bring the plant's work force to a level of technical expertise that had not previously existed.

"It was then the plant really began to change," says Henry Burnett. "By taking on our own end-product charter, we started to become a truly self-sustaining plant. We started building our own support functions and established a sense of permanence by renovating the Armory. The community knew we were there to stay."

Renovation of the Armory presented some structural problems that you don't have in traditional manufacturing facilities, says Burnett. "We converted the Armory into a modern, high-volume manufacturing facility with an efficient materials-handling system. The buildings were not connected, so we had to build passageways between them to keep material flowing. The building also had very narrow halls and doorways—we decided that we could build any storage device with a form factor of eight inches or less in very high volume."

Springfield's success in building tape and 8-inch floppy diskette drives led to plant certification for high-quality storage systems and a major contract to produce Digital's 5¼-inch floppy and hard disk drives, supporting all of Digital's storage needs for PCs, MicroVAX, and eventually large storage systems in the 1980s.

"We got into an attitude that we could do the impossible," says Burnett. "We had a group of wildly imaginative, ambitious people with extraordinary capabilities that had not been recognized at that point. Once we got to the point of understanding that our capabilities were going to be valued and recognized, things just began to flow out the door."

Expanding into Europe

As demand rose "across the pond" for Digital's products, pressure increased for local manufacture to avoid prohibitive tariffs. Limited manufacturing had begun in Digital's engineering-support facility in Reading, England, but expansion there was not approved by the British government. To avoid tariffs in Common Market countries, 50 percent of a product's "value-added" had to be manufactured locally, so a large-scale operation would be necessary. The search for a site concentrated at first on English-speaking countries to simplify language barriers.

"I remember driving all through Ireland, zigzagging up and down across the country," says Peter Kaufmann, "and when I got to Galway Bay on the west coast, it had a good feel. It was a beautiful place, all farms and pastures; the people were wonderful and they needed jobs. We did the analysis and all the numbers worked out, but it was more a matter of instinct. I knew things would work out well there."

Although Ireland's application to the Common Market had yet to be accepted in 1971, Digital began to set up a large manufacturing facility in Galway to produce complete PDP-8 and PDP-11 systems for the European market. The gamble worked, as Ireland was accepted into the Common Market shortly after operations began, and the 50 percent value-added quotient was accepted by inspectors.

"Galway brought the manufacture of our whole product back together again, which hadn't been the case since everything was in the Mill," says Dave Knoll. "From the beginning, Galway did all the operations from module building to FA&T and order processing. They made CPUs, printers, disks, power supplies, and options. Galway people met with the European subsidiaries to resolve customer issues and with product engineering people in Massachusetts to help design products for Europe. This allowed them to be a tightly connected plant."

"New products were introduced into U.S. Manufacturing first, and then we would send our people over there and they would learn about the product and bring it back," says Bud Dill. "We ultimately became excellent at introducing new products, and we developed a very competent manufacturing-engineering group to do that. The manufacturing culture was just about exactly the same as in the States—you could walk out of Westminster, Massachusetts, one day and into Galway the next and feel right at home. We became the largest manufacturer west of the Shannon River, and we had a way of dealing with people that was unique in that area. We were the only nonunion shop around, we paid well, and we did a lot of employee training so people could move up to

Solidarity Forsooth

"We had a little problem in Galway with the parents who didn't want their girls working in a manufacturing environment. What they had in mind, I'm sure, was the old sulphur-match factories. They didn't realize what we were doing there, so we invited all the parents to come down to the plant and served a buffet. They went through the plant and saw the people at work. It went very well, and the problem sort of went away.

"Most everything in Ireland was unionized at that time, and we agreed from the start that if any of our employees ever felt they needed to be represented by a labor union, we would recognize it. After a while the union started getting a bit nasty, so they put up posters and invited themselves into the lunchroom one afternoon at the close of business. I remember seeing my whole test department coming down the street en masse and saying, 'Here's Fuzzy and his boys, and oh God, here we go.' So they sat down, and this red-haired fellow stood up and said, 'Who invited you people down here?' They said, 'Well, they didn't really invite us, we asked to come.' The kid said, 'We'll send for you when we need you.' Another one jumped up and said, 'You know, when I came to work for this company I was a guard on the door, and now I'm an electronics technician.' Another one jumped up and said, 'I've got a sister who works down at Lyden's Bakery. Why don't you go down there.' They gave them a terrible time, and the union went away and never came back."

— Cy Kendrick

Empty Suits

"One of the things I found hard to adjust to was the informality of the place—calling everybody by their first name. It didn't come easy; it took a while before I called people Mike or Cy. The informality was even more difficult for the rest of the community in Galway to get used to. I dealt with a lot of local people who would come to the plant, and the casualness of dress and style there really contrasted with all the businessmen who would come dressed in suits. As the community got to know us, they developed an appreciation for that style. A lot of what the people from the States brought with them in style and culture stayed in the plant: the openness, the feeling that this was a team effort, to be good at what we did, we all did it together."

— Kay Tighe

higher-paying jobs very quickly. The hierarchy between workers and management was invisible. But the craziest thing was our policy of giving away turkeys at Christmas time. To the Irish, that was real unusual; one guy came to work for us one day, and the next day he was handed a turkey—he went into every pub in Galway showing off that turkey. It was a big deal."

"When we built Galway, we included a very large PDP-10 computer in the MIS department—much larger than was needed to run the plant, and one of the biggest computers in Ireland," says Dave Knoll. "This became a beacon that helped attract people and customers to the plant, and greatly enhanced people's learning. We soon had stronger customer connections and a larger market share in Ireland than we had in any country."

"With the success of Galway, setting up new manufacturing plants started to become a marketing tool," says Ed Schwartz. "Soon Britain wanted in on the action, so we started our facility in Reading, England, and put in a major new facility in Ayr, Scotland, for computer and peripheral manufacturing to supplement Galway's production for the European market." The Ayr facility evolved to be a major manufacturing center for low-end systems and VLSI chip production.

"The same pressures for local manufacture also came from Germany," says Dave Knoll. "Although we had analyzed manufacturing in Bavaria, the infrastructure costs and the language challenges were not palatable until the late 1970s, when we opened up a plant in Kaufbeuren. We were initially concerned with our ability to bring our culture to a German-speaking plant, but it worked out quite fine." The Kaufbeuren plant specialized in manufacturing storage products and peripheral systems, and increasingly became a showcase for manufacturing and high-technology transfer in Europe.

Eventually, other European manufacturing operations were started in Valbonne, France, for terminals and printers manufacturing; in Nijmegen, the Netherlands, for software manufacturing and distribution; and in Clonmel, Ireland, for network systems manufacturing.

Competition Among Plants

As the number of manufacturing facilities increased, so did competition among the plants. Just as Digital itself had broken into independent product lines, manufacturing plants were semiautonomous and entrepreneurial entities funded by their own product lines. And just as the product lines competed against each other, manufacturing plants competed against each other for new business, tied tenuously to common goals and cooperation through a matrix management structure.

"Starting in the late 1960s, manufacturing operated under a very strong management matrix," says Jack Smith. "We were growing very fast and we started forming specialized manufacturing groups—for example, for processors, power supplies, or tape units. Then we said, how are we going to manage them? So we decided to build a strong centralized manufacturing organization, with high expertise in manufacturing functions such as materials management, production management, and so forth. The materials manager was expected to oversee and support all the materials functions in the individual manufacturing groups and help them manage their businesses. The idea was that we were growing so very, very rapidly, there was a concern that each new group wouldn't be able to build the expertise fast enough in all the manufacturing functional areas it needed."

"Manufacturing plants had a complex reporting matrix in which you might have two or three bosses," says Dennis O'Connor. "The manager of your group would report both to the site boss and to the functional group in corporate manufacturing. The site boss—the plant manager—had the profit and loss responsibility and provided the entrepreneurial fire to grow and to take on new businesses. The functional group would provide support and try to maintain some consistency and economies of scale between groups, between plants, and between geographies. That worked well for a number of years, as long as the functional management would spend their time nurturing groups and not trying to control them too much."

"Risk taking was with the individual plants," says Lou Gaviglia. "And the competition was fierce. Each plant was trying to beat each other. We'd compete for customers and for new business. We'd compete on metrics about whose plant was better, we'd compete for resources, for people, for support, for scarce materials and equipment. Even so, we'd always help out each other at the end of the month or the end of a quarter. We'd swap people or swap material, take on extra work, whatever it would take. Because it wouldn't do the company any good if I succeeded and another plant failed. As much as we'd compete, we'd always cooperate for the good of the whole."

There were constantly changing product mixes at each of the plants, and changing pipelines of supplies from one plant to the next. Generally, any other plant was viewed as either a supplier or a competitor. It was at the systems business level—the competing Final Assembly and Test (FA&T) plants in Westminster, Westfield, Aguadilla, Marlboro, Salem, and Galway—where the pressures were most dramatic.

"The thing about FA&T was that it took care of the whole customer order," says Lou Gaviglia. "Whatever was on the order—not just the system configuration and peripherals, but also things like software and documentation, cables, and supplies such as extra paper—was put together by FA&T. It made accountability very simple. Everything the customer needed came from one place. You physically took the order and put the customer's name on a frame, and then you built the machine, and it just grew and grew and grew.

"In FA&T, all of the systems were laid out on these huge manufacturing floors—Salem itself was 13 acres of floor space under one roof—and each system was fully configured and fully tested on the spot," says Dennis O'Connor. "All of the software ordered by the customer was loaded, and every system component, from tapes to terminals, was connected and fired up. Then we'd run diagnostics software on the system for days and days on end. It wasn't uncommon for systems to spend anywhere from 8 to 12 weeks on the FA&T floor to complete the whole assembly and test of the system."

"The beauty of FA&T was in providing a single link between Engineering and the customer, and we had to work closely with both, especially when introducing new products or dealing with special order configurations," says Lou Gaviglia. "It became the hub of what was happening at Digital, providing

A Balancing Act

"There was a constructive tension between manufacturing functions, manufacturing plants, and the company's business units. Manufacturing acted as a balancing and integrating force among the different product line and engineering groups."

— Dave Knoll

Like the Shoemaker's Kids

"We learned a lot from each plant. When we built the first FA&T plant in Westminster, the computer room was an afterthought. There were thousands of computers on the floor, but we never thought much about using them except for maybe time cards or payroll, that type of thing. Even though we were a computer company, it took us some years to foresee the tremendous use of computers in the manufacturing environment. As we grew, we started designing the plants around the computer room, with wiring drops and networks and automatic testing systems."

— Lou Gaviglia

the basic linkages between all of Digital's organizations, and we used to draw it at the center of a wheel. And while it seemed simple on paper, understanding both the products and what the customer purchased, how you make them fit, and just the logistics of how you execute an order could be very, very difficult."

"At the end of each quarter, things would get pretty hectic," says Bud Dill. "FA&T was at the very end of the engineering and manufacturing process, and no matter what went wrong, it became your problem. The end date for customer shipment never moved. So you'd end up doing all these Herculean tasks to meet that customer delivery date."

"Our mind-set was: I have the customer order. I own that. It's my job to get that whole thing to the customer. So I'm going to go work with the rest of Digital to make that happen," says Gaviglia. "I had all the customer orders in my desk drawer. And my job was to empty the drawer by the end of the quarter. Not 90 percent of the orders or the line items . . . 100 percent. That drive still exists in the plants today—do what's right for the customer, do your own thing to make it happen. A lot of the customer satisfaction processes we have today, and a lot of today's philosophies and managers, came from the people who worked down in FA&T."

Peripherals Manufacturing

With the success of the PDP-8 and PDP-11, the idea of being a vertical manufacturer of complete minicomputer systems began to take shape. Up until 1970, virtually all of the "mechanical" peripheral systems Digital shipped, such as tape and disk mass-storage systems, terminals and printers, were bought from other vendors.

"We started making our own peripherals because there were simply none available that were appropriately cheap enough for our minicomputers," says Jim Cudmore. "In those days, you could buy an entire PDP-8 for the cost of a single disk drive. Also, we thought there might be some economies of scale in developing our own."

"The first peripheral we made was the famous DECtape," says Cudmore. "It wasn't that hard because tape technology was pretty easily understood. Then we thought we ought to get into making disks because they were so much faster than tapes. People would shake their heads and say, here are companies like IBM with ten thousand times your resources just struggling with this tough technology. But we bought some head components and some platters and just started building disks. We barely understood mechanical systems, let alone recording technology, physics, particle counts, clearance requirements, and the like. I think it was what we didn't know that kept us going. . . ."

Similar efforts began on developing printers and terminals. "We were buying thousands and thousands of Teletypes," says Dave Knoll. "So we started trying to make a dot-matrix printer to replace the Teletype. The LA30 printer design had a 9-wire print head, and there were terrific problems getting the reliability of the head to a reasonable level. Up until this time, mysterious electrical problems with computers would be solved by the technicians in FA&T by reworking modules and rewiring backplanes. But with the new printers and disks, the problems would be mechanical in nature, and that approach no longer worked. Reliability was the key issue, and it had to be designed in right from the start."

"We started establishing reliability requirements completely arbitrarily at first," says Jim Cudmore. "We felt if a printer couldn't run continuously for 96 hours without crashing, we shouldn't ship it. It seemed like a modest requirement. After a couple of weeks, we hadn't shipped a single printer, and there were hundreds and hundreds of them running round-the-clock in every corner of the plant—there were even 300 in the cafeteria because we had run out of room. So we thought maybe 96 hours was a little too much. We talked with customers, who by and large were pretty happy with the printers, started examining their usage patterns, and decided that 96 hours in fact was an inappropriate test. It had more to do with checking how each machine would print out certain character combinations, because of the way the solenoids interacted. But at this point, we still didn't know anything about root cause analysis or reliability methodologies—it was all trial and error, luck and happenstance."

"Making the first peripheral of each type was painful," says Dave Knoll. "Our first printer (the LA30), first disk (the RK05), and first terminal (the VT05) were not successful. We soon learned that in each case, it would be the second or third follow-on product that really took off—the LA36 printer, the RS disks, and the VT100. We learned on the first attempt and sold on the second. It just took some time to get the bugs out."

New facilities were purchased to manufacture specialized peripheral systems. Printer and terminal manufacturing moved to Phoenix and Albuquerque. Data Memory, a producer of magnetic plated disks in Mountain View, California, was acquired, and operations were expanded to include disk manufacturing. Additional manufacturing of disk systems, disk and magnetic tape heads was moved to a leased facility in Natick, Massachusetts, along with a new business in memory modules, in Digital's most significant acquisition— RCA's core memory manufacturing business.

Core Memories

Even though Ken Olsen had helped pioneer the development of core memory at MIT, Digital had not manufactured its own core memory modules because they were extremely labor-intensive to make and more easily purchased. "By 1971, we were the largest consumer of core memories other than IBM," says Jim Cudmore. "The PDP-10s each used quite a bit of core memory, and we needed huge quantities for the PDP-11s and smaller machines. We had some concern about lowering costs and relying on vendors for such a critical component."

"We realized that if we were going to be big, we needed to produce our own memory," says Ed Schwartz. "RCA had developed a core manufacturing business in Needham, Massachusetts, and a large core stringing operation in Taiwan in one of their television plants. Then, in 1970, RCA decided to leave the computer business, which presented us with a terrific opportunity." For two years, Schwartz negotiated the acquisition of RCA's memory business as

Cultural Differences

"We ran into some sizeable cultural differences in managing the core manufacturing operations in Taiwan. The Digital culture was very aggressive and full of ambiguity and constant change. The product line requests and production requirements would change every week, and these would be significant fluctuations that would affect everything involved in the manufacturing schedule. The Chinese culture was basically very conservative and rational, very structured and quality-oriented. Most everyone had also come from RCA, which was also a very conservative, hierarchical organization. It was very hard for them to accommodate.

"They wondered how, in God's name, could schedules change so frequently and fluctuations occur so randomly? It was like being on a yo-yo string. It was a major culture shock, and took them a rather lengthy time to adapt to the swings and our very flexible organization.

"At the same time, they taught us something about the notion of delivering what had been committed to, both in performance and schedules. In the Oriental culture, when you say you will deliver something, you deliver it. If what you deliver doesn't work, you lose face. Manufacturing commitments in the U.S. had always been a bit too aggressive, and they'd always fall short of what they committed to. The Eastern notions of quality started to show up on the bottom line; at the end of the quarter, Volume Manufacturing would tend to have a negative variance, and Far East manufacturing would have a positive variance. We started to work on achieving a better balance."

— Frank Cassidy

well as their large headquarters building in Marlboro, Massachusetts, in what was called "the deal of a lifetime."

"We were able to hire RCA's technical gurus back in Needham and acquire their equipment assets," says Schwartz. "RCA also encouraged us to hire the 400 women who were stringing cores in Taiwan, as well as their entire management team. We set up operation in Taiwan in a new building nearby in the town of Tachi, which was renowned for its exquisitely handcrafted furniture. We built dormitories for the women because there were few places nearby to rent. The women would come in during the week to work, stay in the dormitories, and go back home to their families on weekends."

The magnetic cores themselves were made in a facility Digital leased in Natick, Massachusetts, using equipment purchased from RCA. "We have 19 presses and are running 14 at a time," said one Natick employee in 1972. "We pump out millions of cores a day and are looking to make several billion a year." In a few years, production increased to 30 billion a year. Each doughnut-shaped core was slightly smaller than the head of a pin; 20,000 cores weighed less than one gram.

The cores were extremely fragile, easily damaged, and difficult to produce. The process consisted of pulverizing iron and manganese, pressing them into individual cores, firing them, and then testing each one for thickness and performance. Cores were shipped to Taiwan for manual stringing.

A single memory module might involve stringing thousands of cores, putting four wires through the center of each in a matrix configuration. The wires were mounted on a frame, and stringing was done more by feel than by eye. Occasionally cores would become chipped from a needle sliding through, necessitating starting over from the beginning. The finished assemblies of strung cores, which were called "stacks," were shipped back to Natick for testing and assembly into memory modules.

"The women who strung the cores in Taiwan were typically 15 to 25 years old, with very good eyesight," says Frank Cassidy. "It was a lot like weaving a rug, only you used tiny little metal doughnuts and wires. A typical stack required about 70 hours of labor plus about 10 hours of testing. We paid more than the going rate for labor in Taiwan, and we provided free dormitory housing and a boardinghouse-style cafeteria."

"In 1975, we needed to increase capacity for core manufacturing," says Cassidy. "We expanded into Hong Kong so that we would have multiple sources in case of difficulty. We combined the Taiwan and Hong Kong facilities into a new Far East manufacturing organization, which at its height employed 3,000 people, mostly stringing core memories."

The Far East core memory operation allowed Digital to decrease prices significantly for its computer systems. "The investment payback was actually less than a year," says Cassidy.

"We also did a fair amount of innovating, both in the chemical makeup of the cores, which allowed us to decrease their size by a factor of five, and in designing three-wire stacks, which meant you had to put only three wires through each core instead of four, so we could use even smaller cores," says Jim Cudmore. "We got very, very successful at making core stacks and became the largest core memory manufacturer in the world for a number of years, even selling them to our competitors, which caused a bit of controversy."

However, along with the growth of Digital's core memory operations, semiconductor technology was advancing to the stage where memories could potentially be produced more cost-effectively on semiconductor Dynamic Random Access Memory (DRAM) chips—thus sounding the death knell for core memory. "We had been investigating DRAMs for several years, and as early as 1972 it was clear that the semiconductor memory was going to work," says Jim Cudmore. "Not necessarily as fast or as inexpensively as people were predicting, but we saw it was going to be the future."

Digital assembled a small team of memory designers to work on developing DRAMs, working with Mostek, a semiconductor vendor in Worcester, Massachusetts. But other companies were ahead of the game, and prices for DRAMs fell fast on the market.

"Actually, throughout the 1970s we were achieving a 30 percent reduction in costs per year in the core operation through new core and process techniques," says Jim Cudmore. "So curiously enough, in spite of the semiconductor revolution, our costs for producing certain kinds of core memory remained lower than semiconductor DRAMs up until about 1978; in fact we were still making core memory up until 1980."

Digital began designing and manufacturing memory modules using DRAMs, purchased from vendors, in ever-increasing volume in its module-manufacturing facilities. Digital never manufactured its own semiconductor memory devices, since they became a commodity that became available from a number of specialized vendors and were much cheaper to buy than to make.

"In a way, the transition to making semiconductors instead of core memory modules was trivial; you'd just replace the core stack with some chips on the circuit board," says Frank Cassidy. "But when we were involved in it, it did not seem so trivial. First of all, there was the need to develop relationships with suppliers who could deliver volumes of chips with consistently high quality. Second, unlike core memory, DRAM chips don't retain their values when you turn the power off—they need to use refresh circuitry, which meant that a significantly new set of test equipment had to be developed. Third, a great deal of effort needed to be spent to ensure that the new DRAM modules developed were compatible with the core modules in terms of electrical signals and response time to prevent timing errors—and that required constant manufacturing process adjustments."

"The most important part of the transition though, of course, was that suddenly we had 3,000 people, trained to be the best core stringers in the world, with absolutely nothing to do," says Cassidy. "Making the DRAM modules was a very machine-automated process, and we were tempted at first to keep it back in the States. But we decided that the Far East manufacturing team already had more experience in memory manufacturing than anybody, and since they'd been a great success before, they could be a great success again. So we invested in a module-manufacturing line in the Hong Kong facility and made them responsible for manufacturing DRAM modules. Within a year, their output had risen twentyfold in terms of raw bits of memory capacity. Since Taiwan was already the world capital of television production, we

Counting on Miracles

"With the development of the ceramic core memory, the minicomputer business spurted forth and became practical because we could make inexpensive, powerful, large machines for very little money. As miraculous as the cores were, the miracle of semiconductor memory is much more so: now we have computers in our automobiles, in our microwaves, in our washing machines. It comes about because memories are so cheap."

— Ken Olsen

transformed the Taiwan operation into a video-monitor production plant that eventually made all of our terminal and personal computer monitors—without having to lay off anyone. So I think the effects of the first wave of the semiconductor revolution were to everyone's benefit—frankly, I have to think that anything would be more interesting than stringing cores."

Semiconductor Manufacturing

While Digital chose not to manufacture its own DRAM chips, the initial semiconductor design and process work done with Mostek provided a foundation for other chip development efforts, specifically, putting PDP-11 processors on a chip.

"Mostek was started up by a bunch of engineers from Texas Instruments, and they had developed a leading-edge MOS process capability in Worcester, Massachusetts," says Joe Chenail. "After we'd been working with them on MOS (Metal Oxide Semiconductor) memory designs for about a year, the company decided to move back to Texas. The head of Mostek called us and asked if we'd like to hire some of the top people in their group who wanted to stay in New England, and if we'd like to take over the facility in Worcester. Even though we'd decided not to produce the DRAMs, we said sure, because we'd already started to get some semiconductor expertise going, and we felt that someday we'd need to draw on that expertise. In the semiconductor business, you have to keep investing and developing your expertise or you'll go stale and fall behind and never catch up."

A half dozen of Mostek's top engineers joined Digital and began to set up a MOS production capability in the leased Worcester facility. "Even though we had no designs to build at that time, it was a terrific opportunity and, as it turned out, very fortuitous," says Chenail. "Engineering had developed a MOS design for a complete PDP-11 chip set, the LSI-11, and had contracted the production out to Western Digital, a relatively small company on the west coast. But Western Digital started to lose their process. They were getting extremely low yields on the chips they were building and started to get into financial difficulty."

Engineering asked the MOS group in Worcester if they could investigate making the LSI-11 chips to provide a second source of supply. "We began production and in a very short time we started getting very, very good yields—to the extent that we were soon overproducing and had several months' worth of backlog, something we were very, very proud of," says Chenail. "They even wanted us to shut down, we were making so many! But in his wisdom, Ken said, 'Don't worry, we will sell them, keep producing,' which we did. They cancelled the Western Digital contract and we became a serious contender in the semiconductor manufacturing business. It was a great experience."

Another reason the LSI-11 success was fortuitous was that MOS was the cutting edge of LSI semiconductor technology. Up until then, Digital engineering had developed a number of semiconductor designs that used bipolar TTL technology, an older and more conservative technology whose production could easily be contracted to outside chip fabricators. The MOS process was at that time ill-understood, quirky, and prone to low manufacturing yields—but MOS chips could be made more dense because of their lower power consumption. As a result, MOS chips increased performance significantly over the years.

Putting a whole 16-bit minicomputer on MOS chips was a big deal, something nobody else in the industry had yet accomplished, and it set the technical foundation for Digital's growth and leadership in processor chip design over the next 15 years. Digital added bipolar fabrication lines for a few years for manufacturing custom and semi-custom gate array chips but would phase them out in 1982. Instead, the company concentrated chip manufacturing on the next six generations of MOS technology, which was to enable the manufacture of future chip designs with simply amazing performance characteristics.

The success in manufacturing the LSI-11 in 1975 foreshadowed a multitude of strategies that would contribute to Digital's success in the 1980s. First, manufacturing came to realize that semiconductors were the future, so future investments should be put into chip manufacturing facilities, not more facilities for producing the modules that chips replaced. Also, Digital realized that it would be necessary to develop semiconductor manufacturing capabilities in-house to retain proprietary chip designs. If chip fabrication continued to be contracted to other semiconductor companies, Digital's proprietary technologies would surely leak out to competitors.

The result was a major commitment to advanced semiconductor production, realized in the decision to create a state-of-the-art chip manufacturing facility in Hudson, Massachusetts, in 1977.

"Hudson was the single largest investment the company ever made," says Jim Cudmore. "It was more than a bit of a risk. For one thing, the short-term payback didn't look promising because we could have kept contracting out production to other vendors, and semiconductor technology was changing so quickly that the long-term payback was up in the air. Also, everybody said it was a really dumb idea to build it in New England because there were no semiconductor people here. We had a lot of concerns, not just whether we could get the technical talent, but also whether there was enough of an infrastructure in the region to supply all the equipment and materials and specialty gases and things you had to buy to run the operation."

At first, Hudson started out as a fabrication facility for chips that were developed by remote engineering groups. The existing fabrication operation was moved from Worcester to Hudson, and the team "began struggling through the early chip sets," says Cudmore. "The most complex of the first efforts, the F-11 microprocessor, was an attempt to put the LSI-11 set of chips onto a single chip. It was successful, but took a terrific amount of time to do. Back then, you wouldn't know if you had a good chip until you produced it through the manufacturing process, which took about 20 weeks. Then you'd go back and do some redesign and put it back through the manufacturing cycle, and so forth. That meant that in the course of a year, you'd only get one or two chances to fix something."

The F-11 took five design cycles, or about three years, to develop. The next two microprocessor chips, the T-11 (or Tiny-11) and the MicroVAX I chip set, also took about the same number of cycles and development time. "That was reasonable performance, but not really competitive," says Cudmore. "We began to develop a new game plan of integrating chip design with process

No Guarantees

"We had some struggles in starting up the Hudson manufacturing operation initially. We hired a lot of outside expertise, people who could technically do the job, but some had a bit of difficulty dealing with Digital and the attitude and beliefs of the internal clients. We went through several plateaus of management and operations, bringing in new people and developing new processes, like a series of stepping stones. The good people would attract more and more good people and cause new refinements to the process. Our performance went from marginal, to reasonable, to almost competitive, to very, very competitive, but it took time.

"A lot of the early investments were made on faith. The microprocessor projects involved a lot of money and a lot of risk. At first it was very, very difficult to show the payoff to the company, and we had trouble loading the facility. But by the early 1980s, we had the opposite problem; microprocessor-based products had taken off, and we could not make enough. It became an extraordinary success."

— Jim Cudmore

Working Apart

"As Manufacturing expanded ever farther and farther away from Engineering in Massachusetts, new product introductions became more and more complex. All of a sudden, engineers were not eating in the same cafeteria as the manufacturing people. People gradually became names rather than faces. Products had to be cleaner, and problems took longer to diagnose, duplicate, and fix. Focusing group charters and responsibilities on products in the early 1980s helped to move Engineering and Manufacturing closer together again."

— Dave Knoll

technology. Up until that time, design was limited by the previous manufacturing processes we were using. What we needed to do was develop our process capabilities in parallel with design."

It became apparent that a closer integration between engineering and manufacturing was needed. Turning the complex geometric layout of a new chip into a manufacturing process that will yield a high volume of a quality product requires a massive team effort. It requires the tight coordination of efforts among literally hundreds of people—circuit and software designers, physicists, chemists, process engineers, fabricators, test technicians, and many others. The Hudson facility began to bring together all of these people in the same place to make it easier to integrate efforts. But more important, a new manufacturing organization structure was put in place, along with a new relationship between Engineering and Manufacturing, to facilitate working together.

Manufacturing Decentralizes

Throughout the 1970s, Manufacturing had been operated as a centralized organization in much the same way that Engineering had been centralized in 1973. But Manufacturing as one unit—with 25,000 people, dozens of plants dispersed around the world, and thousands of different products to produce—was growing so big it was becoming unwieldy.

The problem was that different types of manufacturing operations had developed very different types of needs. Making chips required highly automated processes and close interaction between engineering and manufacturing specialists. Making systems, on the other hand, required numerous general-purpose people who could deal with high-volume production. Manufacturing terminals, memories, and storage systems required different types of skills, each concentrated in different geographic locations. Some operations faced primarily cost pressures, others primarily technology or time-to-market pressures—each requiring different management skills and trade-offs.

The new structure that was put in place in 1980 decentralized the Manufacturing organization into six operating groups focused on manufacturing: systems, chips, memories, terminals and printers, storage systems, and Far East operations. "The effect," says Jack Smith, "was to decentralize decision making to optimize each group's different needs and goals." It was a major shift in manufacturing organization towards a product focus, as opposed to functional specialization.

With decentralization, much closer links were formed between engineering and manufacturing groups. "What we began to move toward was more of a focus on special product requirements that brought together the specialized engineering and manufacturing resources required," says Bill Hanson. "It was driven by the new roles of the semiconductor group and the storage systems group, who needed to tightly link their engineering and manufacturing activities. This led to something called the 2 by 2 process—working two in a box, two peas in a pod."

"The traditional relationship between Engineering and Manufacturing was for engineers to throw designs over the wall to be made," says Bill Hanson. "It was a mind-set that followed from the separate organizations; Manufacturing was separate from the product lines and from the engineering groups."

"As the company grew and more and more engineering groups and manufacturing plants formed, it became harder to solve problems," says Ron Cajolet. "Engineering groups would do a design, not knowing what plant would manufacture the product. Manufacturing wouldn't be involved until designs were complete. Good long-term relationships weren't being built up. We needed to start setting up some processes that would make the introduction of new products less of a traumatic and more of an organized event, with the goal of it being less costly and quicker. Two-by-two teams let us be a lot more interactive with design earlier in the process, so we'd know what was coming, when it was coming, and the kind of new process we'd have to put in place."

"The 2 by 2 process was formalized in the phase reviews for new product introduction," says Lou Gaviglia. "We had to work in parallel to meet the goals for phase 0, phase 1, and so forth into the beginning of volume production in phase 4. Engineers would send us early drawings and little models, and the manufacturing people would say this is good, this is bad, and trade information back and forth at each phase. Engineering would visit the manufacturing plants, and Manufacturing would go back and visit them in the Mill. It helped us to get products out much faster because now you had two sets of people working on the same new product introduction."

"Then we added customer service to the team, so you'd have the people who designed it, made it, delivered it, and serviced it as part of the team," adds Gaviglia. "So it became 3 by 3, and then it became 5 by 5 almost overnight, adding the marketing people and everyone else. That new mold became the beginning of a long string of successful product introductions, on the day we said we were going to be ready."

Getting the FA&T Out

Since 1971, each complete system shipped had been configured and tested on the floor of Digital's huge Final Assembly and Test (FA&T) facilities. The ability to test and integrate individual customer orders, in their final system configurations, was at first a major factor in customer buying decisions.

But this integration and testing process was costly. System components, which were becoming more reliable, were designed from the start to strict architectures that would allow them to "plug and play" with different configurations. As this happened, the need for testing system configurations began to disappear. "By 1985, we found that we were able to achieve the same systems quality—and in many ways better quality—by eliminating the FA&T process from most orders, shipping the major system components directly to the customer for final assembly on-site," says Lou Gaviglia. "Not having to test the final system saved an entire manufacturing cycle and allowed us to work with less inventory, lower costs, and more predictability."

The ability to eliminate FA&T in 1985 was the culmination of a series of programs designed to improve manufacturing processes, quality, and systems reliability. The first step, in the mid-1970s, was to develop consistent test strategies across systems and plants. "The technicians at each FA&T location

Meeting Customer Demand

"We used to pride ourselves on how much inventory we had, and how much testing we had to do. We would bring customers down and say, 'Look how big our warehouse is!' never understanding that eventually the game would be inventory turns.

"When we were growing at 40 percent a year, the only thing that seemed to matter was trying to fill customer demand for products. Eventually, we started to pay more attention to manufacturing as a science, understanding how costs, delivery performance, flexibility, and quality management also contributed toward customer satisfaction."

— Lou Gaviglia

would pull together their own set of diagnostics for system tests, according to their personality," says Dennis O'Connor. "There was no consistency in the tests that were run from machine to machine. A customer might have six systems of the same model shipped to their site, and each of the six might have a different problem because different tests would have been used on each."

A new testing process, called ACT and later APT, was developed as a result, allowing consistent diagnostics tests to be downloaded automatically to each system on the test floor. "That was the beginning of 'let's try to do things so we don't have to test everything on the system,'" says Lou Gaviglia. "We figured that there must be pieces of the product that we could test separately, as a unit, and then trust that it's been tested correctly. For example, it didn't make that much sense to take terminals, printers, and tape and disk peripherals out of their boxes, test them with the system, and put them back into the boxes in FA&T. So we decided to just merge certain of the boxes on the FA&T shipping dock without opening them in the first place—what we called 'Dock Merge.'"

"With Dock Merge, we started to change the validation point for quality from the FA&T floor back to the volume manufacturing plants," says O'Connor. "It put the onus for component quality back on the suppliers." A program was put in place to certify plants for different products. To become certified, the volume manufacturing plant had to pass a variety of stringent tests of its manufacturing practices and management controls. It needed to demonstrate that it could consistently produce high-quality, error-free products. Plants typically would celebrate getting certified for a product; it became a source of pride and allowed them to better compete for new business against other plants.

With the confidence that came from certification, peripherals could be dock-merged in their boxes and need not be retested in FA&T. "Dock Merge was not too popular at first," says Lou Gaviglia. "The systems types felt we were taking their jobs away, and the volume manufacturers didn't like having to get certified by an outside force. But it worked much better! The feedback was phenomenal, and the stuff ran great—it even ran better because the suppliers' quality got much better real fast. So we said, 'We might be on to something . . . why don't we just send every system component to a distribution center, not to FA&T, and ship to the customer from there?' We started up some pilot programs that became the beginning of POM (point of manufacture)."

The goal was to have all the parts that go to make up a system shipped directly from the point of manufacture (POM) to the customer's site, eliminating the need for FA&T warehousing space and inventory. However, doing that would bypass a key element—FA&T's order configuration experts—without whose expertise the probability of successful POM shipments would be quite low.

Digital's price book in the early 1980s contained 36,000 line items. Some combinations of those items would result in a complete system configuration, but most of the possible combinations, by far, would not. "The orders sent in by sales were often incomplete, or would have a wrong option line item number that simply was incompatible with the rest of the system," says Dennis O'Connor. "We had hundreds of technical editors in FA&T who would spend up to an hour editing each order to make sure that it was a complete and validated configuration."

Previous efforts to automate the configuration process using traditional programming techniques had failed because of the difficulty in keeping them complete and up-to-date. Working closely with Artificial Intelligence (AI) researchers at Carnegie Mellon, O'Connor developed an experimental expert system called XCON (for eXpert CONfigurator) that would incorporate the configuration rules of thumb employed by the technical editors. "No one knew whether the AI system would fit until we tried it, but there was no other way to help cope with the complexity," says O'Connor. But with the immediate success of the XCON prototype for configuring VAX-11/780 systems, he added, "more and more expertise was built into XCON, to the point where XCON itself was more expert than the design engineers. Over time we added more and more systems, software, and peripherals as they were introduced; now XCON can configure any current system, out of 100,000 possible components, in under two minutes, and do it accurately 98 percent of the time." XCON enabled the POM concept to grow and work: components could be shipped directly from the volume manufacturing plants to the customer.

Quality Consciousness

More than organizational changes had taken place by the mid-1980s. The shape and direction of Digital's manufacturing growth was affected by innovations in the computer industry and by new manufacturing technologies. No longer was it reasonable to take weeks to build and ship orders to customers. No longer could current processes support new technologies. Costs and competition were becoming key words. Plants had to become very flexible and competitive, not only with one another but with external competitors. Improving the quality of manufacturing processes became critical.

"The excitement in the early 1980s was a combination of major new products coming out and major enhancements to the manufacturing way of doing business," says Lou Klotz. "Everything from new manufacturing information systems that were linked to engineering systems across the network, to new materials-handling and quality-control systems, to the process technologies down on the floor itself, to the automation in production and testing, everything had to be enhanced."

Much of Digital's advanced manufacturing technology development group moved to Andover, Massachusetts, in the early 1980s to help develop new manufacturing technologies and transfer them to the plants. Some of these technologies involved automation machinery and processes for making, for example, solderless backplanes, surface mount and multilayer boards, robotics, and computer-aided visual inspection systems. "Andover was like a sandbox in which process engineers could play in order to understand and develop new and better manufacturing techniques," says Lou Klotz.

"The idea was that Andover would be to the modules world what Hudson was to the silicon world, a one-stop shop where engineers could come in through the front door with their schematics and walk out the back with a fully designed, fully tested module, ready for production," says Joe Chenail. "It combined a lot of the knowledge we've developed in 33 years of

Bigger Screws

"When we first started shipping computers to Japan, they would take them all apart and then put them back together again with bigger bolts and screws because they didn't like the way we made them. It's sort of an insult to American manufacturers, but they were probably right in some ways. We went through difficult periods in which quality wasn't what it should be, and it was hard to integrate that back into manufacturing.

"Quality is a built-in thing. It wasn't like you could inspect it in or test it in, you had to do each little thing right.

"We wanted to be a quality company always. Treat our people in a quality way, treat our customers in a quality way. We're not going to lie to you and we're not going to tell you we're going to do something when we can't. That was part of the mystique, part of being different."

— Peter Kaufmann

Field Service, M.D.

"In the mid-1970s, DOAs were running at about 25 percent—one system out of four a customer received would be Dead On Arrival. There was a huge field service organization in place to go out and fix them. Some of the problems were process problems, some were things we didn't know about yet like electrostatic discharge problems.

"Quite honestly, we were much more sensitive to production targets than quality targets in those days because of the explosive growth in customer demand. The natural human instinct is to push that stuff out and get the revenue. It's also hard to train people properly when you're growing at 35 percent a year and have an enormous backlog of orders to meet.

"Customers were so anxious to get their hands on the DEC products that the level of negative feedback wasn't sufficient to make the company change its approach to quality until much later, in the early 1980s.

"Once you got those old -8s and -11s up and running, though, they just kept running and running and running forever."

— Tony Tynan

experience in making modules—design and simulation tools, materials and thermal evaluation, processes, and so forth."

"A key strategy was to use our own computers to make our own computers throughout the manufacturing process," says Dick Clayton. "We began deploying everything from office automation systems, to information systems, to automated systems for materials handling, shop-floor control, inspection and testing, and sophisticated computer numerical control, and robotic tools."

Simple automation was one answer—but not the whole answer. "We were aggressive in using our own latest technology to keep us competitive," says Dick Clayton. "Sometimes that meant automating production; sometimes doing things manually; sometimes using new information systems. There was no hard and set rule."

One of the most automated manufacturing plants in the industry, for example, was an experimental module production facility started in Enfield, Connecticut, in 1984. The experimental emphasis, though, was far less on using automation than on developing new organizational and team structures—high-performance people systems. "Module technology hadn't changed much in 15 years, but the organizational model hadn't changed at all," says Bob Puffer. "Given the new perspective of international competition, it was time to rethink the traditional."

"We talked about the Japanese and competitive weapons," says start-up plant manager Bruce Dillingham. "We wrote up 32 Visions that nobody could argue with—they were all motherhood. The first, for example, was Never Ship A Bad Product—100 percent Quality Yield. Enfield would become the leading edge for Digital in improving cost and competitive position, but it was developing the social skills for participative, self-management that took the most time. Our process was integrated into our organizational design—it can't be seen from a purely technical point of view."

The new technologies introduced to manufacturing in the 1980s supported the designs of new, competitive products. "We began to establish a relationship with Engineering around designing products with consideration for how they would be tested later—Design for Manufacturability," says Lou Gaviglia.

Other critical technologies that were developed included reliability techniques, such as root cause analysis and statistical modeling methodologies. Many of the enabling quality technologies were administrative in nature, such as the development of advanced MRP II and MAXCIM material control systems to support Just-In-Time manufacturing and fast, reliable time-to-market for new product introductions.

Manufacturing plants started judging themselves on standardized productivity and quality measurement scales. The first introduced was Digital's Product Certification program. After achieving certification for different products, plants would go on to try to achieve Class A MRP II national certification—which meant achieving 95 percent compliance in 16 critical quality parameters. Twenty-six facilities were certified as Class A manufacturing sites. Manufacturing introduced a new Continuous Improvement award for the Class A sites to continue to strive for.

The practices and achievements necessary for certification and awards were simply the use of good quality systems and manufacturing practices that led directly to improved productivity, less scrap and rework, and lower overall manufacturing costs. Indirectly, they also contributed to lower inventory and customer service costs for the company as a whole.

With the rise of competition in the computer industry, the concept of quality began to expand to include all measures of customer satisfaction. "Manufacturing succeeded when it guessed right," says Jack Smith, "but failed when it guessed wrong on customer order volumes. We needed to develop intelligent market data and demand forecasts, and accurate customer feedback to succeed."

Corporate programs instituted to increase product quality such as Just-In-Time, Six Sigma, and Benchmarking, and the use of Contextual Inquiry and Quality Function Deployment focused plants on continuous improvement in achieving corporate goals of customer satisfaction. No longer was quality solely in the hands of the QC test inspectors. Quality became a way of life, a fundamental and basic attitude that was part of day-to-day operations.

Manufacturing in the '90s

The days of having 3,000 people stringing memory cores or 1,000 workers on a line assembling parts into modules are gone, their roles displaced by semiconductor devices and new manufacturing technologies.

To remain competitive, Digital became the world's second-largest consumer of VLSI chips, only 5 percent of which are developed and manufactured in-house. Yet it is that 5 percent production of state-of-the-art proprietary (and primarily microprocessor) designs that gives it a competitive advantage today.

The combination of the semiconductor revolution and new engineering and manufacturing technologies has driven the cost of Digital's computer systems to all-time lows. Chips are inserted in modules with automated equipment that is very efficient and has high yields.

From 1977 to 1990, the number of Digital's manufacturing employees decreased from 60 percent to under 35 percent of the total employee population. The semiconductor revolution simply eliminated the need for most traditional manufacturing jobs. "We've improved processes to the point where we don't need the capacity we have today," says Lou Klotz. Some facilities were slowly phased out, and others consolidated to reduce operating costs. Programs were instituted to retrain excess manufacturing employees, but for the first time, Manufacturing had to resort to layoffs in 1989 to reduce the work force, and some familiar places started to be closed.

By the late 1980s, manufacturing at Digital reached a pinnacle of success, ironically, by fading away in importance. Manufacturing had become so efficient and dependable that it was no longer the source of the company's business challenges.

Manufacturing had become a world-class operation and a major competitive advantage to the company. Cycle time for introducing new products into production had fallen from three years to three months. Shipment times from customer order to delivery had fallen from months to days. Inventory-carrying requirements had plummeted with the development of a reliable

Round and Round

"Many of the most interesting advances in manufacturing technology in fact were developed by our customers, particularly OEMs, who built our systems into their products and applications. It was quite circular: we worked closely and shared expertise with our computer customers, we became major customers of our customers, which in turn helped us build better products for them."

— Dick Clayton

Just-In-Time supply network for components, with certain inventory turns approaching 100 per year. Zero-defect quality goals were nearly met, Problem Free Installations were above 98 percent, and reliability/availability for some systems rose to 99.98 percent—systems might be down only an hour or two over the course of a year on the average.

Manufacturing also was transformed into a sales tool. "Other manufacturers know that we've dealt with a lot of hard problems and beat them," says Bill Hanson. "The knowledge we've gained in working problems such as time-to-market, inventories, gross margins, and downsizing is something customers want to learn from us. And we welcome the opportunity to share it with them."

"We've had to reevaluate the role of manufacturing today," says Joe Chenail. "We're starting to be a major components supplier for chips and subassemblies. We're moving our manufacturing expertise into the field, becoming a major Systems Integration supplier in open systems environments, with which we have a lot of experience. Many of our customers are finding that there are areas where we have more expertise than they do. We're offering our experience in the form of consulting and services engagements. We have a lot to offer."

7 Buying Faith

Sales and Service at Digital

Edited by Patrick Pierce

"I got to know Digital when it was a seven-person start-up in 1958. It was through a graduate school project. In our report, my partner and I projected that the company could sell $1 million of modules in the coming fiscal year, but only if they created a sales force. So they made me an offer.

"I went to Maynard to reject the offer. I was going to go back to California to work for a bigger company at twice the salary, but Ken was in Maynard to meet me. He had so much confidence about my returning to California in a year if I wasn't the sales manager that I was bowled over. Especially since there were no orders in hand. When I joined the company, there was zero backlog. Zero. Zip. They had sold to three customers and that was it. So I became the only salesperson.

"I joined the same week that Jack Smith and Bob Reed did. We spent two weeks—it was supposed to be three months—on a training program. I had gone to one of the top engineering schools, but we didn't learn anything about digital techniques; it was all analog in those days. So I patched modules together in a back room for two weeks and then I went out on a sales call. All three of the top managers expected me to come back with an order on my first day.

"I can't remember the first sales call. I just picked up a bunch of bingo card leads, got in the car, and set sail up Route 128. I'd go up to a receptionist, and say the name of the company. Some thought I was selling heart medicine— 'digitalis' was the only word that came close. There really weren't very many people who knew enough about transistor logic, so the real prospects were few and far between.

"It was a very dry summer, and I'm sure they were questioning the wisdom of having hired me, but then, in September, the orders started rolling in at about $100,000 a month. That's the first sales experience I ever had, except selling ties."

— Ted Johnson
Vice President, Sales, 1958–83

Welcome to Maynard: Ted Johnson with PDP-8s to go

Laying Foundations

Archeologists of the future will focus on the industrial shift catalyzed by the entrance of digital computers into the mainstream. Computers were narrowly viewed as counting machines during the 1950s, and using them for tasks such as data collection and manipulation was relatively novel. Enshrined within data processing departments, they were not designed for direct connection or use by engineers.

There were customers who needed a different computing environment, but the challenge of finding those able to work with limited support was the key to Digital's early strategy. Although the company's founders knew how to build high-speed computers with transistors, few people, especially investors, saw new opportunities in the computer industry. Only IBM was making a profit. Nevertheless, a real opportunity existed not by copying IBM, as the big companies were doing, but by staying away from IBM's market.

In 1957 two companies adopted this strategy: Control Data Corporation and Digital Equipment Corporation. Both avoided the IBM commercial market. CDC jumped right into building scientific machines. Digital, with no commercial experience and scant capital, learned to build them from the ground up. Some engineers were prepared to use computers in new ways, wiring them directly into their systems, or to use them for unmediated data collection and manipulation. But finding smart customers was a challenge. Few customers knew how to use computers, let alone program and maintain them. So from the very early days, sales, service, and customer training were all interrelated.

Fred Gould, hired as a technician after leaving the Navy in 1959 recalls, "No one understood computers. I never bothered telling anybody about what computers did because it was too abstract an idea for most people to deal with. Even less was known about digital logic design. We did a lot of bingo cards—an ad with a little card and check-off box. So we'd get these leads. And we'd go to specialized trade shows. Physicists were vanguard users, so we dealt a lot with high- and low-energy physics as an early market for our lab modules and training equipment."

The twin necessities of self-financing and making a profit demanded innovation in products and selling. "We developed a consultative, listening approach, and we grew by finding customers we could satisfy," says Ted Johnson. "We encouraged our customers to be self-sufficient, but tried to collaborate with the most innovative and technically capable users so that we could assist them, and learn from them what their real needs were. Growth came as more people began to understand computers and how they worked."

Missionary Work

Although the original business plan and the founders' intent was to build a computer company, Digital was primarily a circuit modules manufacturer for the first seven years. This bread-and-butter product line proved to be a very profitable repeat-order business, and it provided the revenue base for moving into computers.

> "I built up good relationships with people. I learned that people were buying faith, and trust, and respect. And that's the way I sold. They were buying that as much as they were buying the product."
>
> — Ted Johnson

Showtime

"The first trade show was very interesting because we had to build the booth ourselves. We couldn't afford very much, so we had burlap covering the bottom of the table. Then Ken and I got this clever idea: to silkscreen 'Digital' on it, at an angle. Sort of 1940s modern! It was really a very homemade-looking thing. You could have sold pies there!"

— Aulikki Olsen

But if modules were a means to an end, the sales engineers didn't act that way. They had an intense drive to develop this business, though there was little idea of the magnitude of future growth. The company did so well with modules that DEC (as it was always called then) soon came to dominate what had been a fragmented and half-hearted industry. Digital modules became the standard for labs and system builders and provided the first example of nurturing, redefining, and dominating a market niche. This entrepreneurial and marketing model later was expanded and formalized through the product line structure.

Memory testing was the initial, clear market opportunity for lab modules, and Digital supplied several manufacturers. Expanding from this base, Digital began to sell a concept that was really new: hooking up standard module building blocks to create test patterns rather than using conventional test equipment. It was a standard products approach—easy to buy and use without help.

As the only sales engineer, Ted Johnson travelled to customer sites with a brown leather bag. "It had a relay rack filled with the nine lab modules and flashlight batteries, all taped together. With an oscilloscope, I'd show how easy it was to patch them together and demonstrate the speed of the circuits. The great thing was that you could really be an engineer. You'd take their problem and show them how to solve it. It was a lot of fun. The customer could order the modules, wire them together the way you had it on the blackboard, plug them in, and that was it. A new customer."

These close working relationships let technical customers feel that they were dealing directly with Digital. And they were. Sales engineers focused on educating and working with customers, impressing them with on-the-spot solutions to logic problems. The success of this approach during the formative years helped determine the character of Digital's later marketing and selling style.

With its memory testers, the company encountered a clear international market. Jon Fadiman, a magnetics expert who spoke fluent French, played an important early role in helping to establish Digital in the international area. Jon says, "The first tester went to RCA. The second one to New Jersey. The next one went to Philips in the Netherlands. And the next one went to Siemens in Munich, and the next one to France. After that, Japan, and then Hong Kong, and now you begin to understand how soon Digital got into the international business." In the U.S., enthusiasm spread beyond the memory tester field to labs such as Lawrence Livermore, the Jet Propulsion Lab, Honeywell, and Lincoln Lab.

Harlan Anderson and Stan Olsen shared sales management during these first seven years. Reflecting on the company then, Gerry Moore observes, "We were extremely informal in those days. Salesmen didn't have goals—there was no quota. Success certainly meant selling, but how much was success was anybody's guess. Salesmen were not taught how to sell and a lot of us came there not having a prior sales experience. I had been an engineer up until the day I joined Digital. We had a course on the products and how they worked so we could talk about them to customers, but we were left on our own in terms of sales technique."

This gave individuals a great sense of initiative and freedom. John Jones affirms, "I always felt in those early days that I could do as much and take on as much as I could possibly care to. There wasn't a lot of organized support, but certainly nothing stood in the way of my succeeding. It was up to me."

Educating the Customer

Module orders continued to roll in, spurring further growth. Dick Best joined the company as chief engineer and began development of a range of industrial modules for building systems. These were for pre-OEM system builders who used them in products. As a transistor circuit expert, Best immediately understood the need of Sales for good product information, so he wrote a book on digital logic to explain what it was and how to use it. Based on working examples brought in from the field, the tutorial information gave the book tremendous value.

One of the early applications engineers was Barbera Stephenson. Along with Dave Denniston, she played a major role in providing educational application-focus material. Her expertise was analog-to-digital and digital-analog design. She designed a set of modules and provided a handbook with it that became a very successful sales tool and a popular giveaway on its own.

Education was an inseparable part of the selling cycle. Talking to people, listening to their views, making suggestions, designing possibilities. Digital was very much in education mode, trying to move the simple principles of designing with digital logic into the engineering world.

This led to a key marketing innovation, recalls Johnson. "We had the idea that, with a modules handbook, we could reach the fragmented engineering market by putting Digital on every engineer's reference shelf. We first distributed the handbooks at an IEEE show in New York City. They were hardcover but inexpensive and we stacked them up in front of the booth and handed them out freely. This was electrifying, and the competitors never recovered from this show of confidence and commitment.

"With this success, Stan Olsen decided to print handbooks on newsprint so we could be profligate in their distribution. Salesmen would drop them off in bunches in engineering offices, and during trade shows we would do 40,000. You could see pages blowing around the floors of subways."

Digital later followed this same pattern with small computer handbooks, which introduced computers to many of today's technologists.

"Go Sell a Computer!"

One day Ken Olsen opened a letter from a Naval Laboratory in California. It was a request for a quotation, and it propelled Digital into the computer business. It was April 1959, says Johnson. "When Ken opened the letter, his face lit up, and he said, 'That's the machine I had in mind! Go sell a computer!'"

Harlan Anderson took on the job. Ben Gurley was brought into the company to design and build the machine, and Johnson moved to Los Angeles to open the first sales office. Ben never built the machine specified in the letter; he designed and built a smaller prototype. Development time was brief, in part because of the company's modules expertise. The PDP-1 was demonstrated in Boston just six months later at the Eastern Joint Computer Conference.

Paperback Writer

"We had the concept of putting a catalog and a handbook together. But our advertising people wanted to do a real slick book that cost well over a dollar, probably three. I said, 'That costs too much money.' 'Then why don't you limit the number you print?' 'No, that's not the idea!' So I went to the paperback bookstore and came back with three paperbacks selling for something like 50 cents apiece, and said, 'Here's what we really want.' They said, 'No, we don't want anything to do with that.' I said, 'This is what we're going to do.'

"I think it cost 17 cents apiece to print our catalog and logic handbook together. We produced about 60,000 of them. We would go to the IEEE show, the event of the year for us, and we'd hand out thousands at one show. The secret was, when somebody was walking down the aisle, you stick it in their stomach, and as they'd double over, they'd have the book! When they first saw it, our engineering people rolled over with laughter because they'd never seen anything so different from the real slick stuff.

"Then I had to go out and sell our salespeople on the idea of the book. The people in selling like to have variable prices. We said, 'No. The product is complicated enough; everything else has to be simple. So our product has to be presented very simply—a Sears, Roebuck catalog.' The catalog had the prices in addition to the tutorial information. People could read the tutorial information and figure out exactly what product they needed and know the price. We didn't need mastermind salespeople. The customer could order by mail."

— Stan Olsen

Everyone Had to Do a Little Bit of Everything

"When I started at Digital, I was twenty-one years old. The company was young, too; it had shipped only two computer systems. There was a PDP-1 at Bolt Beranek and Newman and another at the Itek Corporation. Then in August or September 1961, we delivered the third to MIT.

"I worked in Engineering; but back then, with less than a hundred employees in the whole company, the few of us in Engineering did a bit of everything. Maybe you'd work on design one day and test the next, and then you might be called on to do installation or servicing. People in Manufacturing helped out in Engineering and vice versa. It was a closely knit group, and everyone wore a lot of hats.

"As it turned out, I and a few others ended up handling more service calls than the rest of the people did. After a while our names naturally came up when customers called needing help.

"I was asked to go on loan for three months to set up the service organization. At the end of the three months I was asked to stay in the job.

"Jack Smith used to run a piece of manufacturing. He and I sometimes had to get together to work out shipment schedules because the service organization couldn't handle all the products he could build and ship, or because he needed some help from my people to get more systems tested. Once the systems were tested, manufacturing people would go out with us in the field and help install them."

— Jack Shields

The company divided into roughly three sections. The module section was headed by Dick Best and the memory test section (which later became special systems) was headed by Jon Fadiman. These two supported the computer section, headed by Gurley.

In the West, two dominant markets developed for the new computer. The Jet Propulsion Laboratory used the PDP-1 for online data collection from the NASA Mariner space probe, and the Lawrence Livermore Laboratory used it for particle-physics research. In the East, ITT wanted to use the PDP-1 for message switching. They ordered 19 and became the first OEM. This was a volume of hardware to sophisticated customers who could provide their own applications and support. Finding customers who could succeed without much support became a key part of the strategy.

Computer Controls was the initial modules competitor, but the strongest computer challenge came from Scientific Data Systems. SDS knew the NASA market well. Unlike Digital, they stressed commission selling and aggressive growth. SDS also offered more software, such as FORTRAN, but they couldn't break into the physics area, where Digital had already established strong loyalties. They tried to lure away Digital salespeople, but they were too proud of their company and their roles to leave.

Additional field offices were set up in Chicago with Tom Quinn, in New Jersey with Dave Denniston, in Washington, D.C. with Jim Burley, and in San Francisco with Ken Larsen. Many new employees were brought aboard: bright PDP-1 users from MIT, technicians and young engineers, people who had an interest and maybe some experience with computer logic. The emphasis was to hire people with integrity and commitment to the long term; smart people who would understand the products and help the customers, letting the products pull the company, who would not try to over-sell.

Dick Poulsen remembers his interview with Jack Shields. "It went on and on, all these technical questions, I was just whipping out the answers. Finally he stumped me on one. Then he took the time to explain it to me and that was the end of it.

"He was a very technically oriented guy. When he serviced PDP-1s when he joined the company, I was told that he would never have the blueprints in front of him; he'd tell the guys in the field, 'Go and put the scope and check the pulse here, check it there, check this pen down here,' just from memory. So he obviously could see the whole circuit in his mind."

Russ Doane had a similar experience. He remembers his interview with Dick Best. "He impressed me by asking a lot of detailed questions and really listening to what I knew. So it became obvious to me that this was a place that cared about my capabilities, a place where I could really contribute."

It was a goal to find and satisfy the most self-sufficient, challenging, and influential customers, and from the outset, Digital cultivated good customer relationships. There was a solid rapport with scientists and engineers, and those who didn't need high levels of service support. With this intense focus on helping customers be successful, sales engineers were very careful to avoid customers they couldn't help to succeed. The guiding strategy was to establish successful reference sites by maximizing the opportunity developed in each market field or niche.

Bill Lennon, of Lawrence Livermore Lab, was an early Digital customer. "What we discovered in the dim past was that, unlike a lot of companies, DEC made very strong commitments to its existing customer base. They received some criticisms from competitors as a result. Nonetheless, we all appreciated the notion that you weren't throwing your money away when you bought stuff from DEC. We definitely felt that was not the case with a large number of other companies. And I think that in itself has had a lot to do with DEC's success."

Customers appreciated that Digital designers came directly to them to learn about their needs, and customer loyalty remained very high. Ted Johnson says the focus was long term. "The biggest mistake we could have made would have been to overextend ourselves—to ignore the customers we could satisfy and reach ahead too far for those we couldn't, despite the temptation of big sales and bigger markets. We developed the unique ability to support new pockets of sophisticated users." This meant, for instance, that government special business was avoided in favor of standard commercial products and markets. Meanwhile, IBM and others did well by serving the data processing industries.

Despite the sophistication and self-sufficiency of most customers, Digital's growing customer base required an expanding, skilled, service capability. Under Jack Shields, service had been considered a profit-making concern from the start. He and Ken Olsen figured that a customer who valued good service would be willing to pay for it. By 1963, Digital had 12 field service engineers who worked together to cover a territory that included the United States, and installations in West Germany and England.

In those early days the service organization was spread thin. Dick Poulsen remembers how it was in Canada. "There were guys in Edmonton who would drive two thousand miles a week. The interprovincial pipeline from Edmonton to Chicago was controlled by PDP-8s and in those days computers weren't as reliable as they are today. They used to drive the whole length of the pipeline fixing things. So a couple of thousand miles a week driving wasn't particularly uncommon."

Going the extra mile is what customer service is all about. This was demonstrated when a fire swept through an office in the U.K. As Geoff Shingles puts it, "Buildings are destructible, but service excellence need not be. We lost a center that was critical to our service operation. Fortunately, no one was hurt. The initiative and skills of our people were quickly engaged to solve the problem, and we had the whole operation up and running again in less than 24 hours. For some months our people were spread around other offices within a 50-mile radius of their former home. But it was business as usual, because they were still able to communicate freely, and still able to use the same core information—regardless of location."

Making that extra effort is a tradition in the service organization. Dick Poulsen remembers when Jack Shields put Don Busiek in charge of software services. He told Don that his goal was "a billion dollar sure thing, B$ST." Busiek recalls, "We were all engineers ourselves. We used our experiences in installing, training, and repair to build greater reliability into later Digital computers. Customers purchased only the level of service they needed. Some hardly needed help at all.

Toolbox and White Socks

"In the early days, the idea of making money in the computer service business was unusual. It may seem strange now, but at that time much of the industrial service business was viewed as a necessary evil. It was the guy with the toolbox and the white socks. Many people felt it was immoral to make a profit from the misfortune of a customer with a broken machine. Service was often something thrown in to help close a sale.

"Service people learned that if you understood how to make a profit and keep your customer happy, you knew you were adding value.

"There was also a theory that if we made a profit on service, we'd have less happy customers. We learned the opposite was true—that if you had to visit a customer too often to fix a problem, you couldn't make money—and the customer wasn't pleased. We had to learn how to fix a problem so it stayed fixed!

"Those were great times! We had an environment where there were great growth opportunities for people. What do you need to win? You need the skills, motivation, and opportunity. We had all three."

— Ken Senior

Doing Hard Things Well

"I think everyone felt very strongly that DEC was our company, whether we were inside or outside the company, and that DEC's goals were not that different from customers' goals. They were trying to get interesting and hard things done, and done well.

"The organization came across as very open. You knew that people were there just trying to learn what you needed to get done, because they realized that if you figured that out, it would lead to a rational product. If it took care of one sophisticated user's needs, there would be many users out there that would benefit. We tended to buy what we needed, and we explained what our needs were going to be two to three years ahead, and DEC would try really hard to respond. We felt comfortable when we could have an impact on future directions.

"By combining customers from apparently diverse organizations and coming up with some common requirements, we were able to communicate the importance of those requirements to Digital. From the earliest days, DECUS was an important marketing and communication tool for Digital."

— Bill Lennon
Lawrence Livermore Laboratory

"As the field engineers struggled to stay up with the latest designs, we'd go to some customer sites, and they would know more than we did. They'd let us sweat it out in front of them, and then they'd tell us what spares we needed."

Given its deep academic roots, Digital clearly saw that education was a two-way street, and learned early to value the support and feedback from customers. Stan Olsen points out that software was Digital's weak suit for many years. "People were writing their own software out of self-defense. So we brought in some people from the Model Railroad Club at MIT. They wrote a lot of software for the PDP-1 that helped users write their own applications, including a debugging program called DDT, and one called Edmund the Editor. DECUS was formed; it was really a case of necessity being the mother of invention. We didn't have the money, and people insisted on making profit, so we limited ourselves to selling to people who were able to do these things themselves."

Elaborating on this strategy, Ted Johnson says, "It limited the size of the market; it limited support requirements; it caused us to learn how to sell to people like that. To me, that was the secret of Digital's success right there. We basically understood and related to a whole enormously growing, and enormously underserved, segment of marketplace."

Bill Lennon went to Hanscom Field in Bedford, Massachusetts, for the first DECUS meeting. "At the first meeting, the really important, burning issue was whether one society could support both the PDP-1 and the PDP-4 computer. We spent a lot of time discussing whether that was possible."

Later on, when Digital started offering volumes of software, the tone of DECUS changed from being a protective association to more of an information exchange among the users: how they were using a product, what was wrong with it, enhancements, and so on. It became a way for Digital to introduce products and get some gross feedback.

More product input to engineering came from DECUS than from any individual customers; yet, customers really were a vital part of the organization. Johnson recalls, "We created access for customers, and some of those customers certainly felt like they worked for Digital, they were so loyal to us! Some of them felt obliged to criticize constantly everything we did. Those are the ones that loved us the most. Facing them regularly was a real challenge and an absolutely critical learning experience."

"Go Over and Do the Best You Can, Let Us Know What You're Going to Do, and We'll Build a Company Around That"

The markets for Digital's early products were inherently international, and the management view embraced the long-term importance of international opportunities. In 1963, operations were started in Germany and Canada, and in 1964, Australia. A small trading company was hired in Japan. Jon Fadiman says he hired Rikei as the Digital distributor in Japan for the memory test business simply because "they got two orders and nobody else did. It seemed like as good a reason as any other." For a time Digital dominated the world in the magnetic testing business. Ninety percent of all core memories that went into computers were tested either on Digital's core testers, memory exercisers, or memory test machines.

One of the first large computer deliveries was to Perth, Australia—about as far from Maynard as it was possible to be. Ron Smart joined the company via contact with Gordon Bell. Robin Frith had been hired to sell modules but switched to computers when a PDP-6 was sold to the University of Western Australia. Smart established the office in his house. "Unfortunately, it was a new house, which meant that there was no telephone. I had to go down to the telephone box on the corner, because there was no other way to call back to the United States. I mostly dealt with Harlan Anderson, so I always reversed the charges. He said the bill was always the same. Apparently we went up to the limit of the meter each time, and it stopped!"

"It was actually two or three years before we started to get a stream of orders," continues Smart. "The main sales tool I had was the *DECUS Proceedings,* because in the DECUS reports you found all of the applications that were being done in the leading labs around the world. The PDP-6 started to be used in nuclear physics applications, bubble chamber analysis, and so on. That helped to give Digital an air of competence. If you were going to be doing some particular research, then you'd better use the latest that everybody else was using. We were written up in these *DECUS Proceedings,* so it was a strong entree."

In Canada, Digital modules and basic computers were in heavy demand among the labs and the physics establishment. Denny Doyle, a Canadian customer, was so impressed with Digital's modules line that he joined the company and led the way in building the successful subsidiary there.

Stan Olsen sent Ted Johnson to Munich to help in the start-up office there, because nothing much was happening. "My role was very fluid, very informal, and very ill-defined. That was good because I had a lot of freedom, but there weren't any clear goals. It was, 'Go over and do the best you can, let us know what you're going to do, and we'll build a company around that.' That was typical Digital—I was trusted and expected to figure out the right things to do."

Johnson went to Basel, Switzerland, and worked to put a show together with Jack Shields, who was then the U.S. field service manager. They shared a clear recognition that sales and service needed to be better organized. Johnson recalls, "We had a long meeting on a boat on the Rhine River to discuss it, and we formed a kind of partnership right then and there."

"At that time, I discovered that I could relate to these people just like Americans. That excited me, so I took a bunch of leads and headed for Sweden, Denmark, the Netherlands, and back down through Germany. Two PDP-7s and a bunch of modules came out of that trip," continues Johnson. Trips to Italy, Paris, and CERN [Center for European Nuclear Research, Geneva, Switzerland] followed, with a lot of focus on building relationships between the Europeans and Maynard.

Stan Olsen brought back Ted Johnson to run North American sales in 1964. Jon Fadiman was sent to establish the Paris office and John Leng went to start an office in the United Kingdom, operating at first from a bingo hall in a Reading church. Shortly thereafter, when the organizational structure changed, Leng became responsible for European sales. Gerry Moore went there later to work under Leng and took responsibility for Germany, Austria,

Feedback

"When we started DECUS, a lot of people said we were crazy! Don't ever do that! It's a disaster, because the customers will pound on you. They'll drive you out of business. Customers are bad! We decided to risk the negative to find the positive. Nobody is bright enough to design something perfect for a customer without talking to them."

— Stan Olsen

and the Benelux countries. "In Europe we tended to be highly integrated with the U.S.," Moore recalls. "While I felt a large degree of freedom, there were, nevertheless, a lot of telephone communications with the people who were running the business in the U.S.—conversations over the terms and conditions I would be negotiating with a customer."

Working Smarter: Product Lines

The Digital sales force numbered in the twenties by 1964. There were several lines of computers: the PDP-4/7; the small, new PDP-5; the large PDP-6. Modules were a highly profitable product line, and the PDP-7s were doing well. But the informal structure of the company was a problem. Differences about strategy and direction caused severe stress. The PDP-5 had sold very few units but opened new opportunities, and the PDP-6 was demanding a lot of support, pulling resources away from other areas. It was a big computer for a small company.

The PDP-8, an outgrowth of the PDP-5, changed everything. It was a breakthrough in size, price, and performance. Ted Johnson remembers how it was managed by Nick Mazzarese. "He let SDS and Computer Controls announce their new low-end products first. Then he hit the market with our lower price. The competition didn't believe we could make a profit. The speed, price, and packaging hit exactly right. During announcement week, our sales thermometer chart went over the top in two days. It was a great product for salespeople, who could master it and become expert. We felt it was the Model-T of the industry. The ads showed a Steiff teddy bear perched on the console, and with its transparent plastic cover, the PDP-8 seemed a truly approachable, hands-on computer."

The new computer was also a natural for OEM business. Entrepreneurs and existing companies saw opportunities to use it in applications products. They bought volumes of hardware at heavily discounted prices, added their own software and hardware, then sold them through their own sales team. This greatly expanded the sales force promoting Digital.

With the explosive market response to the PDP-8, Ken Olsen made an intuitive decision to change the organization—to resolve the struggle for the strategy and control of the company. In 1964 he established four product lines. Each was to have profit and loss responsibility. The company would now be the sum of the parts. For the next 18 years, this concept determined the structure and development of Digital. Ken Olsen later said that he realized he was in the position of having to make all the decisions, and he didn't want to be in that position. Nick Mazzarese took on small computers, Stan Olsen moved into modules, Harlan Anderson managed the PDP-6, and Win Hindle managed the memory test and LINC group. All the corporate functions, including sales, became services to the product lines. Field service was to be both a product line and a service.

The implicit charter for Sales was to build a corporate sales force while figuring out how to maintain close working relationships with the product lines. Fred Gould thought it was a marvelous system. "It gave us clear responsibility for the markets with some overlap, which was healthy. The relationship that product lines had with the field was the secret to our astronomical growth.

The product line managers were a very special set of people; they tended to be the brightest and the best." Tremendous growth is always challenging, and there was also much to be learned about issues such as delegation, trust, and testing the limits of the new organization. It was a company of specialists learning to operate as a team.

When Stan Olsen took over the modules business, he proposed that Ted Johnson become worldwide sales manager. Johnson knew it was vital to keep Sales and Service together for the customer, and welcomed Jack Shields as the new field service manager. "We had a lot to learn about building commercial-quality equipment," recalls Johnson, "and a disciplined service organization was key to maintaining our reputation and feeding back product improvements. It was a challenge to achieve real collaboration because, typically, the metrics for sales and service are very different, as is the environment. Accordingly, Shields was given a lot of room, which allowed the service organization to grow.

In Shields' words, "Quietly, without a lot of fanfare, Digital changed the way companies view service. We took an activity that companies have always thought of as a nuisance and a problem, a necessary evil, and we made it into a profitable business. We started showing a profit way back in the early 1960s, and over the years we were able not only to provide high-quality service, but also to develop new techniques which allowed us to become more productive and cost-effective and pass those savings on to customers. We created a new way of approaching service that today the rest of the computer industry is trying to emulate."

Shields saw that there was a lot more to service than simply fixing things when they broke. Services included many different activities: Hardware Product Services, Computer Special Systems, Software Product Services, Customer Training and, in more recent years, Desktop Services and Systems Integration. Eventually services would account for more than 40 percent of Digital's revenues.

While the service organization was organized by function, the sales force was specialized within the product line structure, providing a virtual sales force for each product line. John Leng observes, "The product line structure is the most aggressive marketing organization you can have. Everybody is very narrowly focused on their segment; they become expert at their products and markets. This is very tough on the competition, because they don't have that intense customer focus. When you go to a functional organization, you get more generic products; you don't maintain that structure in the same way, and you lose that expertise." In the sales offices, setting and achieving personal goals was highly valued, allowing everyone to feel equally important despite widely varying goals for the three basic types of specialists. The product lines defined strategy, with feedback coming from the field, and provided active sales support and control of individual customer pricing.

Ron Smart and Margaret Rand joined sales headquarters as key support people. A simple budgeting process and reporting tools were instituted. By repeating this formula, opening branch offices became simpler, and with 40 percent annual growth, it was necessary. Contracts were established with

All the Rest Was GIA

"We had an algorithm for opening offices in countries, a systematic approach to looking at the size and makeup of the economy, and the relationship between that and the same thing in the U.S. One by one their number would come up: there would be enough business to put in an office or an agent or a roving technical salesperson.

"By the end of the sixties, each product line had a separate P&L for each of the three areas. Canada was with the United States, called North America, Europe, and all the rest was GIA—the General International Area. By and large, Digital was attractive to those countries, and we were able to bring the capability that they would read about in other places, especially in computer applications in the technical markets.

"We had few OEMs in Australia because they tended to buy from us and build their own applications. Japan was quite different; we converted several instrument manufacturers who were into computers and persuaded them to become OEMs. It was a good strategy. It was helpful to them, because they could then sell their applications around the world on our platforms.

"We tried the same approach in Latin America, especially in Brazil, but it didn't work. They thought that the OEM relationship was one in which we gave them all the problems and walked away with the money.

"In India, they understood this approach, and we had several Indian government OEMs, who bought our machine, built something on top of it, and sold it.

"By 1976, we had 17 countries. We grew faster than the other two areas, enjoyed higher profitability, and suffered no major losses."

— Ron Smart

each product line for bookings, yields (bookings per person), cost per person, and manpower. High priority was given to information sharing—direct, raw input from the company out to the field, and from the field back to the company. The biweekly Sales Newsletter was sent to all sales and marketing people. With all groups regularly contributing, everyone could stay on top of developments in products, markets and product line policies.

Smart recalls an interesting lesson. "At first we had one P&L for each product line at the area level, but no P&Ls by country. The country managers would always argue they needed more salespeople, so we decided they had to learn how to run a business. We took the GIA P&L by product line, and made a P&L for each of the countries and geographic groups. When the managers learned how to run a business, they managed themselves in terms of profitability and growth—the same measure that the Operations Committee applied to the product lines. So the product lines' interest and the country manager's interest were different dimensions of the same thing. This compatibility between the country and the product lines' performance measures made it possible for the area to grow, with little management by the central staff."

With John Leng managing Europe, operations there continued to progress. Geoff Shingles took over the United Kingdom subsidiary. But finding managers was often difficult. Nationals were sought whenever possible, but competence and character came first. "We were looking for the brightest people, people we could trust," says Leng. "We found young, energetic, intelligent people who could really build the company." Gerry Moore was managing Germany, and Jean-Claude Peterschmitt was asked to manage Digital's operations in France. When Harry Mann joined the company as chief financial officer, he brought some order and became a mentor in the international area. By this time, Digital's market was global and varied. "When we went public, in our tenth year, I was struck that our major asset was the terrific customer base we'd established," says Johnson.

Compensation and Culture

"Without commission, a salesperson has to be motivated by growth—like buying a stock without dividends. Growth was not only promotions and higher earnings but individual satisfaction from doing a bigger, better job. My first manager said, 'You make your goals and I'll take care of your career.' In order to make those goals, I had to do better at my job through professional development. When I became a manager, I turned the coin, and figured if I developed the people, the goals would take care of themselves."

— Dick Fredrickson

"To this day, ex-IBM managers can't resist asking how we could have succeeded without sales commissions," says Johnson. "To them, setting sales points and quotas to determine level of income is the key to their process and to their culture."

Digital's salespeople were hired and paid just as other professionals were, for the most part. People joined for the long term, trading riskier short-term opportunities for ongoing career opportunities with fair compensation. Direct compensation fit the company's ways of operating and thinking. It offered many advantages and was rarely questioned. It allowed flexibility and creativity in new product and program introductions, and in job assignments. Digital's cost of selling was competitive, post-sales service was better, and salespeople enjoyed a more compatible relationship with the rest of the company. Customers trusted the salespeople to do the right thing for them, uncompromised by personal motives.

The hiring and salary review practices were a major factor in building the sales and marketing culture. Typically, a candidate would interview with as many as 15 people, not only sales managers, but service managers, personnel, product line managers, and others. "We looked for drive and spark, for real interest in the company, for people who would persist and win," says Johnson. "We wanted people who would develop in harmony with the rest of us, feeling comfort and trust, people who would be fun to work with. We programmed out people who couldn't function without boundaries. We wanted people who would go around walls."

People were trusted to do the right thing for the customer and encouraged to get help or blow the whistle on whatever prevented doing the best job. Fixing the customer problem took priority over everything, including sales. In return for freedom and responsibility, much was expected. Irwin Jacobs was in the Cambridge, Massachusetts, office. "There weren't a lot of rules—just what specialization people would have, and which products and/or markets we would try to cover. Most of that we did ourselves, locally. We tried to minimize the contact we had with Maynard by solving our own problems. So we all became loyal to the sales organization." Open communications and enthusiasm fostered a vibrant culture, even in remote international sites, that could be noticed over the Telex.

For years, every salesman and marketing professional, and every field service manager was reviewed annually by the Operations Committee. This provided visibility and critical feedback about individual performance and future prospects with the company. It was important to salespeople to feel they were known and seen. In such a promising company, promotion was a powerful motivator. As a result, turnover was extremely low and commitment to ongoing career development was extremely high.

Under the direct salary system, managers played a strong role in nurturing team efforts and encouraging individual growth. In 1972, this means of compensation was challenged. An extensive review, however, reaffirmed that direct salary was right for Digital. Instead of changing the system, Sales leadership focused on the need for public recognition of salespeople as a way to encourage spirit and enthusiasm. Field managers took great care to work with salespeople in setting goals and recognizing performance. DEC100 was established to honor those who defined and fulfilled their goals 100 percent. Later, the DECathlon program was added to reward the top 10 percent of the sales force.

In both Sales and Service, customer satisfaction surveys were a key metric in determining performance and compensation. If your customers thought you were doing a good job, you probably were. And both Sales and Service were doing the right things. By the end of the 1960s, Digital had become the leader of a substantial minicomputer industry, with accumulated experience

Culture versus Competence

"I've always felt that if you have the minimum level of sensitivity and the competence to do the job, it's much more important than being part of the local culture, provided you have an infrastructure, which is local culture. That was an important point: our objective was to have local culture infrastructure, as many Germans in Germany, as many British in Great Britain, as many French in France. But when it comes to making a compromise between somebody who is the right cultural person or the right person from a knowledge, competence, managerial view, I would always make a decision in favor of the competence."

— Jean-Claude Peterschmitt

Up and Up

"I would say it cost the company a significant percentage of business to hang on to the PDP-8 too long without having a 16-bit alternative. Our sales yields—the average sales per man—were down. When we introduced the PDP-11, our sales started climbing again and rose to new heights, compared with what they had been before. I used to plot the sales yield, and saw it drop off precipitously after '67, '68. When the PDP-11 was introduced and was gradually fleshed out, and more and more enhancements became available, sales yields began going up and up. It put the company on a real drive upward that, apart from an occasional hiccup in a bad economy, just kept going."

— Gerry Moore

in almost every marketplace, including education, government and industrial labs, manufacturing and medical. The PDP-10 was developing another base of service bureaus, computer science labs, and even commercial data processing. The company enjoyed a broad and loyal base of end users and OEM customers, and a strong reputation among technical users.

Reinforcing Leadership: The '70s

"By 1970, Digital was a mystique. We had led in the creation of a market where Digital became a virtual cult, especially among engineers and scientists. DEC handbooks for computers and modules were status symbols on bookshelves. Many of our customers acted like they were part of Digital, and they were proud of that relationship."

— Dick Fredrickson

With the introduction of the PDP-11 in 1970, Digital reinforced its leadership in the minicomputer business. The increasing complexity of the market and expansion of the company brought a period of intense regrouping and growth to sales and marketing. In the next eight years, the business grew from $150 million to almost $2 billion.

Andy Knowles and Julius Marcus were hired to develop the PDP-11 product line. Along with Roger Cady, the engineering manager, they canvassed the field, selling the sales force on the PDP-11. "Getting the PDP-11 out was the biggest challenge for the team. We had to do everything," Andy recalls. "We finished the design in December, announced it January 5th, and shipped the first one by March 31st to an outfit in California.... We figured we were a year and a half or two years behind the three major competitors. If we didn't hit it right and the thing didn't work, the company was probably dead, because the PDP-8 wouldn't have carried it through."

Before long, the sales force proposed a new definition for sales specialists: reorganizing by market or industry lines. It made little sense to have separate PDP-8 and PDP-11 sales specialists, and the company needed to do a better job of reaching a variety of users. The product lines reacted strongly, insisting that they needed to maintain their individual relationships with salespeople.

Ultimately, the minicomputer product lines were restructured. One outcome was the creation of a separate OEM product line under Bill Long. Data General, the leading competitor in minicomputers, had begun to capture too many start-up OEM accounts. The product line had to understand the need to reshape the discount price curve to turn the tide. A very sophisticated terms-and-conditions package was developed. From then on, Digital was unbeatable as an OEM supplier.

Stan Olsen took on the challenge of developing nontechnical markets, which evolved into commercial OEM business to handle small business applications. The modules business was facing a new kind of competition as a result of the shift to microprocessors. Digital responded by starting an LSI business, managed by Knowles.

The industrial market for computers, particularly in control applications, had developed contrary to forecasts. Growth did not depend on solutions from giant suppliers; rather, it was the increasing confidence and competence of engineers to implement computing solutions for specific applications that drove the market. Digital was well-positioned to provide the tools for the customers' engineers. In this sense, Digital grew as the market grew, working with customers as they developed the ability to build their own solutions.

Up to this time, Digital had been considered largely a hardware supplier. But with the PDP-11 and the DECsystem-10, the power and complexity of Digital software operating systems became dominant. Digital developed into a leading software company at the operating systems level. Larry Portner became a key player in helping to develop the software services business. The field service organization worked closely with Portner's organization to achieve the necessary support. Software licensing and planning, and supporting the complex installation of the first DECnet nodes was a whole new world. DECnet had been announced at a DECUS symposium in 1975. The company's growing involvement in software and networking, coupled with the large field service operation and its sophisticated logistics capabilities, was a powerful force in winning business. It had taken Digital 19 years to reach the billion-dollar level in sales. Two years later, in 1978, sales doubled.

Although this period started with a recession, several important lessons emerged. Digital could gain market share even during a recession. This was one by-product of the salaried approach. Under siege, salespeople could fully focus on selling, not worrying about pay. Outside, some of the best-commissioned salespeople felt the pressure of lower earnings to leave their companies. Sales leadership learned as well to adjust the sales resource planning to set lower yields during a recession. Logically, the same effort or even greater effort resulted in less output in a tough market. This led to the argument to add salespeople, even during tough times. Digital did—and gained further market share and unseated the competition. Even customers noticed the phenomenon.

VAX and Change

The VAX was introduced in 1977. Like the PDP-11, it was another step up in computer power. Where the PDP-11 had evolved multiple operating systems, the VAX had only one, offering even greater compatibility and protection of the customers' software investments.

The company's experience with the DECsystem-10 and DECSYSTEM-20 was very important in introducing the VAX into the marketplace. The two systems lines could be integrated; however, with the move to cluster the VAX, further development of the DECSYSTEM-20 was discontinued. The product and its engineering, marketing, and selling had made an invaluable contribution to Digital's evolution, so it was a difficult and sad day for many when it stopped. Win Hindle calls it "the hardest ethical decision that I had to make, because we had led people to believe we were going to continue developing it. But as we examined the question in the early 1980s, it became clear to me that it would not be doing the right thing in the long term for our users. In our view, the right thing was to move them to the VAX, where we could do a far better job, especially in software. So we worked hard on it, and developed a plan. Rose Ann Giordano very skillfully went, customer-by-customer, and worked out the plan for everyone."

The OEM Business

"At the time of the PDP-8 we recognized that there was an opportunity to sell lots of computers to customers who would stick our computer inside of a larger system that did a specialized job, whether it was word processing or gas chromatography, then resell it. There was no end to applications. That was the OEM business. We were running about a $60 million PDP-8 business when the PDP-11 started to come into its own. We just redefined the marketing activity and created the OEM business.

"Unfortunately, the OEM business was very closely tied with the economic cycles. When the economy was booming, the OEM business boomed. When the economy went bad, so went the OEM business. It was very difficult to forecast. If we could have figured that out, we could have run for president. But it was a good business, and a lot of good people came into it and then moved into the rest of the company as a result of the fast growth."

— Bill Long

Painful

"We had engineering problems with the follow-on to the DECsystem-10/20 in the early 1980s. It became obvious that we were not going to be able to fix them in any reasonable time frame. Even if you put tons of money into it, would the customers wait another two years for a product that was already late? The rational decision was no. It was painful for me and for the company. The large systems users were our most valued customers. We had told people there would be a follow-on, so it became more than a product cancellation. It was our word, our image, and our commitment to customers.

"The decision to halt the product line's development was made five days before a DECUS symposium. Facing these users, for whom the 10/20 products had become a love affair, with our decision and asking them to trust us, was a horrifying thought. By the time Win and I arrived at the symposium, the word was out. There was anger, and I remember consciously wearing a white suit with the hopes that I'd give a 'good guy' message.

"Yet there was no question that VAX was the future, so we put plans in place for each account to protect the customer's investment while migrating, on a one-on-one, very personal basis. I think we saved practically 70 percent of the customer base."

— Rose Ann Giordano

In 1978, with sales of $2 billion, the company had a strong worldwide sales and service organization of 15,000 people. Digital's unique field culture had grown in Europe and GIA, and Digital had steadily strengthened its ability to service large worldwide customers.

"We felt very good about our field organization," says Ted Johnson. "We had a worldwide grid of seasoned field managers and product lines that focused on individual accounts and markets. We had grown fine managers who had developed strong local teams. Their stability and loyalty and the open communication and trust between them and the product lines were tremendous strengths."

During this period, network capability expanded. Digital began to elaborate a concept of distributed computing architectures. This set the strategy for software development efforts. By the end of the decade, this distributed architecture concept, along with the ability to openly interface with and service other vendors' systems, proved to be a key distinction.

But in the industry at large, challenging transitions were taking place, largely driven by the application of new standard microprocessors. Apple and CP/M machines entered the market and monthly District Manager reports pointed out losses of Digital multiuser systems to batches of personal computers, starting in the education market.

Considerable emotion, confusion, and stress attended the development and introduction of Digital's personal computer products. These were largely developed outside of the mainstream responsibility of the product lines. Skepticism about the competitiveness of the Professional 350 was balanced by the introduction of the Rainbow, built around the CP/M and MS-DOS operating systems. Office automation intensified the stress. Wang was growing very fast. The market wondered why Digital wasn't doing better. The success of IBM's personal computer changed the rules and rapidly shrunk the market for special-purpose word processors.

A major paradigm shift was occurring with the rapid transition to more powerful micros and the evolution of third-party software to run on them. Ted Johnson reflects, "Just as IBM had been blind to minicomputers and their complex impact on the market, we were confused by our past superiority in these areas. We sometimes had difficulty appreciating how decisions to buy were actually made in the nontechnical office market."

Major organizational changes occurred. An Office of the President was created to strengthen planning and control. Win Hindle oversaw operations, assisting product lines with their operational plans. Andy Knowles took on marketing, developing a more formal system for product planning, and Bill Long headed up the corporate planning function. Sales was separated from Service, with Software Services moving under Jack Shields in a combined services group. Domestically, sales managers were still nominally team leaders. In the international areas, the result was to diminish the country managers' role.

The product line organization came under attack. Cumulative inventories had become large. Some of the group definitions had become contentious and ambiguous, particularly in large accounts. The sales organization focused on account management, trying to coordinate sales and service activities in large accounts and to enable the customer to experience Digital as one company, despite the connections back to multiple product lines.

Ted Johnson recalls the time when the product line organization was dismantled, in 1983. "I could only reflect on the pluses, and I hoped that Digital would retain the same intense focus on customers and the same great spirited atmosphere of learning, competition, and collaboration that made 18 years of success possible."

"Digital's consistent success and steady growth perplexed many outside observers. They often failed to appreciate the scope of our knowledge and success as a marketing company. Yet, from the outset, we had identified a customer base to ensure profitability. We had created a product—the mini-computer—for that customer base, and it became a standard . . . an industry, in fact. We used unique education and relationship-building approaches, such as handbooks and user groups. Our users were the brightest and the best. We established new channels of distribution through our OEM groups. We visualized the international market from the start, developing extraordinary organizations in Europe, Canada, Japan, Australia and elsewhere. We developed a unique entrepreneurial product line organization, with profitable service counterparts. And, with the largest non-commissioned sales force in the electronics industry, creating a new industry standard for a technical sales force, Digital enjoyed the best customer relations, high and reliable yields, low selling costs, and the lowest turnover. But it was the human achievement more than the numbers. I felt very lucky to have been a part of it all."

Ted Johnson knew how to manage change. From a one-man operation, Sales and Service grew into an organization of tens of thousands of men and women. It is an organization that is still changing. As Dave Grainger said, "Change feels disruptive; but it is unavoidable. To compete effectively in the marketplace, change must be a part of our Digital values. Plans for organizational change should be part of our planning process. We ought to anticipate the kinds of change the organization has to make a year from now, two years from now, three years from now, so we can participate in it fully and be excited about it."

One of Ken Olsen's talents is his ability to anticipate change. In 1985, at a State of the Company Meeting, he said, "The industry is in turmoil. Many computer companies are going into very serious times. We are now in an era where many companies are not going to survive and we have the opportunity to come out on top. We've done the hard part: the products, the networking, the integrating. Now, we have to finish the job."

And finishing the job is the responsibility of Sales and Service. Pier Carlo Falotti summed up Digital's approach to sales and service when he coined the phrase "A Network of Entrepreneurs."

Strong Identity

"There was much more camaraderie in the sales office than there was anywhere inside. There were really two disciplines in the field: the sales people and the field service people. We didn't report to the same organizations. We broke down the barriers, and though we all reported separately, we had just one office. Eventually we had software support people as well, but it took them a long time to build up an identity.

"I still remember Veteran's Day. Half our office were veterans, who had to march in the parade. We closed the office to go watch them in the parade. We had somebody to answer the phone. It used to start somewhere near the Playboy Club, so we'd all take the T [Boston subway] over there and watch our own troops in the parade."

— Jake Jacobs

Part III

How Digital Works

"No longer should a network
be considered as the collection
of machines and the wires that
connect them, but rather as
the collective intelligence of
the people the network brings
together."

— VAX Notes user

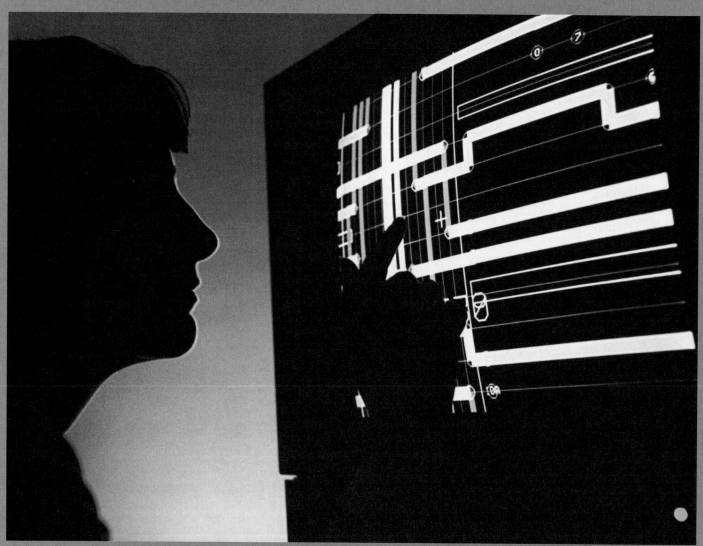

Today's interactive computing

Networking

Now that the ideal of a computer on every desk has just about become the rule, the challenge ahead is to streamline communication between people and machines. This means making it easy to exchange ideas and information freely and quickly between computers and applications despite their differences.

Standards are at the heart of the compatibility that distinguishes Digital computers from the PDP-11 onward. In the same way, standards are a prominent part of the strategy Digital developed for multivendor networking, called Network Application Support, that has contributed to setting Digital apart in the industry.

Networking has come to represent a style of working as much as a communications technology. Over 30 years, the ingenuity of the engineers who started the company has been matched with the ingenuity of the people who followed in their footsteps.

The concept of linking computers in a network first gained attention in the early 1970s. The U.S. Department of Defense used the first packet-switched network, ARPANET, to correlate data from research centers around the country. Telenet, its civilian counterpart, linked seven U.S. cities in a commercial network. Soon after, the X.25 standard was approved internationally for packet-switched networks, and Ethernet developed as the first local area network.

Around the same time, Digital engineers working on the DECsystem-10 developed software to allow computers to exchange data over direct-wiring connections and telephone lines, while another group of engineers at work on DECnet began to use the software to communicate on their PDP-11 systems. As engineer Jim Miller observes, "There is no better way to build a good system than letting the people use the system they built, because if the system doesn't do the job, they fix it."

It wasn't long before the DECsystem-10 engineers envisioned the power and possibilities of linking all manner of systems in a single network.

An Explosion of New Ideas

By the mid-1970s, a number of rudimentary computer networks were in active use at Digital. The Business Data Network circulated financial and administrative information among the DECsystem-10 and DECSYSTEM-20 systems it connected. A network called Easynet was in use in Europe, and engineers were at work on a product called DECnet for connecting PDP-11 systems.

When a group of DECnet engineers moved from the Maynard Mill to a new building in Merrimack, New Hampshire, an hour away, they began to use DECnet to communicate with colleagues back in Maynard. Using the product to develop itself resulted in an explosion of new ideas about how to make networking more useful for Digital's customers.

"Shortly after the opening of the first building in Merrimack [October 1977], we found some 9600 bps modems and data lines on the floor of an empty lab and said, 'Hey, we ought to do something with these things!' So we created a DECnet link between the RSTS development systems in Merrimack and the RSX systems in Maynard. It was the beginning of the Engineering network."

— Jim Miller

Joined Digital 1972

PDP-11/60

"[Digital's network architecture] is beautifully efficient. Neither the computers nor the users ever need to know HOW a message is routed through the network. The network itself finds the best path, simple or complex, depending on what's required, and the paths available at that time. There's no need to try to 'predefine' the best route a message should take. Like water flowing downhill, if a path is possible, it will find the fastest way."

— Bill Gassman
Joined Digital 1980

1990 *Corporate Profile*

Employees	Revenues	Locations
121,000	$12.9 billion	1,200 in 82 countries

Highlights

Digital's first Eastern European joint venture in Budapest, Hungary.
Easynet nodes: 85,000.
Digital ranks 27 on Fortune 500.
Digital eliminates ozone-destroying solvents from circuit-board manufacture.
VMS operating system opens to POSIX standards.

The Best Available Path

From the beginning, Digital's network architecture was based on connecting processors to processors, rather than on connecting processors to terminals. The first remote network link connected two people at two computer systems oceans apart so they could share tasks and resources, communicating back and forth as equals. This kind of networking is called "peer-to-peer" networking, because communications are managed by the members of the network itself, rather than by an outside source. Using the intelligence within the network vastly simplifies moving information from one place to another.

Information is sent on a Digital network with a source and destination. As the information moves through the network and arrives at another computer system, or node, the system reads the destination address, determines the next step in its route, and sends it. This adaptive routing is based on simple routing algorithms, repeated again and again until the information reaches its destination.

Adaptive routing makes it easy to add new users, applications, computers, servers, or gateways to a network. A new system can be added within minutes without affecting the rest of the network.

"In a large network, you can't reasonably expect that all nodes will change to a new phase at once, so whenever we introduce a new phase, we keep backward compatibility to the previous one. A Phase IV network will still support Phase III nodes. Phase III nodes can't do all the things that IV can, but IV can do everything III can do, and they can work together smoothly as part of the same network."

— Tony Lauck
Joined Digital 1974

VAX systems in a computer lab

The Evolution of DECnet Software

Since 1976, DECnet software has been released in phases, with each phase representing an evolution in networking capability.

DECnet Phase I ran only on the RSX operating system for the PDP-11. DECnet Phase II provided communications between different operating systems, as well as protocols for communicating with computers from other vendors and third-party carrier services. But computers still had to be directly wired to one other to communicate. There was no way of routing them through other computers.

By 1981, DECnet Phase III provided adaptive routing, which allowed two computers to "talk" to one another through a third. In addition, if that third computer failed, it could be bypassed. The message then could be recovered and rerouted through other machines on the network.

As networks became bigger, Digital engineers built-in network management to diagnose problems and monitor traffic. Phase III was intended to handle 32 nodes but, in fact, could support a network of 100 computer systems, or nodes.

By 1982, with the development of DECnet Phase IV and Ethernet support, it became possible to link all the networks within Digital in a single network that now numbers 85,000 computer hosts, called Easynet.

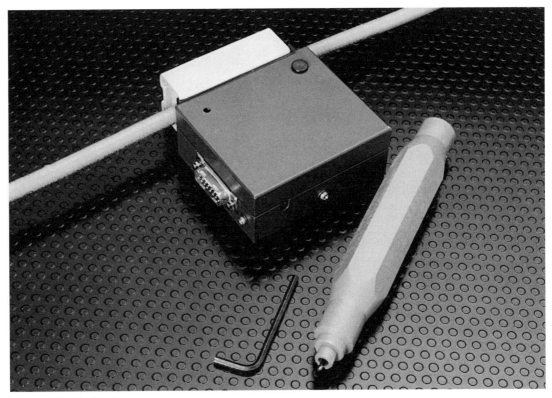

Simple networking hardware

> "The big change in
> networking came in
> the mid-1970s when we
> decided that we'd have
> to network in very stan-
> dardized ways. Everything
> we did used the same
> networking protocols
> and the same networking
> technologies. That really
> made networking a major
> part of our organization.
> It's these standardized
> ways that we've been
> encouraging the world
> to accept so that we
> and they can all work
> together on the same
> network. We've been
> pressing for standards
> to make this possible
> for a long time."
>
> — Ken Olsen
> *Smithsonian Interview*
> *September 1988*

Standards

Digital has based its networking on both international and de facto industry standards to help integrate the different systems customers use into effective networks.

DECnet has become integrated with Open Systems Inter-connect (OSI) and TCP/IP protocols in Digital's ADVANTAGE-NETWORKS. Coupled with Network Application Support services, ADVANTAGE-NETWORKS incorporates the standards required to connect personal computer, local area, and public packet-switched networks, for communicating with UNIX and IBM systems, and for transmitting over telephone networks.

Simplifying Connections

Connecting more than a few systems to one another in a network creates complex problems. Point-to-point wiring is expensive and hard to change, and the software required to manage and mask the complexity demands vast stores of processing power and is difficult to develop.

Digital had simplified a similar connection problem before, *inside* the computer, with the UNIBUS. Would a similar approach—connecting nodes to a single, bidirectional bus, rather than to each other—work for networking one computer to another?

Connecting systems

A powerful technology was required. After careful evaluation of the alternatives, Ethernet, a wiring technology invented by Xerox Corporation, was chosen. Working closely with Xerox and Intel Corporation, Digital helped to develop and refine the Ethernet technology to support sophisticated computer networks. In 1982, in collaboration with these partners, Digital announced Ethernet as its primary local area network standard. Hundreds of companies today continue making products that run on Ethernet.

Local Area Networks

Ethernet allowed Digital to move communications control from individual computers to local area networks. Using Ethernet, systems first are connected into a local area network. Then the local area network is connected via bridges and routers to the larger, wide area network.

"Before Ethernet, you had to make point-to-point connections between machines. We used thousands of DMR11s and miles of coaxial cable. The wiring looked like spaghetti. Ethernet changed all that, providing a simple bus to which systems are attached."

— Jim Miller

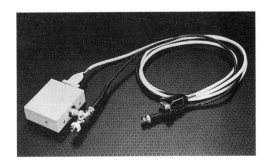

DECWORLD 1986

"In the 1970s, Digital was characterized by enormous growth in facilities, in people, and everything else. Every other week there was a new building being opened. The new VAX computer was being invented. The VAX VMS group moved to Tewksbury, Massachusetts, and we put links in there. The whole thing snowballed. We added sites in Marlboro, Hudson, and Littleton, Massachusetts; in Colorado Springs, Seattle, Palo Alto, and Puerto Rico—and, eventually, in hundreds of other places. The first thing every new engineer wanted was a connection to the Engineering Network, or the E-net, as it was abbreviated. Seven of us managed the growth of the network from essentially nothing to more than 4,000 nodes in six years."

— **Jim Miller**

The Growth of Easynet

In 1982, the development of DECnet Phase IV made it possible to connect the Engineering network and the other computer networks within Digital into one company-wide network, called Easynet. Today, logging in to Easynet connects a Digital user directly to one of 85,000 computer hosts in more than 540 locations in 36 countries around the world.

Up to 200 new computer systems, or nodes, are added to the network every week—doubling the number of nodes on the network every two years. Traffic across the network multiplies at an even greater rate, doubling two and a half to three times a year. Yet the adaptive design of Digital's Network Architecture makes the Easynet relatively easy to manage. Seventy-five staff members are all it takes to oversee the management of the largest private, distributed, peer-to-peer network in the world.

Networking Timeline

1975 DECnet communications software for distributed computing between PDP-11 systems runs the RSX-11M operating system. DV11 synchronous multiplexer, communications pre-processor.

1976 DMC11 network link substantially enhances DECnet performance.

1977 The U.S. Department of Defense selects Digital for the Autodin II worldwide communication network that links U.S. military bases.

1978 Easynet begins in Europe.
PDP-11 Engineering network links Digital buildings in the Mill and Merrimack, NH.
DECnet Phase II permits resource- and capability-sharing between Digital computers and operating systems.
Protocols established for linking to other manufacturers' computers and using third-party carriers.
DECnet first used to diagnose computer faults remotely over telephone lines.

1979 1,000 customers subscribe to DECnet.

1980 Digital, Intel, and Xerox begin to cooperate on Ethernet/Local Area Network project, announced in 1982.

1981 DECnet Phase III includes adaptive routing, network management software diagnoses faults, monitors network traffic.

1982 DECnet Phase IV supports 65,000 nodes, integrates DECnet, Ethernet, X.25 protocols within Digital Network Architecture, DECnet/SNA Gateway.

1983 VAX Notes, electronic conferencing, popularized on internal Digital network.

1984 Digital combines all internal computer networks into one worldwide network, using DECnet Phase IV.

1986 DECconnect
ThinWire Ethernet
Local Area VAXcluster extends distributed computing to workgroups.
Digital initiates software support for multivendor integration (developed as Network Application Support).

1987 Easynet, Digital's internal network—the largest private network in the world—registers its 20,000th node.

1988 Digital's Easynet network adds 27,000th node.
Digital and Apple Computer, Inc., announce a joint development effort to link Apple's Macintosh personal computers and AppleTalk networks with VAX computer systems and DECnet/OSI networks.

1989 Easynet registers its 40,000th node, serving more than 100,000 users at 500 sites around the world.

1990 Network Application Support announced.
Easynet adds its 85,000th node.
FAX Network Gateway enables VAX users to send and receive FAX messages at their desktop computers.
Digital announces plans to "open" VMS with support for the IEEE POSIX standards and branding by X/Open, the nonprofit information system suppliers' international consortium.

1991 The ACE (Advanced Computing Environment) initiative, from Digital and industry leaders, expands the potential of advanced network computing via broad standards-based support.
ADVANTAGE-NETWORKS introduces the fifth generation of Digital networking.
Digital and Microsoft form an alliance to allow Microsoft Windows to share data with LAN servers running Digital's PATHWORKS software.

A connection to the network on every desk

More Responsibility Than Authority

The Digital Organization

Edited by Patrick Pierce

"In the '60s, I was brought in as a consultant to the senior executive group. They were having difficulty communicating. At that time I had been thoroughly imbued with the National Training Lab philosophy. I believed that I knew all about communications in groups and how they should work. What I encountered at the regular staff meetings of this executive group could only be described from an NTL point of view as shocking. People interrupted each other; people shouted at each other; people criticized each other in front of other people.

"I made various interventions concerning how the group might work better and how people should let each other finish talking before they interrupted. But, over time, I could see how little effect I had on anybody. They always agreed with me and said, 'You're right, Ed, we shouldn't do this.' The president even praised me, saying how much I helped them become a better group. But, as a listener, I couldn't detect any real change in their basic communication behavior.

"It was not until years later, when I began to think about organizational culture and to encounter some writings about different concepts of truth, that I began to realize what was happening. I was playing the 'good group' game, and they were playing the 'truth' game. In the context of the 'truth' game, manners were trivial. These staff members were trying to find out when an idea was good enough to be acted upon. They worked in a rapidly changing technological environment where there are no geniuses who know the truth from an individual point of view. Where the only way you can find out if something is true or not is to debate an idea almost to death. If the idea can survive, then, maybe, it's correct enough to act upon.

"From that perspective their behavior made complete sense. They were not interested in good manners; they were not interested in being a team: they were trying to figure out what to do."

— Edgar Schein
MIT Sloan School of Management

"If in reality the vision is the strategy, it never really changed; it's the tactics that change. If you've got a strategy, then your tactics can change according to what's happening in the marketplace, what's happening with the competition, what's happening with the economy, what's happening with governmental changes. The vision is the same, so it's like a strategy, but you're responsively changing your tactics."

— Stan Olsen

"Things were changing so fast—and had to change so fast—that the only thing possible to do was cooperate."

— Peter Kaufmann

How Digital Works

When Digital was founded, very few people actually used computers. Computing technology was primarily used to process large amounts of numerical data. Computing was not active and certainly not interactive. Users brought "data" in predefined forms to computer rooms. Later, they picked up the processed data.

From the first business plan, Digital sustained and elaborated a vision of interactive computing, of back-and-forth dialogue, of open communications. That vision matured through decades of commitment, effort, and discipline. That meant networking—not only the technology, but also the organizational structures that support the process by which Digital people work together. The network evolved naturally from interactive computing as the organization became global.

Jay Forrester describes the roots of the open environment. "In a lot of organizations, people are afraid to take up difficulties, failures, shortcomings, mistakes, or problems with superiors for fear of some kind of retribution. But at MIT . . . the higher administration was there to help if there was a problem. Otherwise, they didn't interfere. There was very little that had to be asked of them in the way of permissions. We would simply go ahead and do our job. Also, there was a very definite hierarchy-skipping system. If you wanted to know what was going on, you might go right down to the person doing it, even though there might be two or three levels in between."

This attitude is alive at Digital today. It is part of the company's legacy; Digital's founders grew up in that environment. Harlan Anderson recalls that Lincoln Lab was in many ways like a corporation, but freed from the traditional restraints of a corporation. And Forrester trained a lot of managers to go out and become entrepreneurs. In fact, Lincoln Laboratory spawned some 50 companies.

The Whirlwind computer, developed at MIT, was unique for a couple of reasons: it was very simple and it was very fast. All the complexity sacrificed to make the machine simple was put into making it fast. It also was an opportunity to make an interactive computer—one that would interact directly with its user through a video or keyboard terminal. This notion—of machinery and people interacting—was the foundation for building Digital Equipment Corporation's product lines and culture.

Whirlwind was developed in an environment where there was a unique way of getting things done, where there was a strong and dynamic group feeling. "There was so much to do," says Bob Everett, "that anybody who demonstrated some ability and initiative and willingness to work rapidly got all he could possibly do." The seeds of change were carried not only in the technology, but also in the experience of working in the lab's open, flat organization structure.

When Digital started, Stan Olsen had the title of Manufacturing Manager, Ken was President and Engineering Manager, and Harlan Anderson took care of Finance and Sales. Stan recalls, "In Maynard they saw us as three wild guys doing something crazy. The first few years nobody could pronounce Digital. Nobody knew what Digital meant . . . but for those who understood our products, the response was tremendous. The biggest problem was to teach people digital logic. You had to tell them what it was, first, then they had to understand what it was, and then they had to understand how to use it. So I'd go around giving seminars on digital logic and then make the sale. Then we came up with the bright idea of having Dick Best, the chief engineer, write a book on digital logic. That wiped me out. I had nothing more to teach because the book told it all. That was really the [company's] original handbook."

Young and Senior

By 1962, when Win Hindle joined the company as Assistant to the President, Digital employed about 400 people. Hindle served as Secretary to the Works Committee, a 20-person precursor to the Executive Committee, and helped in professional recruiting for Engineering and Sales. "I think they were interested in hiring me because I was a business school graduate, not an engineering school graduate. They liked the idea that I wasn't coming here to second-guess any engineering operations."

Many of the engineers at that time had already known Ken Olsen, Harlan Anderson, Dick Best, or Ben Gurley through the MIT lab connection. Tom Stockebrand was among those who came out from the Lincoln Lab to see if they could find jobs with Digital. These engineers all shared a respect for excellence that was summed up by Bob Taylor when he said, "You can't pile together enough good people to make a great one." Stockebrand designed the file system for the LINC, and at Digital evolved the LINCtape into DECtape, so people could have personal filing systems, and write and program directly on the CRT. They could compile and execute programs without going through a central processing facility.

Peter Kaufmann interviewed with Nick Mazzarese, Stan Olsen, Win Hindle, and then Ken. "I walked into Ken's office and Ken and I spent several hours together. I went back to Beckman Instruments. Digital offered me a job and I turned it down. My boss asked me why. I said I didn't think Ken was very bright! He asked why. I said, 'Well, he got on the board and I asked him about his organization and it was all kinds of circles and charts and lines, and I couldn't make it out at all.' He said, 'No man goes from nothing and builds a $20 million business and is an idiot. You better do some thinking.'"

Months later, Digital called Kauffman again. "So I came back, and Ken met me in Boston, and we went up to General Doriot's. He loved production guys. I don't know why; it was something about manufacturing. We spent a couple of hours talking, and then Ken and I spent the rest of the day together. Suddenly I realized, this is a pretty bright guy. We hit it off and I came east.

"The first Operations Committee meeting I went to before I started work—I walked in the door and there were 36 people in the room. There was a chair way down at the end. How does somebody have a meeting with 36 people and get anything done? It seemed a madhouse. All different levels; everybody talking at once. The agenda wandered all over the place. While I sat there an eraser came flying down, and it bounced off the wall and landed on a desk right next to me."

A Generous, Trusting, Challenging Environment

"We also brought some organizational ideas from MIT. There was an attitude and environment at MIT that we wanted to duplicate. It's hard to describe, but MIT was and, I think to a large degree, is a very generous, a very trusting, and a very challenging environment. That environment was one of the things we wanted to capture and bring to our own company.

"We had so much confidence in MIT that we even followed the MIT operations manual. We took the same hours, we took the same vacations, we paid the same holidays. The state came by and said, 'You can't pay on those days, it's illegal.' We said, 'MIT does!' The state said, 'We can't control MIT, but we can control you.'"

— Ken Olsen

The atmosphere was electric. People were creative, enthusiastic, interesting, exciting, and enjoyed working hard. There were very clear goals, so everyone understood what was expected relative to the project they were working on. Their peers also knew, so that increased the pressure for driving hard. And the boss was considered to be relatively unimportant. This had worked well in the research labs, and it was working well in business.

Woods Meetings

"It was very creative, very open. When you wrote a memo you copied everybody, regardless of what you said. There was little of the usual politics of holding things close to the vest and playing games. It was an environment that I really needed to blossom, but it was very rough for lots of people. I was fortunate to have had a lot of outside experience. At Beckman Instruments they wouldn't let me talk, and they sneered at me just because I was educated and I was young. But at Digital, they were all young and were very open. We had a very close-knit organization. There was a lot of yelling and disagreeing, but a lot of mutual respect and trust. And we had a lot of fun."

— Peter Kaufmann

Enter Product Lines

But by 1964 Ken Olsen became very concerned that all the good people were being taken off other projects to help bail out the PDP-6. He felt it might salvage one project, but at the expense of others needed to maintain profitability. So he began to think how the company could be organized so that each product group would be protected from others. All the different product groups could have their own terms and conditions and business models. Each would have a set of resources, and those resources couldn't be moved unless it was proposed and then agreed upon that resources would be shifted from one to the other.

From that concern emerged what came to be called the product line structure. It caused a great stir. Many people who had headed the functions—Sales and Services, Manufacturing and Engineering—were upset about the change in their management responsibilities. Up to that time, Digital had been organized by functional departments, not by business segments. Now, each major project or product was a product line. Each had a budget, a plan, and a marketing plan. Each would be judged on the basis of how well it did compared to the plan the group had submitted.

The pressure to succeed was intense, and quite often the salespeople sold more than predicted, causing manufacturing difficulties. Arguments would erupt. Was the problem that Manufacturing didn't make enough, or that Sales didn't order enough? Ken got so tired of these arguments that he invented a system called Magic Charts. The product lines would project a year and a half ahead how many of each product they had ordered, and then Manufacturing would respond officially as to how many they had committed to. It kept people honest about who said what.

The only real limits arose when dealing with the major functions of the company. Managers had to negotiate with Manufacturing so they would ramp up the product as fast as they could. The same held true with Sales. Negotiations would determine the amount of sales of a new product over the next 12 months. These two negotiations were the most important meetings of the year, because they determined commitments from the functions.

Sometimes several product lines would order the same material. At the height of the product line structure, there were wire cages in the Westminster manufacturing plant, where each product line had its inventory lined up. Rules were established that if inventory was not used in a certain amount of time, then other groups had a right to take the material they needed to meet their customer demand. Jack Smith, as the plant manager, was very creative in making sure that Digital met its shipping goals and maximized the competitiveness of the product lines.

With the overlaps of the product lines, there was constant turmoil. The people who thrived were bright, flexible, and understood movement and change. A lot of the success had to do with the way people treated each other: being honest, being straightforward, being open.

Over the years, important changes were made to the product line, and the organizational structure became a direct function of the business. As the number of products grew, a product line organization became necessary. There had to be a strategic thrust for each line of products, and also an accounting system that tied expenses accountably to the revenue for each product. Only then could it be clear if a particular product was viable.

The early product lines were relatively clear-cut, with products such as the PDP-4, the PDP-6, and the PDP-8. But by the late 1970s, business segments became more complex, changing to the industrial, office, and medical products lines, and so on. The mixture of product lines got in the way of strategy development. For instance, various application areas had product lines, but there also was an OEM product line, a large computer product line, and industry product lines. A sale of a large timesharing machine to a federal government research establishment could conceivably be claimed by three different product lines. If the machine went through an OEM channel, that could be a fourth. In certain cases, product lines that still had operational control were able to gerrymander their boundaries so as to capture revenue and take credit for it, and be able to spend more money. The strategic thrust of some of the other product lines was lost.

New Product Directions

As the product lines changed in character, their responsibilities became market-focused rather than product-focused. With this shift, Engineering was centralized. In 1972, Gordon Bell returned to Digital from an extended teaching and research sabbatical at Carnegie Mellon University. "At that time there was no such thing as Central Engineering. There had always been a central core of engineers, but they were distributed in various product line groups. In 1974, we brought most of Engineering together as a single group," recalls Bell. "From the beginning, we said that Central Engineering would concentrate on basic, rather than market-specific products. The product lines retained small engineering groups, dedicated to tailoring these basic products to meet the needs of their particular markets."

Bell had returned to Digital just as large-scale integrated circuits were becoming available and when the notion of a processor-on-a-chip was beginning to appear. "That was the start of the fourth generation of computing," says Bell. "I came back to start projects based on large-scale integration. It was clear by then that the PDP-11 wasn't big enough. We had to do something else, and I was interested in that next step. We soon got the LSI-11 project going. VAX-11 came later. That's the name I used beginning in April 1975 in the task force to extend the addressing of the PDP-11. It originally stood for Virtual Address eXtension-11, a reminder that we were extending the 11, not starting over. It's a case where the name stuck throughout the project's life and became a major trademark."

Who's Got the Agenda?

"Staff meetings were very overloaded. They had WAY too much to do. Long agendas. I asked how the agenda was created. No one was quite sure. It turned out that when someone called asking for time at the meetings, they would be put on a list. The next caller would be added to the list, and the next below that, and the next below that. It was, quite literally, a completely fortuitous process.

"It became apparent that there were two kinds of agenda items: fire-fighting items and policy questions. At that point I suggested that for the policy questions they might want to have a different kind of meeting. These two-hour-at-the-office meetings would never feel like enough time. So they agreed to take a day or two every month to go off-site and tackle the big questions. That is how I recall the Woods meetings having originated. They grew directly out of examining what they were doing, seeing that it didn't quite make sense, and then inventing their way out of it."

— Edgar Schein

Passionate Responsibility

"It was a great feeling when you were a product line manager because you felt the responsibility to build a product, to market it, to train the sales force, to do everything that was needed to make that product be successful. People who were product line managers really took that job seriously. One of the greatest strengths was that the person or team in charge really felt a passionate responsibility to make that product succeed and to meet their business plan or exceed it. You had the feeling that nothing was hampering you. You could go as fast as your market would allow and your product would justify. There were no artificial limits on what you could do."

— Win Hindle

The idea was to create a new computer family to be "culturally compatible" with the PDP-11. Vice President Bill Heffner, a former VMS project leader, says, "We built the VAX team with experts from PDP-8, DECsystems, PDP-11 and DECnet networking, from Customer Service and from all the operating systems. And we made sure that our key designs were reviewed carefully, in the broadest way possible throughout the company."

The concept was incredibly simple. The VAX architecture provided a set of standards that defined the interfaces among the various components of a system. It allowed changing components to take advantage of new technology without redesigning the whole system. No other manufacturer had anything like that capability. The VAX specifically exploited the fact that most manufacturers had a menagerie of product lines designed to segment the user base, or fill product size and application gaps. Speaking of this development, Bill Strecker, a former VAX project leader, observes, "This architecture made it possible to design a set of systems that would extend from the desktop to the data center. One you start down that road, the natural next step is to tie those computers together so that people can do more than use their own computer interactively; they can work together with other people and other computers in the same way."

Certain aspects of Digital's organization made it relatively easy and natural to assemble a strong ad hoc team to work on the VAX. Since 1966, each product and service group in Digital had been responsible for its own product line. But unlike divisionalized companies, groups in Digital shared major functions, such as Sales, Manufacturing, and Research and Development, on a corporate level. So, while the company had benefited from the competition between groups pursuing different technologies and different markets, Digital's developers and support personnel were used to working together and sharing resources.

After the VAX-11/780's introduction in 1978, Digital adopted the VAX strategy to provide a homogeneous computing environment for a range of interconnected computers. Ethernet was an essential component. It supported different computing environments, allowing users to compute with a cluster of large machines acting as one system, or distributed traditional minicomputers, or distributed clusters of workstations.

Staying Coordinated

In many ways, Digital's approach to networking grew out of business needs that had to be met, in combination with an organizational philosophy that stressed interaction among equals, open discussion, and debate to find the best answer. Networking was a culture before it was a technology. As early as the DECsystem-10, engineers developed software to permit the exchange of data between computers over direct-wiring connections and standard point-to-point telephone lines. At the same time, elsewhere in the company, other engineers were working on a product called DECnet, and engineers began to use the emerging communications product to share information among their own systems. Using the product to design the product was a catalyst for the rapid growth of new ideas. Engineers began discussing the potential of linking together not just one kind of computer system, but diverse systems throughout an organization into a single network.

Bob Taylor once said that only a coordinated system of people can produce a coordinated system of software and hardware. Rapid growth, particularly within Digital's engineering department, created a demand for sophisticated networking. Originally all the DECnet development engineers were in the Mill. Very shortly, space limitations led to the relocation of one of the DECnet development groups to a new facility in Merrimack, New Hampshire, about 50 miles north.

"We had reached the point where we had so much in the state of Massachusetts that we had to develop someplace else in the U.S.," recalls Stan Olsen. "New Hampshire is a very attractive place to bring people and attract talent, so I volunteered to bring the 1,200 people that I had up to New Hampshire. In a short time we were more than 4,000, the largest private employer in the state."

By choice, Digital spread out as it grew, building facilities all over the world. Peter Kaufmann describes an earlier time when decisions were made to expand the plant. "We were at a Woods meeting at Stan's house in New Hampshire. These meetings were very important in terms of pulling the team together. So, we talked about these options. I laid out the possibilities for Puerto Rico, which I had developed, and Westminster, and Westfield, and we were throwing ideas around.

"At the last second, somebody said, 'We should probably do all of them.' Everybody looked around and said, 'Sure.' That was it. Boom. I mean huge decisions were made in split seconds. That was part of what I loved about the Digital environment—it allowed me to use my instinct in a way that almost insisted that you did, because no matter how much analysis you do, you never have all the numbers. And it worked. I was all ready to make these presentations and it wasn't even necessary. So we followed all these options, and all about the same time."

Jim Miller characterizes the enormous growth in facilities, in people, and everything else. "Every other week a new building was being opened. The VAX was being invented, so we put a link into the development group in Tewksbury. The whole thing snowballed. We added sites in Marlboro, Hudson, and Littleton, Massachusetts; in Colorado Springs, Colorado; in Seattle, Washington; in Palo Alto, California; in Puerto Rico; and eventually in hundreds of other places. The first thing each engineer wanted was a connection to the E-net."

"We were inventing new ways of doing things that had never been done before," continues Miller. "It wasn't a structured process. In fact, it was a lot like how most things get done at Digital—through informal teams of excited, interested people. The network helped this approach work even better. Everybody had access to everybody else. Somebody with an interest in an unsolved problem or unexplored technical area with potential could ask around for information, become an ad hoc expert on it, come up with some ideas, and pass them around. Others could respond. In this way expertise was nurtured and shared. People quite naturally took on the responsibilities in which they were capable and interested. There is no better way to build a

You've Got the Model

"As a $14 million company, we were in bad shape for an interesting reason. We ran the company with a Works Committee of 20 people. But it stopped working well. We could only get people involved with the problems of highest interest. Nobody would work on the next level of priority. If we were going to take care of those areas that were not burning issues to the corporation, we had to divide the responsibility.

"One day in 1964 I said, 'We're a new company. You all now have responsibility.' So we broke the company into product lines and service groups to the product lines. Each had a business model that included the cost to engineer, build, market, and sell the product. The measure of success was the product line's profit margin. The first year we doubled our profit without hiring anyone. This came about because someone was held responsible for a given part of the company. We said, 'You've got the model. We're going to measure you every month on what profit you make.'

"We had clear principles. One was, 'He who proposes, does.' If somebody proposes a new product, he or she lays out the plan for the whole product—from start to finish—including the marketing and profitability strategy. When they were telling others what to do, things didn't work out well at all, but when they had the responsibility, it's amazing how smart they were. Things became very clear. They were emotionally committed. They made it work whether their plan was right or wrong. They may have done something stupid, but they fixed it."

— Ken Olsen

Pressing for Standards

"One idea we took from MIT was the idea of networking. The SAGE air defense system was made up of 23 sites; each one had an elaborate, very high-performance local area network. There were a large number of display terminals. Each of the 23 sites was networked to two arrays of radar across northern Canada. It was one very large network. So networking became a theme in everything we did.

"The big change in networking came in the mid-1970s when we decided that we'd have to network in a very standardized way. Everything we did used the same networking protocols and the same networking technologies. That really made networking a major part of our organization. It's these standardized ways that we've been encouraging the world to accept so that we and they can all work together on the same network. We've been pressing for standards to make this possible for a long time."

— Ken Olsen

good system than letting the people use the system they built—because if it doesn't do the job, they fix it!"

Using the Network

The development of Ethernet brought a modular approach to building networks. Ethernet provided enormous flexibility and greatly simplified designing, installing, managing, and maintaining a local area network. Today, local area networks are building blocks for extended computer networks. First, systems are connected in the local area network, then the local area networks are connected, using bridges and routers, into one larger wide area system.

As more applications were introduced on the network, network use grew, and more applications became possible. "The beauty of Ethernet is that you don't have to plan," said Gordon Bell at the product's introduction. A new phenomenon was discovered. When the network reaches a certain point, it starts to feed itself, achieving real synergy. Bill Gassman, a networking software specialist, thinks there should be a 100 Node Club, because that's when things start to get interesting. "Once you reach the magic 100 node mark, you've got more than a means of hooking machines together. You've created a valuable corporate resource with a life of its own."

Effective, reliable networks embrace new users and new technologies as if they've been planned. Over the years the number of systems using Digital's network has doubled every year. At the same time, the traffic across the network has grown at a much higher rate—by 250 to 300 percent every year. Amazing amounts of technical work and interchange take place with little personal contact. Some engineering teams met as a group as infrequently as three times a year while collaborating constantly over the network.

This was an alternative to using large committees to solve problems. Instead of spending their time in meetings, the engineers found it more effective to use interface specifications and the written word. One of the most complex interfaces that Digital designed over the network was the mass-storage control protocol to link mass-storage devices with VAX systems. That was worked out very precisely among engineers in Colorado and VAX VMS engineers in New England, exclusively by written specifications. When it was plugged together, it worked.

While this was developing, the product lines across the company were responsible for customer relationships, in addition to engineering and marketing. Customer orders would come into each product line's order-processing department. As a result, there were 20 different order-processing systems, confusing everyone, particularly the sales force. The product line managers spent too much time on operations and internal relations with other product lines, and too little on strategy. While the product strategy was the domain of Central Engineering, the market strategy was suffering from neglect.

But the field operations were becoming critical of the product lines. They felt that the product lines were trying to overmanage them. The European groups particularly felt they were not being given enough autonomy to maximize the use of local resources. Although every organizational form has its advantages and its disadvantages, the disadvantages of the product line organization became more pressing in the early 1980s. The company decided that local autonomy in each country would take precedence over instructions from headquarters.

Win Hindle explains, "We really unleashed field operations in that organizational change, and emphasized the importance of each country, and the importance of planning marketing in a local environment. The geographies worked directly with Manufacturing as far as order processing and operational control was concerned. And it was as a result of that change that our European organization started to grow so successfully."

Multidimensional Organization

The product lines were to work on strategy. But the market was a highly complex matrix focused by application, by industry, and by channel as well as by geography. There was a need to focus all the different product segments. It required different areas of expertise to do business with such a wide range of products and in so many markets. The resulting strategy has been called "the multidimensional organization."

Ron Smart explains, "Products were segmented at the component level, the systems level, and the applications level. You have important segments at each of these levels, that require business unit focus. On the market side, there's the OEM channel, industry segmentation, and customer application segmentation and geography. 'Multidimensional' means multiple segmentations, both in levels of product integration and in segmentation of the market. In each dimension you have product lines, or business units, or managers, or teams, or even individuals who focus on that particular aspect of the company's business."

"That was the system we designed for implementation in 1982. We could plan it, but we couldn't agree on how to budget it," Smart continues. "From '83 to '85, every time we did a business plan in multidimensions, the accounting system would destroy it. Then finally we reverted back to the hierarchical approach—one profit and loss statement for the whole company, instead of 100 or so, based on one profit and loss for each business unit. The ability of the business units to craft a realistic business plan was hampered by having to deal with pots of money preassigned by function from the top.

"The disastrous quarter we had in 1983/84 was due, in part, to the loss of the informal system that normally kept the company working. There was a lot of turbulence because people were changing jobs so much. The old buddy network that usually took care of the kind of problem we had was missing. We really struggled to put that back in place fast!"

After the bad quarter, the communications problem began to straighten out. But the effect of that difficulty was to turn managers' attention to the fact that all the different dimensions have to work together. One consequence was that electronic mail use shot up dramatically. In 1982 there were 400 internal network nodes and 900 mail accounts across 39 countries. By 1985 there were 5,000 nodes and 35,000 accounts. By 1990 there were 52,000 nodes and 112,000 accounts across 83 countries. This was not part of a grand design. People scrambled to get on electronic mail so they could deal with all the communications that were essential to their business. The basic infrastructure of technology is in place to implement the necessary multidimensional systems,

It's Yours

"A few years ago, we tried to lay out business units so that they always added up to the corporation. And each business unit would have a group of lawyers make sure that they got their share of the order, because the measurement became the goal. They figured if they earned money, they could spend money the way they wanted. But that's not the attitude we want. We want people to have the drive that results in their being satisfied that they are doing a good job.

"So we sliced up the company in many ways. And in one direction, the pieces have to add up to the entire corporation. But you can break it up in many ways and measure each part for the satisfaction and motivation of that group; and sometimes you can have groups compete, without saying that the pieces always, mathematically, have to add up to the entire corporation.

"When my kids were young, we used to walk along the railroad tracks in northern Maine and visit with the workers on the railroad tracks. The workers seemed to spend all day sitting in this little shack drinking coffee, complaining that they were understaffed and couldn't get all the work done. In years past they were given a section of track, and it was theirs, and they took pride in making sure that those tracks were in good shape. Now they got job orders, and they had no motivation whatsoever. There's a difference between being motivated for the job because it's yours and you're trusted, and just being told what to do all the time."

— Ken Olsen
State of the Company Meeting, 1987

A Product Line Manager's Story: You Go in and Beg

"Our group charter in '72 was to get the company into the commercial market. It put a different set of demands on the company. The computers were packaged in five-foot-tall enclosures. The fans sounded like jet engines, not suitable for any kind of office environment. They looked like hell. The panels didn't match. The backs might have sides, or not. We had to do something, but you can't get engineering to do something when no one else had ever complained about it before.

"So you'd have to go into engineering and beg. Beg for resources. You beg this guy who's in charge of enclosure design. You may get a positive answer. You may not. You keep at it. As a last resort, you get the idea, 'We'll fund it.' So you go back to this person and say, 'I'll pay you to solve the problem.' Even though we ended up funding it, they were failing. Finally it begins to dawn: 'What's going on with engineering?'

"One day I stomped into engineering. I was mad. There were six people on the project. I hired five of them and left the manager there. We started our own engineering group. You can imagine the people we were able to attract! We got a lot of the misfits, the mavericks. It's like one of the Phil Silvers movies, where you take all these guys in the wrong slot in the wrong job, and watch them bloom when you give them some creative things to do. Because we were looked at as different from the rest of the company, the group became very tight. We ended up redesigning the cabinets ourselves. Eventually the company took over our design. The cabinet families are in existence today."

— Jake Jacobs

but a question keeps recurring: How do you exploit the network technology in order to improve the business performance of the company? The answer lies in the necessary behavior changes, changes to the original way of working together.

Within Digital, ideas rattle around inside the network all the time. It's often said that the best ideas come from the bottom—sometimes from Engineering, sometimes from Sales, sometimes from Software—from those who are working regularly with customer needs. If an idea lasts in the system, and the person backing it perseveres, the idea becomes a proposal, asking for funding or other decisions. Then the idea is taken more seriously and gets bombarded even more by opinions. Good ideas move ahead based on their merit, and they rise to the top of the pile. Top-level managers do not impose these ideas.

Working Digital

In such a context, many things are called inventions when, actually, they were inevitable. Ken Olsen remarks, "Most of the advances have been made by people whose names will never be remembered. It's more than the work of a few brilliant individuals. There's always a lot of development work done by a lot of people. This goes for ideas of organization, motivating people, how you do things mechanically, how you do things electrically."

Digital is a complicated organization because the business is complex. To find out and create the new knowledge needed to be able to plan and manage the business, Digital is actually breaking new ground in terms of organizational design and testing it in real-time. There are no existing, ready-made models about how to do it. The vision driving the technology is also driving the development of organizational forms and methods to conduct business based on these new possibilities. To use the system requires management styles that complement the network capabilities—delegating authority, and encouraging independent thought and initiative to take advantage of distributed computing.

Russ Doane, senior engineer, observes, "Products always reflect the institution that designs them. If we have been able to operate as one company with one strategy, it's because people are able to network. They can find the message; it doesn't have to go through a hierarchy where it gets distorted or lost. I once got a copy of a speech Ken gave at MIT through the network. It had been 25 places before it got to me . . . I passed it around again. Everything is passed around, shared. Networking is really using everyone's contribution. The hierarchy is weak, partly because the network is strong."

One might say that the company values have been built into the network—the free interchange of ideas, giving people responsibility, trusting people. But obviously, much more than organizational culture and technology is involved. Rapid change and accelerating complexity demand simultaneous evolution not only in products and services, but in processes, resources, and markets. Digital's original contributions in modules and components evolved to further contributions in systems, in pioneering software for timesharing and networking, and in bringing small computers to people where they needed to work. As the world's need for value has moved beyond hardware and MIPS, it has focused more on the promises of converging information technologies. The company is moving with it. Demands for integrated systems and comprehensive business solutions reflect how value for customers continues to evolve to higher levels. While Digital is mapping to the market's evolving needs, the delivery of this higher level of value requires a matching organizational transformation. The structure that worked well to deliver volumes of hardware and software requires change to deliver the high-level business solutions and services the market increasingly requires.

"We picked a business in which things come fast and go fast. We are in a business where things move faster than we ever predicted. Where things two years ago we said were impossible, today we're doing. We're in a business in which many of us haven't even grasped completely what's going on," said Ken Olsen during a 1991 State of the Company Meeting. To respond effectively to manifold changes, the company continues to evolve, to invent itself anew. "The Digital culture is a learning culture," says Edgar Schein, "and the most hopeful thing about it is its ability to learn and adapt, and to draw from its strength in collaborative coordination."

The early product line organization empowered people to create their own organizations and ways of working together. This worked well because the company was small, and people all knew each other. "The way the company worked was all on personal relationships and trust," says Jake Jacobs. But in the 1990s, people don't all know each other personally. It is different to negotiate and get buy-in from strangers than it is from friends. And buy-in is not just a nice phrase. It's a way to test ideas, pushing back to find the flaws before deciding whether to proceed with a plan or not. "When negotiating with a stranger," observes Edgar Schein, "you don't know whether you can trust him or not, or how much, so maybe you withhold a little more information, or start fudging the figures." Cumulatively, this can have a stultifying effect on a company's ability to move where it needs to go. One of the related benefits of Woods meetings is to help build the personal relationships that get the work done.

"We are in the position of going back to do properly what we tried to do in 1982, with networked business units," observes Ron Smart, "to unleash the ability of people to use their creative energy and initiative to contribute to something bigger. People need the freedom to add value, but individual expertise becomes more valuable as it is networked into the larger knowledge infrastructure of the company. Independence matures into more effective interdependence. Despite the complexity of the multiple dimensions, we now have a working understanding of how to manage the company by business units."

The new management system is creating the conditions where Digital's fundamental culture will continue to flourish, and where organizational structure will match business strategy. This emphasizes exploiting key interdependencies among business units, so they complement each other. Each business is viewed as a human network, and the larger enterprise is a network of businesses. Win Hindle points out, "The business units operate off the same base of products, the same base of software, and adapt that to the realities of the market they are trying to serve."

Your Fingers on the Pulse

"When I was a customer, I had an infinite number of opinions on everything that DEC was doing wrong. I would constantly tell DEC these things on the phone. They'd agree with me and try to fix them. It amazed me that any one person could actually have that influence.

"When I joined DEC, I found out how it worked. Everybody has the same size office, a telephone, a workstation. And a terrific freedom to network with anybody else in the company.

"I never know where the next MAIL message might come from. It might be from a sales rep in Hungary or Japan. A customer in Singapore asking me to present a seminar. An announcement from the Open Systems Foundation.

"You have your fingers, not just on the keyboard, but on the pulse of the world. In early 1991 I got a message from DEC Israel asking for some information. I sent it, but said 'Wait a minute, there's a war about to start in your backyard. Tell me what you're feeling.' He sent back an impassioned note about what it was like in Israel at the start of the Gulf War.

"The kind of networking that we do every day at DEC is simply unheard of at most companies. Often we assume that customers are just like us—global, distributed, non-hierarchical, consensus organizations—and that everyone has the same size office, a telephone and a connection to the network. Give me a break! Maybe in 10 years the successful companies will be that way, and the other ones will be out of business. In the meantime, we have a huge advantage because we understand how to use technology to support that kind of organization, and we can show our customers how to do it, too."

— Kathy Hornbach

The network, then, effectively becomes the service delivery vehicle for the evolving knowledge base of the company. And it is here that the greatest values originate, and where the greatest challenges and opportunities are offered.

The constraints are not technological as much as human. Learning how best to use internal information technologies to re-create the company is another form of using the product to develop the product. But unlearning is harder than learning. Stovepipe efficiencies can no longer meet the levels of value the emerging market demands. Edgar Schein observes, "The unique thing about Digital is that such a high value is put on truth. They are willing to tolerate a lot of conflict and emotional turmoil because it leads more reliably to openness and truth. I think it may be a much better model for the organization of the future than anybody is currently aware of. People talk about these flat, knowledge-based, networked organizations. What they're really talking about is Digital! But it's not yet fully recognized or articulated. If we're looking ahead and talking about flat organizations, we have to recognize that they're going to succeed only if they have managers who don't believe that they really have to manage everything, whose job it is to create the right kind of climate, hire the right kind of people, and then let the process work. There will always be some major problem or other, but when bright people get empowered and committed, they learn their way out of it."

Milestones in Digital's History

1957

August   Digital opens in Maynard, Massachusetts, with three employees and 8,500 square feet of production space in a converted woolen mill.

1958

February   System modules go on the market. First fiscal year sales are $94,000.

1960

November   PDP-1, the world's first small, interactive computer, is introduced.

1962

June   Annual sales reach $6.5 million.

1963

March   The first European sales and service office opens with three people in Munich, Germany. The first Canadian sales office opens with two people in Ottawa.

April   The world's first minicomputer, the PDP-5, is announced.

September   The PDP-1 operating system, the first timesharing system, is introduced.

1964

March   Digital begins manufacturing in a woolen mill in Carleton Place near Ottawa, Canada.

June   Subsidiaries are formed in Australia and the United Kingdom.

July   The first European Customer Training Center opens in Reading, England.

October   Digital unveils its first 36-bit computer, PDP-6.

1965

April   PDP-8, the world's first mass-produced minicomputer, is introduced.

1966

August   Digital makes its first public stock offering.

1967

March   PDP-10 is introduced.

June   Manufacturing of PDP-8 computers and peripherals begins in a Reading, England, facility.

Annual sales reach $38 million.

1968

January   Digital stock begins trading on the American Stock Exchange.

July   Manufacturing operations begin in San German, Puerto Rico.

Employment increases 68 percent to more than 2,600 people, including 225 engineers and programmers and 360 field engineers. There are more than 50 sales and service offices located in 11 countries.

1968 (continued)

October   Japanese headquarters opens in Tokyo.

1969

May   Digital stock splits three-for-one.

June   European headquarters opens in Geneva, Switzerland.

July   The UNIX operating system is written on a Digital PDP-7 computer at Bell Laboratories.

1970

January   Production begins at a new plant in Westfield, Massachusetts, producing peripherals and metals products.

April   First deliveries are made of PDP-11/20, Digital's first 16-bit minicomputer and first member of the world's most successful minicomputer family.

June   The total number of installed Digital computers passes 8,000, approximately 1,800 of which are in Europe.

July   A new manufacturing plant opens in Westminster, Massachusetts.

October   Digital establishes its first West Coast manufacturing operation in Mountain View, California, for making disks.

December   Digital stock begins trading on the New York Stock Exchange.

1971

June   The first annual customer satisfaction survey is taken.

July   Manufacturing starts in Galway, Ireland.

November   DECsystem-10 is introduced.

1972

January   Space is leased in a Springfield, Massachusetts, armory to build power supplies and subassemblies.

The Parker Street complex opens in Maynard, Massachusetts.

May   Construction is completed on a new manufacturing plant in Kanata, Ontario.

June   Annual sales reach $188 million. Digital has 7,800 employees.

October   A Taiwan plant opens for core memory stringing operations.

1973

September   Digital purchases administrative and manufacturing facilities in Marlboro, Massachusetts, from RCA.

December   A Hong Kong plant opens for core memory stringing operations.

Manufacturing begins in Aguadilla, Puerto Rico.

1974

March   Digital's 30,000th computer system is shipped.

April   MPS, Digital's first microprocessor, is introduced.

Digital enters Fortune 500, ranking 475th in sales among U.S. industrial corporations.

June   Maynard Industrial Park (the Mill)—19 buildings, 1.6 million square feet—is purchased.

1975

February   LSI-11, Digital's first 16-bit microcomputer, and the powerful PDP-11/70 are added to the PDP-11 family.

1975 (continued)

April	Digital's Network Architecture is introduced.
September	The company's 50,000th computer system is delivered, just 15 years after Digital's first computer was introduced.

1976

January	The 36-bit DECSYSTEM-20, the lowest-priced general-purpose timesharing system on the market, is introduced.
	A new manufacturing plant opens in Ayr, Scotland.
October	Digital stock splits three-for-one.
November	Manufacturing begins in Burlington, Vermont.

1977

May	New manufacturing plants open in Kaufbeuren, West Germany, and Augusta, Maine.
June	Digital breaks the $1 billion mark in sales; has 36,000 employees.
July	The industry's first computerized remote diagnosis is introduced in Colorado Springs, Colorado.
October	VAX-11/780, the first member of the VAX computer family, is introduced.
	Stock is now traded on the Pacific Stock Exchange.
	A new Digital facility opens in Merrimack, New Hampshire.
November	A plant opens in Clonmel, Ireland.

1978

February	Digital ships its 100,000th computer.
April	A plant opens in Colorado Springs, Colorado.
May	A new engineering facility opens in Tewksbury, Massachusetts.
July	Digital's first retail computer store opens in Manchester, New Hampshire.

1979

March	Digital opens the largest industrial training facility in New England in Bedford, Massachusetts.

1980

January	Digital's 200,000th computer is shipped.
February	DECnet Phase III—the most advanced networking in the computer industry—is introduced.
April	Digital opens a state-of-the-art high-technology center for manufacturing semiconductors in Hudson, Massachusetts.
	ULTRIX Engineering is founded at Digital.
June	Digital, Intel, and Xerox cooperate in the Ethernet local network project.
	Digital breaks the $2 billion mark in sales.
July	A manufacturing plant opens in Boston, Massachusetts.
	Digital opens a software engineering facility in Nashua, New Hampshire.
August	A production facility in Tempe, Arizona, for making printed wiring boards is purchased from ITT Courier.
October	VAX-11/750, the second member of the VAX family and the industry's first Large Scale Integration (LSI) 32-bit minicomputer, is introduced.

1981

March	The PDP-11/24 minicomputer system is announced.
June	Digital breaks the $3 billion mark in sales.
September	A Customer Support Center opens in Atlanta, Georgia, offering telephone support for office systems hardware and software.

1982

March	Production begins at the Greenville, South Carolina, printed circuit facility.
April	The VAX-11/730, the third member of Digital's 32-bit computer family, is introduced.
May	A complete range of personal computers—Professional 325 and 350, Rainbow 100, and DECmate II—are introduced.
	Digital ranks 137th in total sales in *Fortune* magazine's annual directory of the largest industrial corporations in the United States.
June	Annual sales reach $3.9 billion. Employee population is more than 67,000.
	Advanced Manufacturing Technology Center opens in Andover, Massachusetts.
	The announcement of RA60 and RA81 disks and Digital Storage Architecture puts Digital at the forefront in storage technology.
July	A new manufacturing plant opens in Singapore.
August	Digital celebrates its first 25 years, during which more than 360,000 computers have been shipped.
September	Japan Research and Development Center opens in Tokyo.

1983

April	Digital announces VAXclusters, a process for tying together VAX processors in a loose processor coupling.
	The company breaks into *Fortune* magazine's top 100 U.S. industrial companies by ranking 95th in sales.
May	Digital donates its largest single gift, $25 million, to Project Athena, a joint experimental program with the Massachusetts Institute of Technology and IBM that will integrate the next generation of computers and interactive graphics into undergraduate education throughout MIT.
June	Annual sales surpass the $4 billion mark.
October	MicroVAX I and VAX-11/725, designed to extend the 32-bit VAX computer family, are introduced.
November	The VT200 family of video terminals is introduced.
December	DECtalk, a text-to-speech system that allows computers to talk, is announced.

1984

January	The Systems Research Center is formed in Palo Alto, California.
March	The Northeast Technology Center for Storage Systems opens in Shrewsbury, Massachusetts.
April	VAX-11/785, the most powerful single computer to date in Digital's VAX family, is introduced.
	The 25,000th VAX computer system is shipped.
June	Annual sales reach $5.6 billion. The company maintains 660 offices in 47 countries with 85,600 employees.
July	The MicroPDP-11/73, a top-of-the-line minicomputer, is introduced.
	ULTRIX Version 1.0, Digital's implementation of the UNIX operating system, makes its debut.

1984 (continued)

October Digital announces the VAX 8600, the first of a new generation of computers within the VAX family and the highest performance computer system in its history.

VAXstation I, the company's first true 32-bit single-user workstation, is introduced.

DECmate III, Digital's lowest-cost desktop computer, optimized for word processing, is announced.

December The PDP-11/84 minicomputer for Original Equipment Manufacturers is introduced.

1985

April For the eleventh consecutive year, Digital increases its standing in *Fortune* magazine's listing of the nation's 100 leading U.S. companies, moving up 19 places to number 65.

Digital signs an agreement with Elebra Computadores, opening the Brazilian market to Digital's minicomputer products.

May Digital introduces the MicroVAX II, which incorporates the revolutionary "VAX-on-a-Chip" and has the highest level of capabilities of any 32-bit processor in the industry; and the VAXstation II, a high-performance graphics workstation.

June Annual sales reach $6.7 billion. The company now maintains more than 900 facilities worldwide, representing more than 29 million square feet of space.

July Digital becomes the first company to register a new semiconductor chip under the Semiconductor Protection Act of 1984 (the MicroVAX II chip).

August Digital ships its 2,000th MicroVAX II.

September DECville '85, an ambitious exhibition held in Cannes, France, underlines Digital's contributions to the European economy.

November The MicroPDP-11/83, the most powerful Q-bus 16-bit-wordlength computer in Digital's history, is introduced.

In Turin, Italy, Digital opens an Application Center for Technology dedicated to the automotive industry.

December The VAX 8650, with a CPU 44 percent more powerful than the VAX 8600, is introduced.

The DIGITAL HAS IT NOW advertising campaign begins.

1986

January The VAXstation II/GPX, Digital's first technical workstation for the UNIX marketplace, is introduced.

The top-of-the-line VAX 8800 and midrange VAX 8300 and VAX 8200 debut.

February Digital hosts DECWORLD '86 in Boston, Massachusetts, the world's largest single-company computer exposition held to date.

The announcement of DECconnect wiring strategy and related products and services extends the company's networking leadership.

April The midrange VAX 8500 is introduced.

Digital stock splits two-for-one.

The company rises in rank to number 55 in *Fortune* magazine's listing of the 100 leading industrial companies.

June Annual sales reach $7.6 billion. The company now employs more than 94,000 people, occupying more than 31 million square feet of space.

The Networking Center is dedicated at King Street in Littleton, Massachusetts.

1986 (continued)

August   The VAX 8550 and VAX 8700 systems are introduced.

September   The VAXmate, a networked personal computer that can combine the resources of the VAX VMS and MS-DOS operating systems, is introduced.

Digital acquires the technology and other assets of Trilogy Technology Corporation in Cupertino, California.

October   *Fortune* magazine declares Digital founder and president Kenneth H. Olsen "arguably the most successful entrepreneur in the history of American business."

November   Digital introduces Local Area VAXcluster systems, extending distributed computing to the work group.

1987

January   Digital introduces VAX 8978 and VAX 8974, its most powerful systems to date, offering up to 50 times the power of the industry-standard VAX-11/780.

February   Digital ships its 100,000th VAX computer system.

VAXstation 2000 and MicroVAX 2000, Digital's lowest-cost workstation and multiuser computers, respectively, are introduced.

April   Digital cracks the Fortune 50, climbing to number 44 in the magazine's annual listing of the largest U.S. industrial corporations.

Business Week magazine ranks Digital eighth among "America's Most Valuable Companies," based on a market value of $21.6 billion—a 128 percent increase from the previous year.

The VT330 and VT340 signify the introduction of a new generation of video terminals, with twice the resolution, up to five times the speed, and significantly lower prices than their predecessors.

ULTRIX Version 2.0 is released.

June   Digital and Cray Research, Inc., the leading producer of supercomputers, announce a cooperative agreement to market and develop products that link their respective computer environments—beginning with the VAX Supercomputer Gateway.

Annual sales climb 24 percent to $9.39 billion for the 1987 fiscal year, with net income up 84 percent to $1.14 billion. Return on shareholder equity rises to 19 percent in fiscal year 1987 from 12 percent in fiscal year 1986.

August   Thirty years after its inception, Digital has 110,500 employees, occupies 33.6 million square feet in 1,057 buildings, and does business in 64 countries.

September   DECWORLD '87 draws 48,500 people to Boston's World Trade Center over a nine-day period, with the ocean liners Queen Elizabeth 2 and Star/ship Oceanic serving as floating hotels and conference centers.

Digital unveils a new generation of its MicroVAX computer family with the introduction of the MicroVAX 3500 and MicroVAX 3600 systems. Also announced: VAXstation 3200 and 3500 workstations, and Phase V of the Digital Network Architecture, migrating DECnet products to full compliance with the OSI (Open Systems Interconnection) model.

1988

January   Digital and Apple Computer, Inc., announce a joint development effort to link Apple's Macintosh personal computers and AppleTalk networks with VAX computer systems and DECnet/OSI enterprise networks. Digital also extends its Network Application Support (NAS) facilities to integrate MS-DOS, OS/2, and UNIX systems into the open DECnet/OSI network environment.

1988 (continued)

Digital and Hinditron of India announce an agreement to form Digital Equipment (India) Ltd., a joint venture to manufacture MicroVAX computers and market Digital products in India.

March Digital introduces its most powerful VAX computers to date—new members of the VAX 8800 series of systems, which utilize VMS symmetric multiprocessing.

April Digital jumps six notches to number 38 in *Fortune* magazine's annual listing of America's largest industrial corporations.

The VAX 6200 series of compact, high-performance network computer systems is unveiled. The new systems are the first to combine symmetric multiprocessing with the high speed of Digital's VAXBI bus and the low cost and reliability of CMOS (Complementary Metal Oxide Semiconductor) technology.

Version 5 of Digital's VMS operating system is introduced, with enhanced speed and functionality.

Version 3 of Digital's ULTRIX operating system is released, with significant enhancements.

May Digital and six other leading computer companies announce formation of the Open Software Foundation, intended to develop and provide an open software environment.

June Annual revenues rise 22 percent to $11.5 billion for the 1988 fiscal year, with net income up 15 percent to $1.3 billion. Digital now employs 121,500 people in more than 1,100 facilities worldwide.

July Digital introduces DECtp, a systems environment that integrates the capabilities necessary to build large-scale transaction processing applications, effectively enabling Digital systems to process up to 100 transactions per second.

September Under the theme, "Integrating the Enterprise," DECWORLD '88 is held in Cannes, France, and 11 U.S. cities, welcoming more than 20,000 customers and prospects to the world's largest single-vendor information systems symposium and exhibition.

Digital forms a subsidiary in the People's Republic of China. Digital Equipment (China) Ltd. will include sales and service centers in Beijing and Shanghai and a manufacturing plant in Shenzhen.

Digital formalizes its strategic direction as a major systems integrator with the introduction of the Enterprise Services and the Network Enterprise Management Program.

Digital and MIPS Computer Systems, Inc., announce a comprehensive technology exchange agreement for RISC (Reduced Instruction Set Computer) technology, and Digital's intention to purchase a minority share in MIPS.

October MicroVAX 3300 and MicroVAX 3400 computer systems are introduced, doubling the price/performance of MicroVAX II. The systems incorporate the new RF30 integrated storage element, a 150-megabyte implementation of the Digital Storage Architecture.

1989

January Digital announces its broadest set of desktop solutions ever, including DECwindows software, which will enable users to access VMS, UNIX, and MS-DOS applications from anywhere on the network: DECstation 3100, the world's fastest UNIX/RISC workstation; VAXstation 3100, Digital's top price/performance VAX workstation; VAXstations 3520 and 3540, multiprocessor workstations with high-resolution graphics; DECstations 210, 316, and 320, a family of industry-standard personal computers; and six new complementary storage devices.

The VAX 6300 systems, Digital's most powerful and expandable VAX systems in a single cabinet, are introduced.

March DECsystem 3100, Digital's first RISC-based UNIX general-purpose computer system, is introduced.

1989 (continued)

April   Digital climbs eight places to number 30 in *Fortune* magazine's annual survey of the largest U.S. industrial corporations.

The MicroVAX family is broadened with the introduction of top-of-the-line MicroVAX 3800 and MicroVAX 3900 computers.

June   Digital's annual revenues grow to $12.7 billion for fiscal year 1989—55 percent outside the U.S.—with net income at $1.07 billion and a worldwide work force of 125,800 people.

July   In Edinburgh, Scotland, test production begins at Digital's newest and most advanced semiconductor manufacturing facility.

Manufacturing Engineering magazine selects Digital for its 1989 Manufacturing Excellence Award, as one of the 10 best American manufacturing companies at which to work.

With the expansion of Network Application Support (NAS), Digital unveils the industry's most open computing environment for the 1990s.

VAX 6000 Model 400 systems are introduced, with up to 85 percent more performance than the popular VAX 6300 line.

Digital introduces the MicroVAX 3100 system, which lowers the entry-level price of MicroVAX family by up to 40 percent while increasing performance 2.5 times.

Digital adds four new members to its UNIX-based RISC family—the DECstation 2100 workstation, the DECsystem 5400 computer, and the DECsystem 5810 and DECsystem 5820 departmental systems.

September   Digital details the technical breakthroughs it has achieved in the application of semiconductor processing for multi-chip packaging—more than doubling a computer's performance when compared to conventional circuit-board technology.

October   Digital brings the speed and capabilities of a mainframe to the VAX architecture with the introduction of the VAX 9000 family of systems—Digital's most powerful computers ever.

1990

February   In response to political and economic reforms, Digital announces its first direct investment in Eastern Europe—Digital Equipment (Hungary) Ltd., a joint-venture company based in Budapest.

Digital ships its one-millionth VT320 terminal to Barclays Bank in the United Kingdom.

The first major international art exhibition sponsored by Digital, "Monet in the '90s: The Series Paintings," opens in Boston. The exhibition, with Digital as its sole corporate underwriter, will also travel to Chicago and London during 1990.

Adding fault-tolerant technology to the VAX family, Digital introduces the VAXft 3000 system. This is the first fault-tolerant system in the industry to run a mainstream operating system (VMS), and extends Digital's industry-leading range of high-availability solutions for transaction-processing applications.

March   Easynet, Digital's internal computer network, adds its 50,000th node. The largest private data network in the world, Easynet serves more than 100,000 users at nearly 500 sites around the world. Easynet plays an integral role in Digital's business processes and also serves as an engineering testbed and customer showcase for Digital's networking capabilities.

An operations center is opened in West Berlin to prepare for the opportunities created by a unified German marketplace.

1990 (continued)

April   Digital climbs three places to number 27 on the Fortune 500, the 16th consecutive year that the company's position has risen. For the decade from 1979 to 1989, Digital ranked second among Fortune 500 companies in average annual compound growth rate, at 21.7 percent.

Digital announces more than 20 new computers, peripherals, and software products—including the DECstation 5000 workstation and DECsystem 5000 server—that significantly extend the distributed computing capabilities of its RISC-based open systems offerings.

Digital announces a new water-based technology used to clean printed circuit boards that can eliminate CFC (chlorofluorocarbon) solvents that destroy the earth's ozone layer. Digital will allow other manufacturers worldwide to use this technology without charge, as part of its commitment to protecting the ozone layer.

May   The 20th anniversary of the introduction of the first PDP-11 computer is marked by the introduction of two new PDP-11 systems: MicroPDP-11/93 and PDP-11/94. The longest-lived family of general-purpose computers has more than 20 members. More than 600,000 have been installed.

June   VAX 4000 family of servers introduced.

The 1,000th application becomes available for the DECstation and DECsystem family of RISC/ULTRIX systems.

July   The first of four DECWORLD '90 events opens in Boston under the banner, "Innovation That Works." Followed by events in Canberra, Australia; Cannes, France; and Tokyo, Japan; the DECWORLD '90 program draws more than 37,000 Digital customers and prospects.

Digital posts revenues of $12.9 billion for the 1990 fiscal year—56 percent outside the U.S. Worldwide, employees total 124,000.

ULTRIX Version 4 is released.

August   The VT1200 Windowing Terminal is announced.

September   Digital introduces FAX Network Gateway, enabling VAX users to send and receive FAX messages from their desktop.

Volume production begins at Digital's South Queensferry, Scotland, plant, Europe's most advanced semiconductor facility. The plant represents Digital's largest internal investment ever outside the U.S.

The VT1300 Color X Windowing Terminal is unveiled.

October   Digital acquires the financial services business of Data Logic, Ltd., a leading London-based supplier of UNIX-based software for trading rooms.

The U.S. Labor Department honors Digital with its Opportunity 2000 Award for leadership work in addressing issues relating to cultural diversity and equal opportunity in the work force.

Digital introduces the applicationDEC 433MP system, Digital's most expandable system for small and medium-sized businesses, which is based on the popular SCO UNIX System V and the Intel 486 microprocessor.

Digital announces its intention to open VMS—to add to the VMS operating system support for the widely accepted POSIX standards of the IEEE (Institute of Electrical and Electronics Engineers), and to have the VMS operating system "branded" by X/Open, the nonprofit consortium of many of the world's major information system suppliers.

1990 (continued)

December
In its largest external investment ever, Digital announces the formation in Germany of Digital-Kienzle Computer Systems from the Mannesmann-Kienzle Computer Systems Division of Mannesmann AG. Digital owns 65 percent of the new company, to employ 4,000 people developing and selling UNIX-based solutions to small and medium-sized companies throughout Europe.

1991

January
The world's largest company, Japan's Nippon Telegraph & Telephone (NTT), announces its Multivendor Integration Architecture (MIA) to define NTT's basic procurement requirements for general-purpose computers, based on the same multivendor computing philosophy embodied in Digital's NAS (Network Application Support). NTT also selects Digital's ACMS as the basis for its transaction processing interface under MIA.

February
The VAX 9000 series of mainframes and supercomputers is expanded with the addition of 10 server models.

March
Digital continues its push into the emerging markets of Eastern Europe, announcing the formation of a wholly owned subsidiary in Czechoslovakia.

Four new VAXft fault-tolerant systems are announced, extending the range of Digital's high-availability systems.

The readers of *Datamation* magazine name Digital's VAX 9000 mainframe computer "System of the Year" in an industry-wide competition.

April
Digital ranks number 30 in *Fortune* magazine's annual survey of the largest U.S. industrial corporations.

The Advanced Computing Environment (ACE) initiative is introduced by Digital and several other industry leaders to create a broadly supported, standards-based open computing environment that allows the use of advanced networked computing systems to reach their full potential.

Digital enters the emerging market for massively parallel computer systems through a strategic agreement with MasPar Computer Corporation.

Digital and Asea Brown Boveri Inc. (ABB) form a new company—EA Information Systems, Inc.—based on ABB's Engineering Automation Software Division, a leading supplier of 3-D plant design and engineering document management systems to the power, process, and manufacturing industries. Digital owns 80 percent of the new company, and ABB owns 20 percent.

May
The 15,000th VAX 6000 system is shipped. Receiving the system is Switzerland's Generaldirektion PTT, which uses more than 60 VAX 6000 systems to provide postal, telephone, and telegraph services throughout Switzerland.

Digital unveils its broadest set of personal computers to date, all optimized for network personal computing. New models include the Intel 386-based DECpc 333 portable and DECpc 320sx notebook computers, the Intel 486-based DECpc 433 workstation, and the DECpc 433T deskside system.

June
Digital announces The Open Advantage, a worldwide corporate strategy to establish Digital as the industry leader in delivering open solutions that give customers the freedom to choose and the power to use the highest-quality applications available at the best price.

Digital's position as the performance leader in open networks is enhanced with the introduction of its fifth generation of networking.

July
Digital enters into its first private-label OEM agreement for text terminals with Olivetti Systems and Networks.

1991 (continued)

August Digital introduces the DECmpp 12000 system series, supplied under an agreement with MasPar Computer Corporation. The DECmpp systems are a family of computers based on massively parallel processing (MPP), an emerging, high-performance technology targeted at very complex problems of technical, scientific, and commercial users.

September Digital opens a subsidiary in Morocco.

Digital and its most successful distributor in Latin America, SONDA (Sociedad Nacional de Procesamiento de Datos Limitada), announce participation in a joint venture for marketing and logistics support in all 14 of the Latin American countries where Digital has distributors.

Rear Admiral Grace Murray Hopper (USN Ret.), a Digital employee, is awarded The National Medal of Technology by President George Bush.

October Digital introduces the new VAX 4000 Model 500 departmental system—three times more powerful than previous VAX 4000 systems—and VAXstation 4000 Model 60, providing better RISC price/performance. The VAX 6000 Model 600 is also introduced, doubling the performance of previous VAX 6000 systems.

Digital introduces innovative, user-based software licensing, allowing customers to choose licenses to match the way they use software, an example of the Open Business Practices Digital is establishing to satisfy customers' unique needs.

Digital announces the formation of a wholly owned subsidiary in Poland, continuing its strategy of investment and expansion in the emerging markets of Central and Eastern Europe.

Digital launches Project Sequoia 2000, a major research collaboration with the University of California, aimed at overcoming barriers to crucial environmental research.

November Digital and Microsoft announce an alliance allowing Microsoft Windows to retrieve and exchange data with local area network servers running Digital's PATHWORKS software.

Digital acquires the Information Systems Division of Philips Electronics. With this acquisition, Digital announces the formation of Digital Equipment Enterprise (DEE), a new company to manage the small and medium-sized enterprise market in Europe, strengthening Digital's position in this market.

Digital initiates a $5 million equipment grant program for qualified health organizations worldwide dealing with HIV/AIDS or Alzheimer's disease.

December Digital announces its plans for establishing sales and service offices and an educational center in Russia, Ukraine, and neighboring republics.

Who's Who

More than 300 people were interviewed for this book. The biographies listed here reflect only those individuals who are quoted or mentioned.

Alden, Vernon
Director, Digital Equipment Corporation. Director and Trustee of several organizations. Former Chairman, The Boston Company, Inc.

Anderson, Harlan
Digital co-founder from Lincoln Lab. Digital employee 1957–1966. Currently in venture capital investing.

Barnard, John
Director, Digital Equipment Corporation, 1957–1971.

Bell, Gordon
Digital employee, Vice President of Engineering, 1960–1983.

Berg, Lynn
Joined Digital 1977. Currently Manager of Client/Server Computing.

Best, Dick
Joined Digital 1959. Currently Chief Engineer.

Brobeck, Wayne
Director, Digital Equipment Corporation, 1957–1966.

Brown, Gordon
Institute Professor Emeritus, School of Electrical Engineering and Computer Science, MIT.

Burg, Irving
Managed Maynard Mill Complex 1953–1974. Rented Mill space to Ken Olsen and Harlan Anderson in 1957. Digital employee 1974–1988, Facilities and Administration. Retired, Colorado Springs, Colorado.

Burley, Jim
Former Digital employee, Sales. Retired, Toronto, Canada.

Burnett, Henry
Joined Digital 1976. Currently Corporate EEO/AA Manager.

Busiek, Don
Former Digital employee, Enterprise Integration Services.

Cady, Roger
Former Digital employee, PDP-11 Engineering. Currently at Stratham Corporation, Arcadia, NH.

Cajolet, Ron
Joined Digital 1961. Currently Employment Manager, Westfield, MA.

Caldwell, Philip
Director, Digital Equipment Corporation. Senior Managing Director of Shearson Lehman Brothers, Inc. and Director of several corporations.

Cassidy, Frank
Joined Digital 1972. Currently Program Manager, External Research for Manufacturing and Logistics.

Chenail, Joe
Joined Digital 1974. Currently External Technical Manager.

Churin, John
Joined Digital 1979. Currently software consultant.

Clark, Wesley
Developed the LINC and LINC-8. Currently consultant, Clark Rockoff & Associates, New York, NY.

Clayton, Dick
Digital employee 1965–1984. Currently Vice President, Thinking Machines, Cambridge, MA.

Cocke, John
Designer of the Reduced Instruction Set Computer (RISC). Currently affiliated with T.J. Watson Research Center, IBM, Yorktown Heights, NY.

Congleton, William
Director, Digital Equipment Corporation, 1957–1974.

Conklin, Peter
Joined Digital 1969. Currently Alpha Product Office Manager, VMS Systems and Servers.

Cudmore, Jim
Joined Digital 1961. Currently Vice President, Operations Staff.

Cutler, Dave
Former Digital employee, Engineering. Currently with Microsoft.

Demmer, Bill
Joined Digital 1973. Currently Vice President, VAX VMS Systems and Servers.

Dennis, Jack
Professor Emeritus, senior lecturer, School of Electrical Engineering and Computer Science, MIT.

Denniston, Dave
Digital employee 1960–1989. Manager of Australian subsidiary. Retired, Santa Barbara, CA.

de Vitry, Arnaud
Director, Digital Equipment Corporation. Engineering consultant and Director and Trustee of several organizations.

Dillingham, Bruce
Joined Digital 1966. Currently Manager, Organization Technology Consulting Group.

Doane, Russ
Joined Digital 1960. Currently Senior Quality Manager, Manufacturing Education.

Dodd, Stephen
Whirlwind engineer. Retired, Englewood, Florida.

Doriot, Georges
1900–1987. President, American Research and Development. Digital advisor and Director, 1972–1987.

Esten, Dick
Joined Digital 1969. Currently Vice President of European Logistics and Manufacturing.

Everett, Robert R.
Director, Digital Equipment Corporation. Retired President of The MITRE Corporation.

Fadiman, Jonathan
Digital employee 1958–1966. Currently Director of International Sales for CSPI.

Falotti, Pier Carlo
Joined Digital 1969. Currently Vice President and CEO, Digital International (Europe).

Forrester, Jay W.
Served on Digital's Board of Directors 1958–1966. Currently Germeshausen Professor Emeritus, Sloan School of Management, MIT.

Fossum, Tryggve
Joined Digital 1972. Currently Technical Director, VAX Systems and Servers Advanced Development.

Fredkin, Edward
Computer pioneer in the fields of artificial intelligence, physics, and computer science. Professor and founder of several companies, including Information International, Inc.

Fredrickson, Dick
Digital employee, Sales, 1973–1990.

Frith, Robin
Digital employee 1964–1979. Subsidiary General Manager, Australia. Currently proprietor of Computer Images, Sydney, Australia.

Gassman, Bill
Joined Digital 1980. Currently Marketing consultant, Network Management Marketing.

Gaviglia, Lou
Joined Digital 1967. Currently Vice President, Manufacturing Logistics and Administration.

Gilmore, Jack
Joined Digital 1974. Currently Director of VCA Technology, Software Product Group.

Giordano, Rose Ann
Joined Digital 1979. Currently Vice President, U.S. Marketing. Corporate Officer for DECUS.

Glorioso, Bob
Joined Digital 1976. Currently Vice President, Executive Consulting.

Goldsmith, Clair W.
DECUS member and two-term DECUS president (1981–1987). Currently Director of Strategy and Planning for MIS for the University of Texas System and Deputy Director of the Computation Center, University of Texas, Austin.

Gosper, Bill
Affiliated with MIT AI laboratory.

Gould, Fred
Joined Digital 1959. Currently Sales Manager for New England Small and Medium Enterprises.

Graetz, Martin (Shag)
Writer.

Grainger, David
Digital employee, 1969–1991. Vice President, Sales and Service, Corporate Channels. Currently with Xerox.

Greenblatt, Richard
Former MIT hacker.

Gurley, Ben
Digital employee, 1959–1962. Designer of the PDP-1.

Gutman, Mike
Former Digital employee, PDP-11 Group. Currently Chief Operating Officer, PictureTel.

Hamel, Bob
Joined Digital 1981. Currently Educational Project Leader.

Hanson, Bill
Joined Digital 1967. Currently Vice President, Logistics.

Heffner, Bill
Joined Digital 1975. Currently Vice President, Image/Voice/Video.

Hindle, Win
Joined Digital 1962. Currently Senior Vice President.

Hoagland, Henry
Director, Digital Equipment Corporation, 1957–1968.

Hornbach, Kathy
Joined Digital 1986. Currently Manager, CASE Program Office.

Hustvedt, Dick
Corporate Consultant Engineer, Software Products.

Jacobs, Irwin (Jake)
Digital employee 1965–1982. Currently independent consultant.

Johnson, Ted
Digital employee 1958–1982, Vice President, Sales and Service. Currently principal of The Enrollment Collaborative.

Jones, John
Joined Digital 1963. Currently U.K. Insurance Director.

Kalb, Jeff
Digital employee and Vice President 1981–1987, semiconductor engineering. Currently President, MASPAR Computer Corporation.

Kaufmann, Peter
Digital employee 1966–1977, Vice President of Manufacturing. Currently independent process consultant specializing in conflict resolution.

Kendrick, Cy
Digital employee, Manufacturing, 1962–1982.
Retired, Acton, MA.

Kent, Allan
Joined Digital 1966. Currently Senior
Consultant Software Engineer, Systems
Integration Engineering Group.

Klotz, Lou
Joined Digital 1966. Currently Senior
Manufacturing Engineering Manager.

Knoll, Dave
Joined Digital 1967. Currently Group
Manager, Strategic Integration.

Knowles, Andy
Digital employee 1969–1983, Vice President,
Marketing. Currently President and CEO,
Artel Communications.

Kotok, Alan
Joined Digital 1962. Currently Corporate
Consulting Engineer and Technical Director,
Telecom Business Unit.

Lampson, Butler
Adjunct Professor of Computer Science
and Engineering, MIT. Currently Corporate
Consultant, Corporate Research and
Architecture.

Lary, Richie
Joined Digital 1969. Currently Corporate
Consultant, PC Systems and Peripheral
Engineering.

Lauck, Tony
Digital employee 1968–1972, in PDP-10
group. Rejoined in 1974. Currently Corporate
Consultant Engineer, Networks and Commu-
nications Architecture and Advanced
Development.

Learoyd, Cathy
Joined Digital 1977. Currently Group Manager,
Secure Systems Business Development.

Lemaire, Henry
Digital employee 1972–1977. Vice President,
Component Manufacturing and Engineering.

Leng, John
Digital employee 1963–1979. Vice President,
Technical Group. Currently Chairman,
Avex Technologies, Toronto, Canada.

Lennon, Bill
DECUS President 1977–1979. Currently
responsible for future directions, Advanced
Telecommunications Program, Lawrence
Livermore National Laboratory.

Licklider, J.C.R.
1915–1990. Pioneer in human-computer
interaction and networks. Former head of
Engineering Psychology at BBN. Emeritus
Professor of Electrical Engineering and
Computer Science, MIT.

Lipcon, Jesse
Joined Digital 1972. Currently Corporate
Consultant Engineer, Manager of Entry
Systems Business.

Long, Bill
Digital employee 1963–1985. Vice President,
OEM Group.

Mann, Harry
Digital employee 1968–1974. Vice President
and Chief Financial Officer.

Marcus, Julius
Digital employee 1969–1984, Commercial
Group. Currently Senior Vice President, New
Business Development, Xerox Corporation,
Stanford, CA.

Mazzarese, Nick
Digital employee 1962–1972. Vice President,
Small Systems.

McCarthy, John
Currently Professor of Computer Science,
Director of AI Laboratory, Stanford
University.

McGaunn, Paul
Joined Digital 1963. Currently Manager
of Total Quality Management programs,
Manufacturing Support Group.

McLean, William
Director, Digital Equipment Corporation.
Engineering consultant and Director of
several corporations.

Miller, Jim
Joined Digital 1972. Currently Consulting
Engineer, Networks and Communications
Marketing.

Minsky, Marvin
Professor of Electrical Engineering and
Computer Science, Toshiba Professor of
Media Arts and Sciences, MIT.

Molnar, Charles
Designed the LINC with Wes Clark. Currently
project engineer, Dearborn, MI.

Moore, Gerry
Digital employee 1962–1983. Currently
President, Clarity Learning, Inc., Concord, MA.

Nelson, Stewart
Experimented on the PDP-1 at the MIT AI lab
and later cofounded Systems Concepts.

O'Brien, John A. "Gus"
MIT Digital Computer Lab Department
Head; Lincoln Laboratory Group Leader;
SAGE subsystem development manager, The
MITRE Corporation. Currently retired.

O'Connor, Dennis
Founder and director of Digital's Artificial
Intelligence Technology Center.

Olsen, Aulikki
Mrs. Kenneth Olsen.

Olsen, Ken
Founder and President, Digital Equipment
Corporation. Director of several corporations.

Olsen, Stanley
Former Vice President 1957–1981. Currently
Owner/President of Gulf to Lakes Corporation;
Meadowcrest, a planned unit development;
several restaurants; and Black Diamond Ranch,
a championship golf course community, in
Citrus County, FL.

Papert, Seymour
Professor of Education and Media
Technology, LEGO Professor of Learning
Resources, MIT.

Papian, William
Whirlwind engineer. Retired, Shadyside, MD.

Parker, Wayne
Joined Digital 1980. Currently Senior
Hardware Consulting Engineer,
Semiconductor Engineering.

Patel, Mahendra
Joined Digital 1982. Currently Corporate
Consulting Engineer, Technical Director,
Networks and Communications.

Payne, Ron
Joined Digital 1977. Currently Vice President,
Staff Manager, Strategic Resources.

Pearson, Stan
Digital employee, Engineering and Marketing,
1974–1990.

Peterschmitt, Jean-Claude
Digital employee 1967–1987. Vice President,
Europe.

Porrazzo, Gloria
Digital employee 1957–1982. Modules
Assembly Group Manager.

Portner, Larry
Digital employee, Vice President Software
Development, 1975–1982.

Poulsen, Dick
Joined Digital 1968 in Canadian Customer
Services. Currently Vice President and
President, Digital Equipment Corporation
International.

Puffer, Bob
Former Digital employee, Manufacturing.
Currently Director of Manufacturing,
Dennison Manufacturing, Framingham, MA.

Rand, Margaret
Joined Digital 1961. Currently Senior
Executive Secretary.

Reed, Bob
Joined Digital 1958. Currently Operations Manager, Technology Planning and Development.

Rowe, Dorothy
Treasurer and Senior Vice President, American Research and Development. Director, Digital Equipment Corporation, 1962–1989.

Rubinstein, Dick
Joined Digital 1980. Currently Manager of Technology Assessment and Planning in Corporate Research, on sabbatical as researcher at the Cambridge Research Laboratory.

Russell, Steve
Cowrote Spacewar! program for the PDP-1 while at MIT. Currently with X-Ray Instrumentation.

Sage, Nat
Emeritus Coordinator of Research, University of Rhode Island.

Samson, Peter
Former MIT hacker.

Saviers, Grant
Joined Digital 1968. Currently Vice President, PC Systems and Peripherals.

Saylor, Leroy
Digital employee, Manufacturing, 1970–1990.

Schein, Edgar
Sloan Fellows Professor of Management, Sloan School of Management, MIT. Organizational development consultant with Digital since 1960s.

Schwartz, Ed
Digital legal counsel, 1967–1987. Currently President, New England Legal Foundation.

Senior, Ken
Joined Digital 1963. Currently Secretary of the Executive Committee.

Shields, Jack
Digital employee 1961–1989, Vice President, Sales and Service. Currently CEO, Prime Computer.

Shingles, Geoff
Joined Digital 1965. Currently Vice President, Country European Manager, U.K., Ireland, and Nordic countries.

Sims, John
Joined Digital 1974. Currently Vice President, Strategic Resources.

Singer, Bert
Joined Digital 1972. Currently Training Programs Manager.

Smart, Ron
Joined Digital 1964. Currently in Management Systems Research.

Smith, Jack
Joined Digital 1958. Currently Senior Vice President, Operations.

Stephenson, Barbera
Digital employee 1960–1966. Attorney, Albuquerque, NM.

Stewart, Bob
Joined Digital 1971. Currently Technical Director, Workstations.

Stockebrand, Tom
Digital employee 1962–1991. Currently Engineering Consultant, LGK Corporation, Albuquerque, NM.

Stone, David
Joined Digital 1970. Currently Vice President, Software Product Group.

Stone, Ollie
Joined Digital 1975. Currently Manager of Computer Aided Acquisition and Logistics Initiative, and activities in support of Concurrent Engineering.

Strecker, Bill
Joined Digital 1972. Currently Vice President, Engineering.

Supnik, Bob
Joined Digital 1977. Currently Corporate Consultant, Technical Director, VMS Systems and Software.

Sutherland, Ivan
Independent consultant, Sutherland, Sproull and Associates, Pittsburgh, PA. Computer graphics pioneer.

Taylor, Bob
Joined Digital 1983. Currently at Systems Research Center, Palo Alto, CA.

Taylor, Norman
Worked on Whirlwind Project at MIT's Digital Computer Lab; Associate Head of Lincoln Laboratory Computer Division in charge of the Memory Test Computer, FSQ-7, TX-0, and TX-2 computers, and Ken Olsen's supervisor during this period. Later managed SAGE weapon integration. Currently independent consultant.

Teicher, Steve
Digital employee 1969–1990. Currently with Kubota Pacific.

Tighe, Kay
Digital employee, Personnel and Employee Relations, Galway, 1971–1991.

Titcomb, Allan
Digital employee, Engineering, 1962–1990.

Tynan, Tony
Digital employee, MIS, 1974–1991, Galway.

Walter, Skip
Digital employee 1976–1990. Currently Managing Partner, Value Quest Group, Inc.

Wecker, Stu
Former Digital employee. Currently Professor of Computer Science, Northeastern University.

White, Don
Digital employee 1960–1989. PDP-8 modules engineer.

Wieser, Robert
Whirlwind engineer. Retired.

Wiitanen, Wayne
Spacewar! developer, with Steve Russell and Shag Graetz.

Yen, Dick
Former Digital employee, Vice President GIA Manufacturing and Engineering.

Glossary of Computer Terminology

A/D module	A computer component that converts analog signals to digital signals
address	A grouping of numbers that uniquely identifies a station or node in a network or a location in computer memory
algorithm	A set of rules for accomplishing a specific task, consisting of a sequence of detailed, unambiguous executable steps
analog computer	A computer that operates on analog signals
analog signal	An electrical signal that can assume any of an infinite number of voltage or current values, in contrast to a digital signal, which can assume only a finite number of discrete values
ARPANET	An acronym for Advanced Research Projects Agency Network; a computer network designed to share resources and to support dissimilar systems at separate sites
artificial intelligence	A computer program that simulates human thinking in order to solve problems
assembler	A program that converts code written in assembly language to code in machine language
BASIC	An acronym for Beginner's All-purpose Symbolic Instruction Code, a computer programming language commonly used to teach computer programming to beginners
batch processing	A method of processing that requires no human programmer interaction
bit	An acronym for a binary digit: 0 or 1
bps	An abbreviation for bits per second, the speed at which a serial transmission takes place
buffer	A temporary storage space for data
bug	An error in software or a malfunction in a system or device
bus	A group of wires in a computer system that carry related information; common buses are the data bus, in which each wire carries one bit of a word of data; the address bus, used to select sources and destinations; and the control bus, which carries control signals
byte	A binary character string made up of bits considered a unit and usually shorter than a computer word, most commonly an 8-bit quantity
CAD	An acronym for Computer-Aided Design, which facilitates the designing of architectural, mechanical, and electrical systems
CAM	An acronym for Computer-Aided Manufacturing; similar to CAD, CAM supports manufacturing processes
card	A printed circuit board used in a computer that usually provides a peripheral device for the computer system

cathode ray tube	*See* CRT
central processing unit	*See* CPU
chip	*See* integrated circuit
CISC	An acronym for Complex Instruction Set Computer, whose CPU supports an additional element that translates a microprogram into machine-level code
CMOS	An acronym for Complementary Metal Oxide Semiconductor, the technology commonly used in the design of integrated circuits; CMOS circuits are noted for low power consumption
COBOL	An acronym for Common Business-Oriented Language, a computer programming language, in which the programming code resembles English sentences
compiler	Translates a computer program written in a high-level language such as Pascal, FORTRAN, C, or COBOL into machine code
console	A computer component that supports interaction between the computer and the operator, typically a keyboard, a display, and the connections to the computer
core memory	A form of memory used by computers until the late 1970s
CPU	An abbreviation for Central Processing Unit, a computer component that consists of circuits to control, interpret, and perform the execution of instructions
CRT	An abbreviation for Cathode Ray Tube; an interactive input/output device that creates pictures by spraying electrons on a phosphorescent surface; most television and computer displays are CRTs
DCL	An abbreviation for Digital Command Language; DCL is the standard command interface to Digital's major operating systems
debug	To find and correct all errors in a program or computer system
DECnet	Digital networking software that runs on nodes in both local and wide area networks
DECtape	An early block-addressable medium for storing information on small magnetic tapes
DECUS	An acronym for Digital Equipment Computer Users Society, established in 1961 by Digital to create a program library and to exchange information between user and manufacturer
digital	Pertaining to digits or to showing data or physical quantities by digits
Digital Command Language (DCL)	The standard command interface to Digital's major operating systems
digital computer	A computer that operates on digital data
digital data	Information transmitted as discrete electrical quantities
DOS	An acronym for Disk Operating System; used by many computer manufacturers as an operating system for microcomputers
drum	An early computer storage device for storing data on rotating magnetic metallic cylinders
E-Mail	*See* electronic mail
ECL	An abbreviation for Emitter Coupled Logic; circuits that use this type of logic design are very fast but consume a large amount of power

electronic mail	A paperless system of communication between terminals or computers
electrostatic tube	An electronic device, similar in function to a transistor, that consists of a glass vacuum tube
Ethernet	A CSMA/CD (Carrier Sense, Multiple Access, Collision Detection) system that uses coaxial cable and was developed at Xerox Corporation by Metcalfe and Boggs; the initial system ran at 3 MHz, while the system commercialized by Digital, Intel, and Xerox runs at 10 MHz
fixed disk	*See* hard disk
flip flop	A circuit capable of assuming one of two stable states (on or off)
FORTRAN	An acronym for FORmula TRANslator; a programming language used for scientific applications
gate	Several circuits that perform simple digital logic
gate array	A geometric pattern of logic gates contained in a single chip; during manufacturing, the gates interconnect to perform a complex function that can be used as a standard production
hard disk	A disk that can typically store 20 to 200 megabytes of information but cannot be removed like a floppy disk; stores more information with a faster access time than a floppy disk
hardware	The physical elements of a computer system; computers, printers, disks, and devices
Input/Output	*See* I/O
instruction	A set of characters representing a computer operation
integrated circuit	An electronic component consisting of many circuit elements created on a contiguous material
interactive system	A computer system in which the user and the operating system communicate directly by means of a terminal
interface	A shared logical or physical boundary between various entities such as hardware, software, communications components, or humans; or the physical device that supports this boundary
I/O	An input and output function or operation
Large Scale Integration	*See* LSI
light pen	A light-sensitive stylus used to input information to a computer by manipulating data on a CRT
linking loader	A single program that loads, relocates, and links compiled and assembled programs, routines, and subroutines into tasks
LISP	An acronym for LISt Processor; a high-level functional computer programming language developed for use in artificial intelligence
logic	A discrete mathematical operation, or the electrical circuitry that performs such an operation
LSI	An abbreviation for Large Scale Integration that describes an integrated circuit, typically ¼-inch square, containing 100 to 100,000 gates
magnetic tape	A tape with a magnetic coating for recording information
mainframe	A large computer that can support 100 to 500 users at a time
megacycle	One million cycles; *see also* megahertz
megahertz	The measure of a computer's clock speed, where one megahertz is one million cycles per second

memory	The component that stores information in a computer system
microcode	The group of primitive instructions that implement machine instructions
microcomputer	A computer that uses a microprocessor as its central processing unit (CPU) and includes a memory and input/output circuits
microprocessor	An integrated circuit containing the entire CPU of a small computer on one or a few chips
minicomputer	A computer of intermediate size that can support 10 to 100 users
modem	An acronym for MOdulator/DEModulator that transforms digital into analog signals and analog into digital signals for communication
module	A functionally independent part of a computer program, or a component of a computer system
monitor	The display device of a computer or terminal
MOS	An acronym for Metal Oxide Semiconductor
mouse	A small device whose movements are mimicked by a pointer on a computer's display; by clicking a button the user selects text or icons
multiplexing	Any method of sending different signals along the same transmission medium so that each signal is distinguishable
multiprocessor	A single computer system that employs more than one processor in performing operations
network	A communication connection between computers or devices that transmits information
NMOS	An acronym for Negative-channel Metal Oxide Semiconductor
node	One of many interconnected computers in a network
OEM	An abbreviation for Original Equipment Manufacturer; the manufacturer of equipment that is used in another manufacturer's product
online	Pertaining to a condition in which a unit can communicate with the host processor or to equipment or devices directly connected to and under control of the computer
operating system	An integrated collection of programs that manages computer resources and controls the execution of application programs and provides system functions or software that organizes a central processor and peripheral devices into an active unit for the development and execution of programs
oscilloscope	A display that shows fluctuations in voltage as a function of time
paper tape	A storage medium consisting of a narrow, continuous strip of paper or plastic on which data is encoded in punched holes
parallel data transmission	A data transmission technique, generally faster than serial transmission, by which several bits are sent or received simultaneously
Pascal	A computer programming language designed to encourage the creation of modular and well-structured programs
peripheral	A hardware device that is not a functional part for the CPU
personal computer	A computer intended to be used by one person at a time

PMOS	An acronym for Positive-channel Metal Oxide Semiconductor
primary storage	Fast-access memory
printed circuit board (PCB)	A complete electronic circuit etched or wired on rigid material
processor	*See* CPU
Programmable Read-Only Memory	*See* PROM
Programmed Data Processor (PDP)	The first line of computers produced by Digital Equipment Corporation
PROM	An acronym for Programmable Read Only Memory; a computer chip that is manufactured in a blank state, then programmed once permanently
protocol	A specific set of conventions for communications among computers
punched card	An obsolete method of entering programs and data into a computer; cards were punched with holes that a computer could interpret
RAM	An acronym for Random Access Memory, a method of storage in which the time to access a piece of data is approximately the same for all such pieces of data; the access time is independent of the previously accessed data
Random Access Memory	*See* RAM
Read Only Memory	*See* ROM
real-time	Describes systems that operate while the external events that are significant to the system are actually occurring; or the amount of actual time a timesharing computer takes to accomplish a specific task, as opposed to "computer time"—the amount of time spent by the computer on that particular task alone; *see also* timesharing
Reduced Instruction Set Computer	*See* RISC
RISC	An acronym for Reduced Instruction Set Computer; a type of computer whose CPU operates on a limited number of instructions
ROM	An acronym for Read Only Memory in which information is permanently stored at the time of production and is not alterable by computer instructions; *see also* PROM
sector	A part of the track on a disk that is considered one logical storage unit
semiconductor	A material that has electrical characteristics somewhere between those of insulators and conductors
sequential access	A method of accessing ordered data in order
serial transmission	A method of transmission in which each bit of information is sent sequentially on a single channel rather than simultaneously as in parallel transmission
SNA	An abbreviation for Systems Network Architecture, IBM's layered communications protocols
software	A set of instructions that control the operation of a computer
stack	A data storage structure in which the last item stored is the first retrieved

synchronous transmission	Transmission in which the data characters and bits are transmitted at a fixed rate with the transmitter and receiver synchronized, providing greater efficiency by eliminating the need for start-stop elements
Systems Network Architecture	*See* SNA
TECO	A simple text editor developed by Digital, used to store and manipulate ASCII files
Teletype	A system of communication that used keyboard or paper tape as transmitters and printers to receive and display information
TELEX	A system of internationally linked teletypewriters
terminal	A computer component allowing human interaction with the computer, usually consisting of a keyboard and display
timesharing	Pertaining to a system in which multiple-user programs get, in turn, time or use of a computer or computer device
TOPS-20	A Digital timesharing operating system developed for use on the DECsystem family of computers
transistor	A solid state electronic device used mainly as an amplifier or a switch
TTL	An abbreviation for Transistor-Transistor Logic, the most widely used technology for the design of digital logic circuits
UNIBUS	An asynchronous data bus to which all devices can be directly attached, bypassing the processor
UNIX	A popular operating system, designed to be modular and extensible
VAX	The Virtual Address eXtension (VAX) computer, using a 32-bit architecture, developed by Digital Equipment Corporation
Very Large Scale Integration	*See* VLSI
Virtual Memory System	*See* VMS
VLSI	An abbreviation for Very Large Scale Integration, describing an integrated circuit that contains more than 100,000 gates
VMS	An abbreviation for Virtual Memory System, the operating system used on VAX computers
wire-wrap equipment	A machine that wires computer modules, cheaper and faster than human labor
word	A sequence of bits that is considered a single, logical unit by a system; the length of a sequence may vary
word processor	A computer used to create and produce text documents
workstation	A powerful microcomputer typically with graphics and windowing capabilities

Prepared by Aran Anderson and Kenneth Spark, students at Worcester Polytechnic Institute

Sources

Marotta, Robert E., ed. *The Digital Dictionary: A Guide to Digital Equipment Corporation's Technical Terminology.* 2d ed. Bedford, MA: Digital Press, 1986.

McNamara, John. *Technical Aspects of Data Communication.* 3d ed. Bedford, MA: Digital Press, 1988.

Bibliography

The following sources were used during the research of this book.

Bell, Gordon, Craig Mudge, and John McNamara. *Computer Engineering: A DEC View of Hardware Systems Design.* Bedford, MA: Digital Press, 1978.

Fleck, Glen, ed. *A Computer Perspective.* Cambridge, MA: Harvard University Press, 1973.

Levy, Steven. *Hackers: Heroes of the Industrial Revolution.* New York: Doubleday, 1984.

Marotta, Robert E., ed. *The Digital Dictionary: A Guide to Digital Equipment Corporation's Technical Terminology.* 2d ed. Bedford, MA: Digital Press, 1986.

McNamara, John. *Technical Aspects of Data Communication.* 3d ed. Bedford MA: Digital Press, 1988.

Redmond, Kent C., and Thomas Smith. *Project Whirlwind: The History of a Pioneer Computer.* Bedford, MA: Digital Press, 1980.

Rheingold, Howard. *Tools for Thought: The People and Ideas Behind the Next Computer Revolution.* New York: Simon and Schuster, 1985.

Rifkin, Glenn, and George Harrar. *The Ultimate Entrepreneur.* Chicago: Contemporary Books, Inc., 1988.

Schein, Edgar. *Organizational Culture: A Dynamic Model.* MIT Industrial Liaison Program Report. Cambridge, MA: MIT Press, 1983.

_____. *The Role of the Founder in the Creation of Organizational Culture.* MIT Industrial Liaison Report. Cambridge, MA: MIT Press, 1983.

Schein, Edgar, Warren Bennis, and Caroline McGregor. *Leadership and Motivation, Essays.* Cambridge, MA: MIT Press, 1966.

Smith, Douglas, and Robert Alexander. *Fumbling the Future.* New York: William Morrow and Company, Inc., 1988.

Thanks to the staffs at the following archives and libraries for their enthusiastic assistance:

The MITRE Corporation, Bedford, MA
MIT Museum and Historical Collections, Cambridge, MA
MIT Archives, Cambridge, MA
Maynard Historical Society, Maynard, MA
Digital Corporate Photo Library, Marlboro, MA
The Computer Museum, Boston, MA

The following are trademarks of Digital Equipment Corporation: ADVANTAGE-NETWORKS, ALL-IN-1, applicationDEC, BI, DDT, DEC, DECmate, DECnet, DECsystem, DECtalk, DECtp, DECUS, DECUSCOPE, DECville, DECWORLD, DIGITAL HAS IT NOW, the DIGITAL logo, Digital Press, GIGI, IAS, J-11, KA10, KL10, LA, LSI-11, MASSBUS, Micro/PDP-11, MicroPower/Pascal, MicroVAX, MicroVAX I, MicroVAX II, OMNIBUS, PATHWORKS, PDP, PDP-11, PDP-11/70, Q-bus, RA, RSTS, RSTS/E, RSX, RSX-11, RSX-11M, RSX-11M-PLUS, RT-11, ThinWire, TOPS-10, TOPS-20, ULTRIX, UNIBUS, VAX, VAX Notes, VAX-11/750, VAX-11/780, VAX 6000, VAX 8500, VAX 8550, VAX 8600, VAX 9000, VAXBI, VAXcluster, VAXft, VAXmail, VAXmate, VAXstation, VMS, VT50, VT100, WPS.

Third-party trademarks: 1-2-3, Lotus, and VisiCalc are registered trademarks of Lotus Development Corporation. Apollo is a registered trademark of Apollo Computer, Inc., a subsidiary of Hewlett-Packard Company. Apple, AppleTalk, Lisa, and Macintosh are registered trademarks of Apple Computer, Inc. CP/M is a registered trademark of Digital Research, Inc. CRAY-1 is a registered trademark of Cray Research, Inc. IBM and OS/2 are registered trademarks of International Business Machines Corporation. Intel is a trademark of Intel Corporation. MasPar is a registered trademark of MasPar Computer Corporation. MAXCIM is a registered trademark of NCA Corporation. Microsoft and MS-DOS are registered trademarks and Windows is a trademark of Microsoft Corporation. MUMPS is a registered trademark of Massachusetts General Hospital. Mylar is a registered trademark of E.I. Du Pont de Nemours & Company, Inc. Olivetti is a registered trademark of Ing. C. Olivetti. Open Software Foundation is a trademark of Open Software Foundation, Inc. PageMaker is a registered trademark of Aldus Corporation. SCO is a trademark of the Santa Cruz Operation, Inc. System V is a trademark of American Telephone and Telegraph Company. Tandy is a registered trademark of Tandy Corporation. Teletype is a registered trademark of Teletype Corporation. UNIVAC is a registered trademark of Unisys Corporation. UNIX is a registered trademark of UNIX System Laboratories, Inc. Wang is a registered trademark of Wang Laboratories, Inc. WordStar is a registered trademark of MicroPro International Corporation. X/Open is a trademark of X/Open Company, Ltd. Xerox is a registered trademark of Xerox Corporation.

Index